THE DIVINE GOODNESS OF JESUS

In this book, Paul K. Moser explores Jesus's role as God's filial inquirer of those who inquire of him. He also clarifies a method of inquiry regarding Jesus – one that offers a compelling explanation regarding his experiential impact and his audience's response. Moser's method values the roles of history and moral/religious experience in inquiry about him, and it saves inquirers from distorting biases in their inquiry. His study illuminates Jesus's puzzling features, including his challenging question for inquirers of him (Who do you say I am?), his distinctive experience of God as father, his reference to himself as "the Son of man," his attitude toward his suffering and death, his unique role in the Kingdom of God, and his understanding of his allegedly miraculous signs and of his parables and Good News. The book also enables inquirers of Jesus to make sense of evidence for the reality and the main purpose of Jesus, and thereby to avoid prejudice in their inquiry.

Paul K. Moser is Professor of Philosophy at Loyola University Chicago. He is the author and editor of numerous books, most recently *The Cambridge Companion to the Problem of Evil*, *The God Relationship*, and *Understanding Religious Experience*.

The Divine Goodness of Jesus

Impact and Response

PAUL K. MOSER
Loyola University Chicago

CAMBRIDGE UNIVERSITY PRESS

CAMBRIDGE
UNIVERSITY PRESS

Shaftesbury Road, Cambridge CB2 8EA, United Kingdom

One Liberty Plaza, 20th Floor, New York, NY 10006, USA

477 Williamstown Road, Port Melbourne, VIC 3207, Australia

314–321, 3rd Floor, Plot 3, Splendor Forum, Jasola District Centre, New Delhi – 110025, India

103 Penang Road, #05–06/07, Visioncrest Commercial, Singapore 238467

Cambridge University Press is part of Cambridge University Press & Assessment, a department of the University of Cambridge.

We share the University's mission to contribute to society through the pursuit of education, learning and research at the highest international levels of excellence.

www.cambridge.org
Information on this title: www.cambridge.org/9781009013642

DOI: 10.1017/9781009031707

First published 2021
First paperback edition 2023

A catalogue record for this publication is available from the British Library

ISBN   978-1-316-51602-7   Hardback
ISBN   978-1-009-01364-2   Paperback

Who then is this man?

Mark 4:41

Contents

Preface

Jesus attracts controversy on many fronts, and our understanding why he does can be profoundly illuminating
regarding us as inquirers and perhaps regarding God too.
We need, however, an illuminating and focusing perspective for understanding Jesus, and his own perspective on
divine goodness will serve our purpose well. Divine goodness was his focus and his motivation, and we shall examine how it clarifies who he was and is. Neglect of that
perspective has often blocked making good and accurate
sense of Jesus.

This book uses an impact–response model of interpreting Jesus to highlight who he was in his self-understanding
and his redemptive mission in relation to God. Two questions focus the model: What was and is Jesus's intended
impact on his audience, now including *me* as part of that
audience? What should *my* response to him be in relation to
the divine goodness he portrayed as *the divine worthiness of
being valued* above all else, with full commitment?

The model enables us to identify the distinctive kind of
evidence bearing on Jesus's status in relation to God. It also
directs us to the significance of moral experience and conscience for such evidence. The impact–response model
applies not only to Jesus and his audience, including current inquirers of him, but also to God and Jesus in their

interpersonal relationship. In addition, it explains how the intentional impact of Jesus includes *his* morally challenging inquiry of people inquiring of him. This relatively neglected feature merits careful attention from inquirers about Jesus, including scholarly investigators.

The key redemptive impact of Jesus includes his moral power not to control or coerce people but to *attract* receptive people to sympathetic and cooperative reconciliation with God. If perfectly good, God would seek goodness in interpersonal relationships for the sake of building a good human society, and that would call for human reconciliation with God in divine goodness. The intended power to attract people to such reconciliation comes by the manifestation of divine goodness, and it reveals what its audience values, by way of its response to divine goodness. Interpreters of Jesus have failed to give such distinctive power due attention as central to his self-understanding and redemptive mission. This book corrects that omission, by portraying Jesus through divine goodness and its impact on and from him. It explains how he engaged in moral-theological conflict without interpersonal violence for the sake of promoting such goodness.

If we understand persons ultimately by what they value, we can understand Jesus by what he primarily valued: (a) God's perfect responsive and guiding goodness from *Abba*, as the divine worthiness of being valued above all else, with full commitment; (b) being attracted and led by that goodness to cooperate with it, in his life and the lives of others; and (c) encouraging humans to guide their lives for a due cooperative response to God's goodness. Interpretations of Jesus often omit the central role of (a)–(c), and they thereby miss out on the heart of who Jesus was and is. This book fills that omission with a new impact–response focus on Jesus in relation to divine goodness, with special attention to its role in Gethsemane. It explains how such goodness is attractive, responsive, and guiding in its stemming from a redemptive purposive agent Jesus called

"*Abba*." How Jesus understood his purposes in relation to God bears significantly on how he intended to relate to his audience, given God's normative role in his life.

This book gives special attention to the joint relevance of history, theology, and ethics in understanding who Jesus was and is. It also explains how the moral power he offered can serve as distinctive evidence of the reality and the presence of Jesus and of God, even if some people fail to recognize it. The book explores the significance of the variation among humans in their recognition and reception of the evidence in question. In doing so, it makes sense of Jesus's important view of divine hiding at times for redemptive purposes. It also explains the decisive role of human valuation and cooperation in apprehending the distinctive evidence in its intended fruition in agreeable cooperation with God.

Chapter 1, "Inquiry about and from Jesus," identifies the kind of inquiry suited to a reliable understanding of Jesus in relation to his understanding of divine goodness. It acknowledges the intentional impact of Jesus on his audience as a source of relevant evidence that calls for a morally relevant response from inquirers. Chapter 2, "God through Divine Goodness," explains what kind of evidence in experience we should expect from a God devoted to the moral redemption of humans in the kind of interpersonal reconciliation suggested by Jesus. It characterizes the kind of moral impact God would have on human moral experience and the kind of cooperative response God would expect.

Chapter 3, "Divine Goodness from *Abba*," clarifies the center of Jesus's response to God in relation to God's impact on his moral experience. It uses the Gethsemane experience of Jesus to illustrate this center in his filial responsiveness to God as *Abba*, and it presents this experience as normative for his disciples. Chapter 4, "Good News of Divine Goodness," identifies the Good News of God from Jesus in terms of the arrival, in his ministry, of a kingdom of divine goodness. It characterizes this kingdom in terms of a unique moral power aimed at human redemption in divine–human reconciliation, and it explains how such cooperative reconciliation guided the mission of Jesus, including in relation to divine hiding at times.

Chapter 5, "Stories for Divine Goodness," examines the aim of Jesus when he used parables expressive of God's goodness. It locates this aim in Jesus's desire to attract people to divine goodness in a volitionally engaging way. This way not only shows their valuing or disvaluing it but also invites them to decide, voluntarily, whether to cooperate with it. Chapter 6, "Suffering for Divine Goodness," explains the role of Jesus as the suffering "Son of man" foreshadowed in the Book of Daniel. It identifies how Jesus aimed to self-identify with the suffering people of God in a manner that shared their destiny for God, and it finds a ground for this aim in divine goodness – particularly God's moral character and purpose directed toward reconciliation with humans.

Chapter 7, "Kingdom of Divine Goodness," examines the role of Jesus in the Kingdom of God, with a distinction between the two phases of the kingdom. The first phase, postponing divine judgment, seeks the current redemption of humans in divine–human reconciliation, and the second phase realizes the future full society of the people of God accompanied by final divine judgment. Chapter 8, "God's Gambit for Divine Goodness," explains God's gambit as a strategy of risk for the sake of sharing divine goodness with humans in building, with their voluntary cooperation, a society fully reconciled with God. It identifies the central role of Jesus in this gambit, while highlighting his focus on redeeming the evil in conflict with divine–human reconciliation, even when we cannot fully explain such evil relative to God's purposes. The book concludes with a return to Jesus's signature question in search of cooperative reconciliation in divine goodness for his inquirers: Who do you say that I am?

This book has benefited from comments and suggestions from many people. For constructive help, I thank Jacob Andrews, Simon Babbs, David Bukenhofer, Tom Carson, Aeva Munro, Benjamin Nasmith, Clinton Neptune, students in my classes at Loyola University Chicago, and various anonymous referees. I also thank Abigail Neale for her careful copy editing of the manuscript. For excellent help at Cambridge University Press, I thank Beatrice Rehl, Publisher.

Parts of the book make use of revised materials from some of my recent essays: "Jesus and Abba in Gethsemane," *Journal of Theological Interpretation* 15 (2021), "Jesus as Moral-Kingmaker," *Biblical Theology Bulletin* 50 (2020), "Having 'Ears to Hear': Jesus, Gethsemane, and Epistemology," *Evangelical Quarterly* 91 (2020), and "God, Redemptive Friendship, and Self-Reflective Decision," *The Routledge Companion to the Philosophy of Friendship*, ed. Diane Jeske (London: Routledge, 2021).

Inquiry about and from Jesus

Jesus emerges in the history of ancient Israel, and he cannot be separated from it, if we are to understand him as a figure in human history. Israel's ancient history, however, is drenched in the blood of holy war in the name of God, the supposed Father of Jesus. Many people rightly doubt that all of the blood spilled there is redemptive in turning something bad into something good. If real, the alleged good involved often eludes the perception of many of us, through no evident fault of our own.

We should ask how Jesus fits into Israel's ancient history of holy war, if he does fit. Our answer will attend to Jesus's own understanding of his role in holy war, and it thus will clarify the relation of Jesus to the God of ancient Israel. In doing so, our answer will reveal a portrait of Jesus that is neglected by many commentators on his life and work and by many of his self-avowed followers, early and late. We shall see that Jesus's chosen conflict is not military but moral-theological, aimed at divine–human reconciliation in God's goodness. We may understand *moral* goodness broadly in terms of the *supreme* good, bearing on personal character, virtue, and action and thus on value, praise-worthiness, and rightness, individually and interpersonally. Even so, divine goodness is not reducible to moral goodness, because it includes goodness in domains other than the moral domain, including the cognitive and prudential domains.

Why bother with Jesus *at all*? He evidently is second to none in attracting attention from inquirers about human history, inside and outside the academic world, and the range of those inquirers is vast in diversity of perspectives and interests. Why all of this interpretive flurry, past and present, about *Jesus*, an obscure Galilean Jew put to death by the Roman government after upsetting the Jewish leaders by creating a ruckus in their temple? We can approach an initial answer.

1.1 A REASON TO INQUIRE

Different inquirers about Jesus often have different motives and perspectives, with no easy or uneasy means of reconciliation. Let us not miss the obvious, however: Much of the inquiry about Jesus arises from questions about his representing, or relating people to, *God*. His supposed *theological*, or Godward, importance underlies the lion's share of attention to him, and this goes beyond his mere historical, moral, sociological, or ecclesiastical significance and influence. Many inquirers ask about him because they want to ask about *God through him*, if implicitly. Whether they get good answers is, of course, a separate matter.

Inquiry about Jesus eventually leads us to an important feature of his: his *intentional impact* on inquirers. The relevant evidence, we shall see, includes some repeating patterns of literary evidence in the synoptic Gospels. This evidence is best understood in terms of the intentional impact of Jesus himself on his disciples, given that he did not produce writings for posterity.

James D. G. Dunn remarks: "All we have are the impressions which Jesus made."[1] These "impressions" include

---

[1] James D. G. Dunn, *Christianity in the Making, vol. 1: Jesus Remembered* (Grand Rapids, MI: Eerdmans, 2003), p. 329. This observation has antecedents in Martin Kähler, *The So-Called Historical Jesus and the Historic, Biblical Christ*, trans. C. E. Braaten (Philadelphia: Fortress Press, 1964 [1892]), pp. 79, 87, 90, 94, and in Ernst Troeltsch, *Glaubenslehre* (Berlin: Duncker, 1925); Troeltsch, *The Christian*

"Jesus remembered," as Dunn notes, but the impact can extend to past and present readers of the synoptic Gospels. This is plausible if William Manson is right: "The main factor in the formation of the Christian narratives was the initial, specifically religious impression produced upon the mind of the community by Jesus himself."[2] In this general vein, Dale C. Allison reports: "I find it very difficult to come away from the primary sources doubting that I have somehow met a strikingly original character. I seem to have a permanent and vivid impression of who he must have been."[3] This consideration figures, as Allison notes, in a method of historical inquiry that proceeds by abduction, or inference to a best available explanation, regarding our literary historical data.

In general, we seek historical interpretations of Jesus that make the best available sense of the impressions he left on his audience. They will offer the best available answers to such questions as: Why did Jesus leave these particular impressions on his audience rather than some other impressions? Why did he leave these impressions rather than no impressions at all? Such questions are explanation-seeking, and they will guide a historically responsible interpretation of Jesus. They seek explanations that best fit our overall evidence, without neglect, distortion, or extravagance toward it. We thus can agree with E. P. Sanders: "The only way to proceed in the search for the historical Jesus is to offer hypotheses based on the

---

Faith, trans. G. E. Paul (Minneapolis: Fortress Press, 1991), p. 101. See also Paul E. Davies, "Impact and Response," *Interpretation* 18 (1964), 276–84. Davies comments: "All we have from Jesus is the impact he made on [people] and their response to him in hostility, indifference, or faith. The Gospel account was written in these terms and within this limitation" (278).

[2] William Manson, *Jesus the Messiah* (London: Hodder and Stoughton, 1943), p. 45.

[3] Dale C. Allison, Jr., *Constructing Jesus: Memory, Imagination, and History* (Grand Rapids, MI: Baker Academic, 2010), p. 23. See also Allison, *The Historical Christ and the Theological Jesus* (Grand Rapids, MI: Eerdmans, 2009), p. 29. For discussion of some needed constraints on memory in this context, see Allison, *Constructing Jesus*, pp. 435–62, Richard Bauckham, "The General and the Particular in Memory," *Journal for the Study of the Historical Jesus* 14 (2016), 28–51, and Allison, "Memory, Methodology, and the Historical Jesus," *Journal for the Study of the Historical Jesus* 14 (2016), 13–27. See also Dunn, *Jesus Remembered*, pp. 130–4, 327–38.

evidence and to evaluate them in light of how satisfactorily they account for the materials in the Gospels, while also making Jesus a believable figure in first-century Palestine and the founder of a movement which eventuated in the church."[4]

Allison, Dunn, and Manson have used an abductive approach to illuminate the self-understanding of Jesus, with Dunn and Manson identifying historical evidence for Jesus's "sense of intimate sonship before God."[5] In the same vein, Oscar Cullmann has identified the life of Jesus as the basis in two areas for our understanding him: "in Jesus's own self-consciousness and in the concrete presentiment his person and work evoked among the disciples and the people."[6] If we understand "presentiment" broadly as "response to an impact," we can agree with Cullmann, Manson, Dunn, and Allison in favoring an abductive approach sensitive to the impact, including the intentional impact, of Jesus on his audience. Disputes about details can, and will, continue, but we should be able to use abduction thus oriented to fill in much of the striking image left by the impact of Jesus on his audience. In doing so, we will be using a method common to historical inquiry in general.

It would be implausible to assume that people influenced by the impact of Jesus must or even always distort Jesus beyond recognition. William Manson comments:

The faith of the Christian society penetrates and suffuses the matter of the tradition: we see Jesus in the light of the

---

[4] E. P. Sanders, *Jesus and Judaism* (Philadelphia: Fortress Press, 1985), pp. 166–7.

[5] See Dunn, *Jesus Remembered*, p. 762, and Manson, *Jesus the Messiah*, pp. 105–9; cf. Allison, *Constructing Jesus*, pp. 221–304, and Allison, *The Historical Christ*, pp. 64–6. For a recent use of abduction (arguably over-extended at points) to capture the self-understanding of Jesus, see Andrew Ter Ern Loke, *The Origin of Divine Christology*, SNTSMS (Cambridge: Cambridge University Press, 2017). On the broader role of abduction in relation to religious experience and theological belief, see Paul K. Moser, *Understanding Religious Experience* (Cambridge: Cambridge University Press, 2020), chaps. 7–8.

[6] Oscar Cullmann, *The Christology of the New Testament*, rev. ed., trans. S. C. Guthrie and C. A. Hall (Philadelphia: Westminster Press, 1963), p. 317.

community's faith and love. But this glow or aureole in which the glory of the risen Lord blends to some extent with the lineaments of the Jesus of history does not mean that the image of Jesus as he was on earth is so refracted as no longer to appear in its reality ... Within the tradition the "I–Thou" relation of his word to us is maintained with unmistakable clearness.[7]

"Unmistakable clearness" aside, this chapter will return to the "I–Thou" relation between Jesus and his audience, but the point now is that it was a live option for the original hearers of Jesus to convey his impact on them accurately. Indeed, it would be puzzling if that audience had no interest in representing Jesus as he actually was. A concern for accuracy about Jesus would be included in the audience's concern to represent *Jesus* rather than someone else. At least part of that audience gives us the definite impression of wanting to represent Jesus as he was, at least on some matters of importance.

This book uses evidence from history and experience to clarify the impact of Jesus on various inquirers. It attends to a special but widely neglected feature of his intentional impact: *his inquiry of us as inquirers*. In doing so, it puts our inquiry of him in a challenging context, namely, the context of his illuminating inquiry of us. This approach leads to an impact–response model of theological interpretation (we will call it *theistic accountableism*), where interpreters are accountable for their responses, including their ethical and religious responses, to the relevant impact of Jesus and God on them.

C. F. D. Moule notes: "The historian can observe, within the limits set by the data, both the historical figure [of Jesus] and the symptoms of subsequent religious experience [of him], but if he is both properly inquisitive and honest, he is bound to pay attention also to what is implied by the

---

[7] Manson, *Jesus the Messiah*, p. 32.

religious symptoms, although this itself belongs outside the strictly historical purview."[8] He thus asks "whether it is not right and proper to hold the historical and the 'trans-historical' together in a single continuum, albeit without any blurring of the respective limits and frontiers of the two."[9] He also wonders whether strictly historical work about Jesus can be illuminated by religious considerations of a historically transcendent Jesus that cannot be reduced to strict history.[10] We will benefit, from an explanatory point of view, by going beyond a "strictly historical pur-view" to relevant considerations of moral and religious experience, while giving our historical evidence its due.

We shall see that Jesus engaged in inquiry of his inquirers in order to prompt them to undergo moral self-reflection and decision-making *in relation to God*. Apart from such reflection and decision-making, our scriptural and historical interpretations of Jesus will miss his intended impact, omitting how we are to be related to the morally challenging personal subject of our inquiry and his (Jesus's) relation to God. We shall see how this consid-eration yields an effective, experience-based method for human inquiry about Jesus and God.

Our impact–response model of interpretation will be distinctive in making inquiry about Jesus go beyond ordinary scriptural and historical interpretation to a use of abductive, or explanatory, reason based in an inquirer's *moral experience*. This interpretive model matters, beyond historical or academic controversy about Jesus, in relation to questions about an inquirer's moral experience and standing before God and Jesus. This model thus will fit with what we shall identify as a central concern expressed by Jesus. We shall see how our interpretive model is irreducibly interpersonal and ethical, and how it can be

[8] C. F. D. Moule, "The Gravamen against Jesus," in Moule, *Forgiveness and Reconciliation* (London: SPCK, 1998), pp. 105–6.
[9] Moule, "The Gravamen against Jesus," p. 113.
[10] Moule, "The Gravamen against Jesus," p. 99.

self-revealing for persons regarding their moral status in relation to God and Jesus.

How we inquire about Jesus and God matters, because trustworthy inquiry must fit with its subject matter, in a way that allows its subject to present itself (or, in this case, Jesus himself) accurately to inquirers. A use of abductive reason based in moral experience must be added to history and scripture, if we are to represent and know who Jesus truly was and is. We thus shall see that the triad of history, scripture, and experience benefits, in representing Jesus on the basis of his impact, by being grounded in moral experience of a kind to be clarified.

A key issue concerns the impact of Jesus as including *volitional* confrontation with his audience – that is, the power of his manifested moral will or intention in confrontation with an inquirer's will, without coercing the latter will. As Leander Keck has observed: "His good news about the impingement of God's kingdom implied that his hearers *can* respond appropriately, though it is not easy to allow God's character to reshape one into a son or daughter of God."[11]

Seeking divine–human reconciliation, Jesus intended the moral power of his will to *attract* sympathetic cooperation, including uncoerced agreement in action, from inquirers in relation to God's goodness represented by him. He thought of such reconciliation as part of God's redemptive will or intention for a morally flourishing life among humans, and he thought of the moral power manifested as a portrayal of divine goodness, including divine love for humans. In general, we may think of God's *redemptive will* for divine–human reconciliation in terms of God's powerful but uncoercive directedness toward divine goodness in interpersonal relationships.

---

[11] Leander Keck, *Who Is Jesus? History in Perfect Tense* (Columbia, SC: University of South Carolina Press, 2000), p. 103. See also Keck, *A Future for the Historical Jesus* (Philadelphia: Fortress Press, 1980), p. 192.

The Oxford English Dictionary, 2nd edition, offers the following definitions of "reconciliation": (1) "The action of restoring humanity to God's favour, especially as through the sacrifice of Christ; the fact or condition of a person's or humanity's being reconciled with God." (2) "The action of restoring estranged people or parties to friendship; the result of this; the fact of being reconciled."[12] Arguably, the best understanding of Christian "atonement," "redemption," or "salvation" is in terms of human cooperative reconciliation to God as a divine gift. In any case, we see a pattern of attempted reconciliation in the ministry of Jesus, including in his eating with social outcasts and in his calling wayward people to follow him to trust and to obey God.

Inquirers will not experience the reality of the divine moral power on offer for what it is intended to be if they omit their freely given, sympathetic cooperation as a result of either their indifference or their opposition. The intended moral power would be *in cooperative interaction* with God, when a cooperative inquirer is, by uncoerced attraction, led closer in volition to God's moral character and will. Without the sympathetic cooperation, the divine power would not come to its intended fruition, and therefore it would not be experienced by an uncooperative inquirer for what it is intended to be by God. So, the moral response of an inquirer matters significantly, from an experiential, a moral, and a cognitive point of view. As a result, what an inquirer values relative to divine goodness looms large in this context.

Some theologians balk at a role for human cooperation in the divine redemption of humans based on the assumption that such a role would be "Pelagian." This is a serious mistake. A role for human cooperation would preserve a role for *responsible persons* as genuine moral agents, but it would not entail their *earning* or *meriting* divine approval.

---

[12] *The Oxford English Dictionary*, 2nd ed. (Oxford: Oxford University Press, 1989).

It thus would not threaten divine grace. Obeying need not be earning at all. If we omit a role for genuine human cooperation, we will exclude the status of genuine, responsible persons to be reconciled to God. We then will have at most a controlling divine will oblivious to human agency. In that case, commands to humans to obey God, such as those represented by Jesus, will be pointless and even misleading with regard to attracting humans to divine–human reconciliation. God's will then would be the sole relevant cause.

A key issue concerns how Jesus effectively can represent God's moral will to inquirers, against the historical background of how he intended to represent God. If real, God would exist at a level of moral depth deeper than that of typical human existence, given that God as worthy of worship would be morally perfect. In addition, such a God would aim to attract and to lead inquirers toward God's level of moral depth, with their sympathetic cooperation, for the sake of their having distinctive evidence of God's reality and their knowing God. Jesus, we shall see, claimed to have a unique, God-appointed role in that aim, and he acted accordingly. This consideration figures in the astonishing amount of attention he has received from inquirers. Such attention makes good sense in the light of the portrait of Jesus to be offered here. It also fits with what we will identify as his intended impact, in relation to divine goodness, on inquirers about him.

1.2 HISTORY AND THEOLOGY

Where should an inquiry about Jesus begin, regarding who he was and is, and how should it proceed? It may be easier to state where such an inquiry should *not* begin and how it should *not* proceed. For instance, it should not begin with an ahistorical systematic theology or a dogmatic creed about who Jesus is. Otherwise, we easily can end up with the tail wagging the dog, with our theological preferences defining Jesus in ways that obscure the historical reality about him. Instead, we should start with our actual evidence regarding Jesus, allowing the real Jesus to emerge, even if in conflict with our preferences about him. We then shall have an opportunity not to construct Jesus in our own preferred image. We thus shall try to avoid George Tyrell's image of inquirers representing Jesus by seeing their own faces reflected as they peer into a deep well.[13]

What actual evidence of ours regarding Jesus can aid our inquiry? The plot thickens with this question because people dispute what is our actual evidence about Jesus. Some people endorse a kind of extreme skepticism regarding Jesus that leaves us with very little, if anything, to trust about him. We should not *start* there, however, because we first must consider relevant evidence to see if it is trustworthy.

Some inquirers will invoke evidence about Jesus from their religious experiences, and that may or may not be acceptable *in the end*. We shall see the importance of relating any evidence from religious experience to our relevant historical evidence, if only to curb distortion of the Jesus of history. For now, then, we should consider what some of our oldest historical testimonies regarding Jesus have to say and what is their supporting evidence. Included in the New Testament, they merit the close attention of anyone inquiring about Jesus as (at least) a historical figure, because they claim to represent the impact of Jesus himself on his earliest historical audience. C. H. Dodd has remarked: "The first three gospels offer a body of sayings on the whole so consistent, so coherent, and withal so distinctive in manner, style, and content that no reasonable critic should doubt, whatever reservations he may have about individual sayings, that we find reflected here the thought of a single, unique teacher."[14] We shall see that our evidence confirms Dodd's claim.

[13] George Tyrell, *Christianity at the Crossroads* (London: Longmans, 1913), p. 44.
[14] C. H. Dodd, *The Founder of Christianity* (London: Macmillan, 1970), pp. 21–2. Similarly, see James D. G. Dunn, *Jesus, Paul, and the Gospels* (Grand Rapids, MI: Eerdmans, 2011), pp. 10–21.

Talk of "historical" and "history" is confusing without some clarification, given that such talk varies widely in meaning among scholars and others. In general, "history" can be understood simply as *past events* or other past realities; in addition, it can be understood as a *record* or an *interpretation* of such events or other realities. The two categories should not be confused because past events or other realities need not have a record or an interpretation at all. In fact, most past events or other realities are not coupled with a record or an interpretation, even though many are. We often formulate interpretations as a means to make some sense of past events or other realities in response to our explanation-seeking questions about those events or other realities. Some interpretations are better than others, from an explanatory point of view, and some are correct while others are incorrect, owing to agreement or disagreement with the events or other realities in question.[15]

A prominent conception of "history" among biblical scholars is called "scientific history" or "empirical history." This is history understood ultimately in terms of physical and human causes, with no purposes or intentions deeper than human purposes or intentions. Even if human purposes have causal efficacy in history, given this conception, they are not to be explained in terms of any deeper, theological purposes or influences. God is not "historical" in this conception, given that God is not a physical or a human cause in history. God, then, is excluded from undertaking actions in "history" and therefore from intervening in the "historical" life of Jesus and other humans. *Scientific* historical interpretation thus goes against the historical interpretations offered in the numerous biblical narratives,

---

[15] I have argued elsewhere that, as long as we make assertions, we cannot avoid a notion of reality or factuality; see Paul K. Moser, *Knowledge and Evidence* (Cambridge: Cambridge University Press, 1989), chap. 1, and Moser, *Philosophy after Objectivity* (New York: Oxford University Press, 1993), chap. 1.

including those representing the teaching of Jesus, that ascribe causal efficacy to God in historical events.

An influential alternative to "scientific history" aims to accommodate some of the biblical narratives by distinguishing scientific or empirical history and *redemptive* history (*Heilsgeschichte*). God has the option of intervening directly or indirectly in history, according to this approach, but in doing so God would go beyond empirical history.[16] God is not an empirical object or event, and therefore God's causal influence in history, direct or indirect, would not be that of an empirical object or event. Our discerning such divine influence is, of course, no simple matter and definitely is not just an empirical matter. Some other kind of discerning would be needed, and we shall identify how moral discernment on the basis of distinctive moral experience, aligned with God's moral character, can serve. In this matter, we shall take a lead from the teaching of Jesus on apprehending God's intervention in human experience.

If we neglect either redemptive history or morally relevant theology in our inquiry about Jesus, we risk ignoring a historical divine effort toward our moral education in becoming morally fit for God's redemptive purpose. Moral theology matters if God exists and seeks to improve people morally, and redemptive history matters too, if God works in human history, directly or indirectly. So, redemptive history and morally relevant theology can matter together in an inquiry about Jesus. Nothing requires, as we shall see, that they be in opposition or competition.

We have noted that one can define "history" in a way that excludes God from "history," as some historians have done (the list of proponents is long, even in Biblical Studies). That move, however, would be to foster, at least

---

[16] A defense of this approach is Oscar Cullmann, *Salvation in History*, trans. S. G. Sowers et al. (London: SCM Press, 1967). For an overview of the dispute, see Leonhard Goppelt, *Theology of the New Testament*, trans. J. E Alsup (Grand Rapids, MI: Eerdmans, 1981), vol. 1, pp. 263–81.

by implication, a *philosophical* position subject to serious dispute.[17] We have no compelling reason from philosophy as a discipline to exclude God from history, just as philosophy as a discipline does not exclude God from reality in general. At another extreme, we could proceed with theology as if history were irrelevant, as some speculative theologians have done, but that would be to neglect theological recognition of any divine redemptive effort in human history. We are well-advised not to foreclose that option, at least as a matter of principle.

A responsible approach, from an explanatory point of view, considers that history and morally relevant theology can be mutually illuminating. We shall take such an approach seriously. My approach will require that both morally relevant theology and historical interpretation must earn their keep from supporting evidence if they are to survive needed scrutiny. So, not just any theology and not just any history will do. Theological and historical beliefs matter, but they do not matter on their own as *mere* beliefs from a cognitive, epistemic, or explanatory point of view. They call for evidential support to avoid being a matter of mere opinion, and that support can be abductive relative to one's experience: a function of the explanatory power of a claim relative to the whole range of one's experience. We shall outline such an abductive experiential approach and relate it to our evidence regarding Jesus.

We can distinguish between:

(a) *knowing who Jesus is* (or was) in a way that understands his unique identity as a person and thus distinguishes him from other people,
(b) *knowing Jesus by firsthand acquaintance* as an intentional, personal agent, and

---

[17] For criticism of *a priori* exclusion of what is supernatural from history by various New Testament scholars, see Ben Meyer, *The Aims of Jesus* (London: SCM Press, 1979), chap. 2. See also George Eldon Ladd, "A Search for Perspective," *Interpretation* 25 (1971), 41–62.

    (c) *knowing that various facts* (or realities) apply to Jesus
         (for instance, that he was a Galilean Jew).

Knowledge of kind (c), including historical knowledge of that kind, can leave one without knowledge of kind (a) or kind (b). A familiar sense of "knowing a person" involving kind (b) goes beyond knowing that various facts apply to that person. For instance, I can know many facts (or realities) about former President Obama without knowing him by firsthand acquaintance. In addition, even if knowing of kind (a) requires some historical knowledge of kind (c), we should doubt that knowing of kind (c) is sufficient for knowing of kind (a). I also doubt that kind (b) requires kind (a), and I doubt that kind (a) requires kind (b).

Our knowing *who Jesus is* (or was) would depend on the kind of intentional being he actually is (or was), including his purposes in either allowing or not allowing others to know who he is (or was). For instance, he could hide some of his unique purposes from some people for various reasons, such as to save them from misunderstanding if they are not ready to understand.[18] This consideration is typically ignored by historical inquirers about Jesus, but it is irresponsibly uncritical and perhaps even naïve to ignore it. We shall give it due attention in order to maintain a responsible approach to methodology.

We will consider whether restricting historical knowledge about Jesus to his objective teachings and conduct obstructs rather than benefits our having history-based knowledge of who he truly is (or was). We thus will examine whether having knowledge of who he is (or was), given his purpose in allowing such knowledge, requires a special, morally relevant attitude toward him on the part of an inquirer. We should not ignore that he may have had

---

[18] On the redemptive value of a corresponding kind of divine hiding at times, see Paul K. Moser, *The God Relationship* (Cambridge: Cambridge University Press, 2017), chap. 3, and Moser, *Understanding Religious Experience*, chap. 8. Chapter 4 returns to this topic.

such a purpose, even if historical inquirers about him typically ignore this. Some of our evidence, we shall see, indicates that he did have such a purpose. In attending to it, we will give a fair hearing to Jesus as he is represented in our historical evidence.

Baron von Hügel has observed a widely neglected fact about knowing some realities, such as knowing a person.

We get to know [some] realities slowly, laboriously, intermittently, partially; we get to know them, not inevitably nor altogether apart from our dispositions, but only if we are sufficiently awake to care to know them, sufficiently humble to welcome them, and sufficiently generous to pay the price continuously which is strictly necessary if this knowledge and love are not to shrink but to grow. We indeed get to know [these] realities in proportion as we become worthy to know them, in proportion as we become less self-occupied, less self-centred, more outward-moving, less obstinate and insistent, more gladly lost in the crowd, more rich in giving all we have, and especially all we are, our very selves.[19]

Historians typically do not attend to this consideration regarding an inquirer's moral "dispositions," but they should in cases where a personal object of inquiry calls for it. This consideration could figure in the kind of *knowing a person* available to us regarding a historical figure. One can define "historical knowledge" to exclude this consideration, but the result could be a harmful limitation on our knowing a historical person. Responsible historical inquiry does not block this consideration at the start, even if we find that is does not apply at the end.

Adolf Deissmann has offered an observation about historical knowledge that extends beyond the previous consideration (with qualifications needed):

---

[19] Baron von Hügel, *Essays and Address on the Philosophy of Religion* (London: Dent, 1921), p. 104.

The way of historical science is narrow. If one wants truly to grasp Jesus, one must make the way broader. It is the way which Paul called "the more excellent way." "*Tantum Jesus cognoscitur, quantum diligitur*" – "Jesus is known as much as He is loved." I know, even when I begin an academic lecture on Jesus, that there is an unacademical way to Jesus, and that it is the best way, because it is open to all. Jesus lives not only in the historical sources of the Gospel, but is to be experienced by us also, wherever he is manifested in the present day, as living energy.[20]

Deissmann raises the controversial topic of the *present status* of the Jesus of history, and that topic cannot be avoided by responsible inquiry about who Jesus is.

Deissmann holds that the historical Jesus is not *merely* historical, but is still alive and available to be known as alive now, as a powerful intentional agent with "living energy." This should not be a starting assumption for historical inquiry about Jesus, but it may emerge at the end of a careful examination of all relevant evidence. So, we should leave open for now the option of a currently living Jesus, neither rejecting nor embracing it. A living Jesus could have a decisive say now in how human inquirers come to know who he is, preferring to be known not as a *mere* artifact of history but as one who prompts the kind of agreeable response to his moral character suggested by von Hügel. As responsible inquirers, we do well not to ignore that option.

Deissmann acknowledges a consideration similar to that offered by von Hügel:

On one point there is, for the historian, a contact between his historical and his personal attitude to Jesus. Every historian

---

[20] Adolf Deissmann, *The Religion of Jesus and the Faith of Paul*, trans. W. E. Wilson (London: Hodder and Stoughton, 1923), p. 20. For related talk of "energy" from God through Jesus, see H. R. Mackintosh, *The Doctrine of the Person of Jesus Christ*, 2nd ed. (Edinburgh: T&T Clark, 1913), p. 318, and C. F. D. Moule, "The Energy of God," in Moule, *Christ Alive and at Large*, eds. Robert Morgan and Patrick Moule (London: Canterbury Press, 2010), pp. 99–103.

who has more to do than merely investigate old texts, to solve chronological problems and make certain of outward facts, who rather has to deal with the soul of a great man, must in the end, if he wishes to gain an all-round picture, divine by means of intuition. This cannot happen without sympathetic imaginative entry into the life, without *agapē*.[21]

Instead of talking of "the soul of a great man," we may talk instead of how Jesus allows or does not allow one to know him or who he is *if he is alive*. We thus must ask: *Who* gets to say how we may or may not know Jesus or who he is if he is alive? Do we as ordinary inquirers have this authority, or does Jesus? In asking the question, we get a plausible answer: We would not have this kind of authority over the living Jesus, nor should we expect to have it.

As responsible inquirers, we should consider the option of our coming to know who Jesus is on the basis of the manner of knowing him approved by Jesus himself. A living intentional Jesus would have authority and power in this area. Only an uncritical bias, even if called "historical," would exclude this prospect at the start. We will not exclude it, but, at the same time, we will not beg the question of whether Jesus is still alive. In addition, we will not make use of an obscure notion of "intuition"; instead, we will clarify a relevant notion of "moral experience" related to moral "conscience."

Deissmann offers an important distinction for an inquiry about knowing who Jesus is, including the historical Jesus.

Our task, which is only partly to be done by historical methods, is not identical with the study of what is usually called "The Teaching of Jesus." If that were our objective, the theme would be much easier. "The Teaching of Jesus" can be easily set forth, just because the tradition itself is relatively objective. But the teaching which is expressed outwardly is

---

[21] Deissmann, *The Religion of Jesus*, p. 23.

something secondary. It points back to something primary, namely, inner communion with God. Our problem is not the secondary matter, but the primary: not the teaching, but the experience behind it.[22]

The question, then, is whether an inquirer about Jesus will consider anything beyond the "relatively objective" teaching and publicly observable conduct of the historical Jesus.

Some inquirers limit historical inquiry to "relatively objective" matters, leaving out what Deissmann calls the "primary" matter, that is, the matter of the underlying *experience* suggested by the life and teaching of Jesus. Perhaps that matter includes a morally relevant experience of God in some kind of human confrontation by God, and perhaps not. We should not foreclose either option at the start, if we seek to know who Jesus is (or was). Responsible inquiry, in contrast to a distorting bias or prejudice in inquiry, will be open to what our relevant evidence supports, and that evidence could challenge our preconceptions and antecedent beliefs (at least if we are suitably responsive to it). An inquirer's evidence could challenge even a proposed limitation to "relatively objective" historical considerations about Jesus. We shall consider how such a challenge proceeds.

1.3 INQUIRY FROM JESUS

The Gospels of Mark, Matthew, and Luke portray Jesus as inquiring of his inquirers in a morally relevant way.

Jesus went on with his disciples to the villages of Caesarea Philippi; and on the way he asked his disciples, "Who do people say that I am?" And they answered him, "John the Baptist; and others, Elijah; and still others, one of the

---

[22] Deissmann, *The Religion of Jesus*, pp. 24–5.

prophets." He asked them, "But who do you say that I am?" Peter answered him, "You are the Messiah." And he sternly ordered them not to tell anyone about him. Then he began to teach them that the Son of Man must undergo great suffering, and be rejected by the elders, the chief priests, and the scribes, and be killed, and after three days rise again. He said all this quite openly. And Peter took him aside and began to rebuke him. But turning and looking at his disciples, he rebuked Peter and said, "Get behind me, Satan! For you are setting your mind not on divine things but on human things." (Mark 8:27–33, NRSV here, and in subsequent biblical translations, unless otherwise noted; cf. Matt. 16:13–23, Luke 9:18–22)

In Mark's Gospel, this is a turning point in the mission of Jesus because he makes clear the kind of mission from God he has undertaken, and the result is not popular.

Three main factors emerge from the pivotal exchange represented in all of the synoptic Gospels. First, Jesus asks his followers to consider *from their own decision-perspective* who he is: "Who do *you* say that I am?" Second, the apostle Peter identifies Jesus as God's special emissary to Israel: "You are the Messiah," and Jesus evidently approves of this in general terms, or at least he does not reject it whole-sale. Third, Jesus reveals his ultimate purpose in terms of "setting your mind on divine things" (literally, "the things of God"), in contrast with "human things." His self-avowed purpose includes not only his intentionally focusing his mind on God's will, but also his willingly "suffering, being rejected, being killed, and rising again" as part of the "divine things." So, his purpose includes his intentional cooperation with the "divine things," the "things of God," bearing on him and his mission.[23]

---

[23] On the historical basis of the reported exchange between Jesus and Peter at Caesarea Philippi, see W. D. Davies and Dale C. Allison, Jr., *A Critical and Exegetical Commentary on the Gospel According to Saint Matthew*, ICC (Edinburgh: T&T Clark, 1991), vol. 2, pp. 602–23.

"Who do *you* say that I am?" This probing question from Jesus is put in the second person, and, while Mark's Gospel has the plural "you," considering the question responsibly demands a reference to *oneself* – that is, considering it from *one's own* decision-perspective, as the apostle Peter did without delay. Hence, in my case, even if I am part of a social group: Who do *I* say that Jesus is? The intended question from Jesus thus has a *self-referential application* for an inquirer: It prompts one to put *oneself* in the presence of the question of who Jesus is, in order to give *one's own* answer, from *one's own* first-person perspective, even if influence from a social group is allowed. The question in an individual's case is thus not ultimately a question about what others say. In this regard, a person cannot pass the buck to a group but must face the issue directly. Jesus's question thus puts individual hearers on the spot.

In my case, *I* become, if implicitly, the one being interrogated by Jesus, involving what he will think of *me*. I thus become the subject of a self-referential inquiry, courtesy of Jesus. So, my inquiry about *Jesus* expands, in the light of his question, to an inquiry also about *me*, in relation to who Jesus is and whom I take him to be, even if I consult with a social group. This inquiry is morally relevant because my response will reveal my perspective on the moral significance or insignificance of Jesus. It thus will reveal my moral standing relative to him. If his moral significance stems from or otherwise represents God, my response to him may bear importantly on my response to God, in relation to my moral standing with God. At least we shall explore that option. In representing God, Jesus would intend his question to present me with divine goodness in a way that holds me accountable to God. If the resurrected Jesus is contemporaneous with us, his question will have direct importance for us; otherwise, it will have its importance indirectly, in relation to God.

The question from Jesus at Caesarea Philippi yields a self-referential approach to inquiry about Jesus, as an inquirer about Jesus becomes "the inquired of" (by Jesus). An assessor of Jesus becomes "the assessed" (by Jesus). (Who do *I* say that he is, and what leads *me* to my answer regarding him?) These results hold even for those who start out as self-described "merely historical" inquirers. The question from Jesus to his inquirers implicates an inquirer in a way that goes beyond mere history, to the broader intentional perspective of that inquirer in relation to moral standing. An indication of Jesus's seriousness about the response to him is his remark: "Whoever is not with me is against me, and whoever does not gather with me scatters" (Matt. 12:30, Luke 11:23). He had in mind "gathering" people for God and God's kingdom, with their cooperation.

In saying who Jesus is, I would be engaged in intentional action, in an action of saying something about Jesus. I might say that I do not know who he is, and this, too, would be an intentional action. In any case, I am under challenge, from Jesus himself, to give an answer, and this challenge puts me on the spot. It puts me in a position to be assessed regarding my answer, at least in terms of its status as responsible or irresponsible and as morally good or morally bad. Such an assessment will bear on my moral standing, at least relative to the moral status of Jesus and perhaps in relation to God if Jesus represents God.

Whatever I say or do not say in response, Jesus's question implicates me and my decision-perspective by inviting a question about myself: *Am I being responsible* in my response, relative to all of my evidence, whatever my response is and whatever social influence I allow? We can assess this matter of first-person responsibility from the position of my relevant evidence about Jesus.

A striking feature of Jesus, according to the overall portrait of him in the New Testament Gospels, is that he speaks for and represents *God*. E. P. Sanders remarks: "[Jesus] thought that he had been especially commissioned to speak for God, and this conviction was based on a feeling of personal intimacy with [God]."[24] Sanders finds, on the basis of our historical evidence, that Jesus represented himself as the "viceroy" in the kingdom of God, "subordinate only to God himself." Some of the supporting evidence comes from Jesus's remarks about his status of unique authority in the final judgment of humans (Matt. 19:27–9; cf. Luke 22:28–30). Some additional evidence comes from such remarks by Jesus as: "Blessed [by God] is anyone who takes no offense at me" (Matt. 11:6, Luke 7:23; cf. Matt. 13:16–17, Luke 10:23–4; Matt. 12:42, Luke 11:32), and "no one knows the Father except the Son and anyone to whom the Son chooses to reveal him" (Matt. 11:27; cf. Luke 10:22).[25]

Given the conclusion by Sanders about Jesus's presumed relation to God, we may propose that Jesus thought of himself as the human king and judge immediately under God and thus as the human measure or norm for the morally relevant things of God. He considered himself to exemplify and to represent, in actions as well as words, God's moral character of righteous love. In that capacity, Jesus functioned as the human benchmark for the assessment of humans by God's moral standard. He thus could challenge people to seek first God's kingdom and to do God's will (Matt. 6:33, 7:21), while assuming that he himself shows how this is to be done (Mark 14:36). The latter assumption underlies his frequent injunction, "Come, follow me." The initial aim of Jesus was to draw all of national Israel to reconciliation with God (hence his selecting twelve apostles), but the scope of his movement arguably became broader, going beyond Israel, in the face of resistance from national leaders (Matt. 21:43; cf. Acts 11:16–18).

[24] E. P. Sanders, *The Historical Figure of Jesus* (London: Penguin, 1993), p. 239. See also Sanders, *Jesus and Judaism*, p. 153. Likewise, see C. K. Barrett, *Jesus and the Gospel Tradition* (London: SPCK, 1967), pp. 29–30, and Dodd, *The Founder of Christianity*, pp. 51–2.

[25] On the historical credibility of Matthew 11:27, see Davies and Allison, *A Critical and Exegetical Commentary on the Gospel According to Saint Matthew*, vol. 2, pp. 271–97.

Rudolf Bultmann has captured the relevant evidence as follows, despite his deep historical skepticism about the gospel portraits of Jesus: "In his lifetime [Jesus] had demanded decision for his person as the bearer of the Word [of God] . . . It does imply a christology which will unfold the implications of the positive answer to his demand for the decision, the obedience response which acknowledges God's revelation in Jesus."[26] As a result, when Jesus raises, by implication, his self-referential question about me by asking who I take him to be, he puts me in a morally defined I–Thou context. As I stand before Jesus and his question, facing his moral character and responding from my moral character and perspective, what is *my* assessment of *him*? The moral contrast between Jesus and me, including relative moral closeness to God, is so striking that I might be inclined to question my own moral reality, propriety, and authority instead of his. Certainly, it would be misguided for me to assume my moral superiority over Jesus, particularly in relation to his God of perfect goodness, including righteous love for others.

Jesus raised a serious moral challenge in his response to the rich man's inquiry of how to get eternal life. He directed the man to obey God's commandments and, given his attachment to wealth, to sell his possessions. He then added: "Come, follow me" (Mark 10:21; cf. Matt. 19:21, Luke 18:22). Jesus thought of himself as the human model or norm for obeying and pleasing God. He thus presented himself as the human measure for how humans are to relate to God, as indicated in his recurring command to some members of his audience "Come, follow me." His

---

[26] Rudolf Bultmann, *Theology of the New Testament*, trans. Kendrick Grobel (New York: Charles Scribner's Sons, 1951), vol. 1, p. 43. A critical assessment of Bultmann's historical skepticism can be found in Manson, *Jesus the Messiah*. For a critical response to Bultmann's understanding of faith, see Keck, *A Future for the Historical Jesus*, pp. 50–8. Bultmann fails to appreciate the importance both of faith being well-grounded in evidence and of the role of abduction in the historical and other sciences. For evidence for the importance of the historical Jesus to the earliest Christian message, see Graham Stanton, *Jesus of Nazareth in New Testament Preaching*, SNTSMS (Cambridge: Cambridge University Press, 1974).

question, then, raised the issue of how I fare in relation to him as the human measure for relating to God. So, the self-referential question from Jesus is no matter of mere information or intellectual reflection. It leads to the vital issue of my relation to God from a morally relevant perspective, bearing on my actions, attitudes, and thoughts.[27]

The question of *Jesus's purpose* in the self-referential feature of inquiry about him rarely emerges from historical inquirers about him. We shall see, however, that it sheds light on two matters: who Jesus considered himself to be, and who an inquirer, as a moral agent, is in relation to Jesus and God. Jesus considered himself to be called by God to challenge people with the coming of God's kingdom to them, in a way that invites a response, a decision, from each of them in relation to God. Part of this challenge included his showing, in actions and words, who God is, as a righteous and loving Father. As Werner Georg Kümmel notes, Jesus "wanted to preach with specific urgency that God seeks to encounter man [and woman] with fatherly love ... Like a father, God will *care* for his children."[28]

Jesus did not allow for a response by proxy, as if someone else could respond *for me* to the message of God's arriving kingdom. Even if I take input from others, I am responsible for my settled response, all things considered. Given the self-referential feature of suitable inquiry about Jesus, I am challenged to allow myself to be confronted by the message of Jesus and thus by its reported source – God as a morally powerful agent. This approach to inquiry differs from an examination of mere conduct or teachings from history. It brings the inquirers themselves into the current focus of inquiry and assessment. Jesus thought of

---

[27] Jesus did not call all of his audience to follow him in his itinerant ministry. He advised some people who responded positively to go home instead, thus acknowledging that callings from God can differ in detail (Mark 5:18–20). Even so, he typically did call his audience to obey God in keeping with his understanding and presentation of God's goodness.

[28] Werner Georg Kümmel, *The Theology of the New Testament*, trans. J. E. Steely (Nashville, TN: Abingdon Press, 1973), p. 40.

it as the assessment of inquirers *by God* (and himself), with regard to the fitness of inquirers for the kingdom of God. He thus thought of himself as God's authoritative inquirer for the divine kingdom, including for human suitability for entering it.

Jesus's question for an inquirer, say me, prompts me to reflect not only on my understanding of who *Jesus* is, but also on *my* motives in inquiring about him. What do I aim to do with my information about who Jesus is? In particular, do I aim to use my information in a manner guided by the main purpose of Jesus regarding God in his relating to humans? Or, do I have an aim contrary to his purpose? If so, what motivates my contrary aim, and is it suitably grounded in reality rather than in a harmful misrepresentation of reality or of Jesus? In addition, does a contrary aim of mine block me from knowing who Jesus actually was or is and from receiving important evidence regarding him? Such questions are, at least, about me as an inquirer about Jesus, and they merit a fair hearing if we aim to understand Jesus.

Relevant questions about me abound. In facing Jesus's question about an inquirer of him, such as me, do I allow myself to be revealed to myself, particularly regarding how I stand, morally and otherwise, in relation to Jesus and God? In that connection, am I *attracted* to the moral character and purpose of Jesus and God, and if not, is this my moral shortcoming? Do I allow Jesus's question of me to become a mirror of self-reflection where I can be compared to the normative standard set by *his* moral character and purpose, including his obeying God? If so, do I allow myself to be morally convicted, forgiven, reconciled, and redirected by him?

If I am suitably cooperative, I may able to experience firsthand who Jesus really is, in relation to God, and what are his main redemptive purpose and power. Otherwise, I may obscure or block such firsthand evidence of him for myself, including firsthand evidence of his moral goodness, power, and authority. In not allowing his moral power to come to its intended fruition in my cooperative experience, I may obstruct that power in my life and thereby block salient evidence from that power for the reality of Jesus and God. I then may fail to apprehend Jesus's moral goodness, power, and authority in being God's unique representative for humans, including myself. So, my moral response can make a significant difference.

Confirmation of Jesus's self-referential approach for us arises from his response to a question about his authority. His response came after his judgment on certain temple practices.[29] He proceeded obliquely: "Jesus said to them, 'I will ask you one question; answer me, and I will tell you by what authority I do these things. Did the baptism of John come from heaven, or was it of human origin? Answer me'" (Mark 11:29–30; cf. Matt. 21:24–5, Luke 20:3–4). His inquirers chose to plead ignorance, having been challenged to reflect on their own attitudes regarding the spokesman from God who had introduced Jesus as a superior, authoritative representative. Jesus thought of John the Baptist as an Elijah-like prophet commissioned by God to be his forerunner (Matt. 11:7–15, Mark 9:11–13). Jesus thus aimed for moral self-reflection from inquirers, in relation to God's purpose for them, but he typically received resistance from them. Inquiry about Jesus, then, can become a moral clash for inquirers in relation to God.

If we omit the self-referential feature in question, we may be inquiring not about the real Jesus but instead about a more convenient object of our own preference. Much inquiry about Jesus, inside and outside the academic world, seems to have such a defect, and it can lead to a distorted, morally impotent Jesus in our inquiry. We shall begin to correct that problem in order to remove some common bias or prejudice in inquiry about Jesus.

---

[29] For discussion of varying views of Jesus's judgment on certain temple practices, see Simon J. Joseph, *Jesus and the Temple: The Crucifixion in Its Jewish Context*, SNTSMS (Cambridge: Cambridge University Press, 2016), pp. 105–67.

We shall hold together our inquiry about Jesus and *his* inquiry about us as inquirers, thus avoiding a typical one-sided approach to inquiry about him. The typical approach, and any resulting bias in inquiry, will be challenged by a standard set by Jesus the inquirer of us.

The relevant I–Thou confrontation between a human inquirer, on the one hand, and Jesus as God's supreme human norm and God, on the other hand, would have a purpose. The divine purpose would be to confront an inquirer with the personal and intentional *moral power* of God, for the sake of attracting an inquirer to cooperation in divine–human reconciliation. This would be human confrontation not just with an idea, but with an intentional agent with intentional power – that is, an agent with the moral purposes and power to attract and to lead a human toward perfect moral goodness.

Measuring ourselves by the standard of the moral character of Jesus can occur in moral conscience, and it can present a sharp contrast between his moral character and ours. C. H. Dodd thus remarks: "To bring about the awakening of conscience was a major object of [Jesus's] work, certainly the major aim of most of the parables."[30] The intended awakening was an awakening to divine goodness, in contrast with our looking or valuing in the wrong, lesser places. On this basis, we can be convicted of our moral shortcoming before Jesus and before the God he represents. Our being thus convicted by him requires our cooperation with him, but it would not be *self-conviction*. Instead, it would come from an intentional source morally superior to us, a source aiming to lead us toward cooperation with divine goodness.

We should expect God to seek our willing, uncoerced moral conviction, because such conviction would figure importantly in human redemption as moral reconciliation to God. The divine aim here, being redemptive, would be

---

[30] Dodd, *The Founder of Christianity*, p. 62.

for our motivated or involved positive commitment to God and God's redemptive purpose. So, the consideration of how we are best motivated by God would arise.

Helmut Thielicke has remarked on the motivational importance of interpersonal confrontation:

What Jesus is saying is that I want [people] to confront me ... I want the decision to be made in relation to my person ... Mere telling [of a message] which does not lead to involved confrontation with [the person at] the center of the message engenders empty dogmatic formulae and the pseudo-faith which is conventionally called a purely historical faith or *fides quae creditur* in distinction from *fides qua creditur*, i.e., belief [that something is the case] in distinction from faith [in someone] ... [So,] Jesus does not use the title "Messiah" or "Christ" to define his person and mission but handles it socratically, leaving it ambiguous and thus maieutically triggering the question of his person [for inquirers].[31]

We have noted that Jesus raised "the question of his person" at Caesarea Philippi, and we have noted its self-referential application for inquirers of him.

Aiming to elicit human faith and love toward God, Jesus sought sympathetic trust and caring appreciation toward God that go beyond (historical) belief that various truths apply to God and himself (Mark 11:22, 12:28–30).[32] The relevant kind of trust is *cooperative* trust; it includes resolving to rely on and cooperate with divine goodness as experienced. Belief that truths obtain, however well-grounded, does not yield trust in God, even though trust in God is ideally well-grounded in evidence regarding divine trustworthiness and goodness.

[31] Helmut Thielicke, *The Evangelical Faith*, trans. G. W. Bromiley (Grand Rapids, MI: Eerdmans, 1977), vol. 2, pp. 349–51.
[32] See Keck, *A Future for the Historical Jesus*, for needed emphasis on the role of faith as *trust* in God, in the teaching of Jesus.

We need caution toward the position of Van Austin Harvey that "the content of faith can as well be mediated through a historically false story *of a certain kind* as through a true one, through a myth as well as through history."[33] If this position allows for faith in God and Jesus as mere "symbols," without reference to actual extra-linguistic realities (such as the historical person of Jesus), it distorts the teaching of Jesus regarding the causal reality of God in human experience. Such a causal reality could be a matter of causal influence without causal coercion of human wills. It also could elicit and attract faith in God, thus saving such faith from being self-manufactured or self-sustained. The active and voluntary trust component of faith in God, in any case, does not require earning or meriting approval from God.

God would seek human trust and love toward God in order to lead people willingly toward an improved moral character and its corresponding conduct for a divine kingdom. God thus would care about the *motive* behind a person's affirmations (or the lack thereof) regarding God, given the bearing of motive on goodness in the formation of moral character. In addition, the divine leading would include the causal reality of *God*, rather than a mere "symbol," in human moral experience. It is to be leading by and to *God's* perfect moral character, beyond any symbol involved. So, a false myth devoid of a divine causal reality would not serve the redemptive purpose in question. It would misrepresent the central aim of Jesus regarding God.

A motive of willing personal resolve toward trusting and loving God and Jesus could benefit one's enduring in faith and love toward God and Jesus when opposition arises. It could contribute to a kind of personally involved responsibility and ownership toward one's

---

[33] Van Austin Harvey, *The Historian and the Believer: The Morality of Historical Knowledge and Christian Belief* (New York: Macmillan, 1966), pp. 280–1.

commitment toward God and Jesus. So, we should not be surprised by the relevance of an inquirer's motive in coming to know who Jesus was or is. (Chapter 5 examines this consideration in connection with the parables of Jesus.)

The moral gravity of Jesus as inquirer of us indicates that he is not after a parlor game, a spectator sport, or a merely intellectual puzzle for us. His self-referential question puts my moral adequacy and my corresponding adequacy in discernment (about his status relative to God) under question relative to him and to God, in a way that can challenge bias or prejudice in my inquiry. If he or God seeks firsthand acquaintance with me, this kind of I–Thou encounter would be partly up to me as a free agent in this area. I could reject being in God's presence in a morally challenging way, by turning away to other matters. I could refuse the divine moral challenge, such as when I suppress the workings of my conscience or choose to be distracted by something else, perhaps even by truth-seeking of lesser importance.

My properly knowing the challenge of me by God's moral character represented by Jesus would require the kind of ethical knowing suggested by von Hügel. It would require that I acknowledge the sharp contrast between God's moral character and my own, given my moral shortcomings and failures. This acknowledgment could be the beginning of my cooperative turning toward God as a change of my moral direction and purpose, but the actual turning by me would depend on my volitional cooperation. I should not expect to be a divinely controlled pawn for God, if God seeks what is good overall for others.

The self-referential application of the question from Jesus leads to another decisive question. *Whose* question takes priority: Jesus's question of me or my various questions regarding him? Who has authority in this area? This is a matter of *lordship*, and our approach to it will reveal what, or who, has lordship *for us* in this area. We often think of our questions as morally neutral but they actually can be morally revealing about us and our priorities. They show what we value in inquiry, and often in what order of priority. We shall see that Jesus took the matter of God's lordship seriously and insisted on singularity of commitment here (Matt. 6:24, Luke 16:13).

If Jesus has moral authority for us, his morally relevant questions should be acknowledged for their priority relative to our questions of him. Inquirers, in any case, will decide about the moral authority of Jesus for them in how they approach the self-referential question from Jesus relative to their own questions. In doing so, inquirers should consider that God and Jesus could self-reveal commensurate with how those inquirers will respond, in terms of their own cooperative self-revealing to God (for instance, in comparing themselves candidly to the moral character of Jesus). This would include their allowing themselves to be "known by God," in the language of the apostle Paul (Gal. 4:9, 1 Cor. 8:3). (Chapter 2 returns to the topic of being known by God.)

Jesus raises the question "Who do you say that I am?" not just to get our answers but also to prepare for his own answer that reveals his ultimate purpose. That purpose includes his setting his mind, with active cooperation, on "the things of God," in particular, God's redemptive will or mission for him as God's special emissary seeking the reconciliation of humans to God. By this standard, a suitable understanding of who Jesus was or is relates Jesus to God as one who supremely committed himself to God's redemptive purpose for him and who challenges, at least with his self-referential question, other humans to do the same. Our impact–response method of inquiry points us to the central role of that purpose in understanding who Jesus is as a person. We need to consider how such a purpose could be disclosed to us in a redemptive manner.

1.4 PURPOSE DISCLOSED

With regard to "knowing a person," we may think of a person as a conscious intentional agent who aims or wills to satisfy a purpose or goal. A purpose is sought or pursued by the person for it to be satisfied, actualized, or realized. The person thus has *settled* on a purpose with a *volitional* resolve or commitment that goes beyond thought, belief, or desire. (For instance, I do not *simply* think, believe, or desire that I write this paragraph as I *intend* to write it.) Being willing to act, under certain conditions, by a person is central to being a person; without it, we do not have a person or a personal agent influencing human history (even if we have a human body). Understanding who a person is, then, will include understanding intentions or purposes of that person. A person's purposes contribute to who that person is and seeks to be, in satisfying those purposes.

The Oxford English Dictionary, 2nd edition, presents the following as its first definition of the noun "purpose": "That which a person sets out to do or attain; an object in view; a determined intention or aim."[34] One's "setting out" to do something includes one's *settling* on doing it, one's resolving or willing to do it. The "object in view" is *what* one aims or intends to bring about, to actualize, as a goal. So, this is not just one's thinking, believing, or desiring regarding something, such as a merely intellectual plan; instead, it includes one's willing to actualize an outcome.

Whatever persons are, they are not *mere processes* or *mere things*. Their purposes distinguish them from such processes or things. They have a distinctive kind of *goal-directedness* that is lacking in mere processes or things. They thus are intentional agents irreducible to mere events. They have distinctive power to act, to implement a will toward a goal. This is *intentional* power, and it is foreign

---

[34] *The Oxford English Dictionary*, 2nd ed. (Oxford: Oxford University Press, 1989).

to the world of mere processes or things. Mere causal power can be found among mere processes or things, but intentional power is not *mere* causal power. Instead, intentional power is casual power *directed* or *guided* toward a goal. I now am exercising, for instance, the intentional causal power toward finishing this paragraph, regardless of whether I succeed in finishing it. The world of mere processes or things does not exercise such power, whatever else it exhibits.

Some intentional powers are positive moral virtues and others are not. For instance, the intentional power to love a person unselfishly for that person's good is a positive moral virtue, but the intentional power to hate a person is not. From a moral point of view, the power to hate, in aiming to harm an undeserving person, contradicts morally virtuous power that aims to bring about what is morally good for persons. So, the intentional power central to being a person need not be morally virtuous, and it can be immoral.

Our understanding Jesus as a person requires our having a purposive understanding of who he was or is, and not just an understanding of his merely physical features. The needed understanding will identify purposes that guided or guide his thinking and his behaving, and it thus will entail that he was or is irreducible to a merely physical process or thing. It will characterize him as a *psychological agent* with purposive features irreducible to physical features. We thus will identify what Jesus *aimed to accomplish* in his earthly mission. In doing so, we will clarify some of his goals for his life. This effort will make some sense of who he was or is as a person in relation to his ends. We shall postpone for now the question of whether he is currently a living person, but that question will emerge in due course.

We now can see the bearing of our impact–response model on inquiry about who Jesus was or is as a person with identifiable purposes. It seeks a distinctive kind of knowledge of a person on the basis of identified purposes of that person. This method isolates and assesses our available evidence for the ultimate and the instrumental purposes of Jesus. It relies on abduction as a best available explanation of our overall experience and resulting evidence to isolate which claims about Jesus and his main purposes are credible relative to that evidence.[35] The claims that figure in a best available explanation relative to our overall experience accrue a positive epistemic status, in the absence of defeaters.

According to our best available explanation, Jesus's ultimate purpose included his pleasing God from wholehearted love of God (Mark 12:30), and this purpose underwrote his aim to fulfill his redemptive mission from God for advancing divine goodness among other humans. His mission included his probing question for his inquirers: Who do you say that I am? This question was prompted not only by that explicit formulation but also by many of his striking nonverbal actions. We see this, for instance, in the case of his disciples' response to his saving them from panic in a storm. His nonverbal actions prompted the question from them "Who then is this man?" (Mark 4:41, my translation; cf. Matt. 8:27, Luke 8:25). Nonverbal actions can have an intentional interrogative impact on people, and the question prompted can be: Who is this? We shall see that Jesus acted in ways that raised that question as his audience's response to his impact in word and in deed.

The redemptive purposes of Jesus identifiable in the New Testament can play a role in saving us from what we may call "the excess of a third-person perspective" in inquiry about Jesus. This excess would leave Jesus as a *mere* historical object, an object merely talked about in the third

---

[35] For epistemological details on abduction oriented to empirical experience, with special attention to nonbelief foundational evidence and defeaters, see Moser, *Knowledge and Evidence*. For misgivings about some familiar alternative standards for historical authenticity, see Dale C. Allison, Jr., "How to Marginalize the Traditional Criteria of Authenticity," in *Handbook for the Study of the Historical Jesus*, eds. Tom Holmen and S. E. Porter (Leiden: Brill, 2011), vol. 1, pp. 3–30.

person, without purpose-oriented confrontation with an inquirer. *Perhaps* he is a merely historical person, but the New Testament writers tend to suggest otherwise. According to Paul, for instance, the risen Jesus "became a life-giving spirit" at his resurrection (1 Cor. 15:45), and thus he can work now, and even be met now, in human experience.[36] In particular, his self-referential question of us can be an opportunity for an I–Thou confrontation that challenges and convicts us to turn cooperatively to God for the redemptive purpose of divine–human reconciliation.

A key issue becomes: Do some humans actually confront Jesus at times in his redemptive question and message, perhaps via their conscience? If so, are they willingly convicted by him and his main purpose to conform to God's redemptive will? These two questions raise two more questions *for us* bearing on whether *we* would cooperate with a redemptive disclosure from God and Jesus. First, are *we* as inquirers willing to take seriously a redemptively significant question from God and Jesus about our response to them? Second, if so, are *we* as inquirers willing to cooperate with a challenge, on the basis of suitable evidence, to follow Jesus as the supreme human norm for God?

Our questions resist easy answers from us for two reasons. The first reason is that the self-referential question from Jesus includes his setting a demanding standard for a cooperative response – taking up one's "cross" to follow Jesus in redemptive obedience to God (Mark 8:34). This is no casual, merely intellectual means of cooperative response; instead, it calls for one's *life* being committed to God in cooperation. The second reason is that a cooperative response demands *wholehearted* commitment to God, in keeping with the commitment of Jesus to God, as expressed in his primary command to love God fully. These demanding expectations can lead us not to welcome a confrontation

---

[36] See James D. G. Dunn, "The Spirit of Jesus," in Dunn, *The Christ and the Spirit, vol. 2: Pneumatology* (Grand Rapids, MI: Eerdmans, 1998), pp. 338–41. Chapter 4 returns to this topic.

with God or Jesus and even to try to avoid it, especially if
we prefer to remain mere spectators without personal
moral challenge. As a result, we easily could direct our
attention elsewhere, to less demanding matters. In that
case, we would raise an obstacle to our being confronted
by God or Jesus with intended reconciliation to them.

H. R. Mackintosh has identified how Jesus could function as more than a merely historical object of our inquiry.

Is he more than a dead Jew, who perished about 30 A.D.?
Now, when we look away from books to actual life, we discover that Christ remains past only as long as he is not faced in
the light of conscience. So long as we bring into play our
intellect merely, or the reconstructive fancy of the historian,
he is still far off ... The change comes when we take up the
moral issue. If we turn to him as people keen to gain the
righteous, overcoming life, but conscious so far of failure,
instantly he steps forward out of the page of history,
a tremendous and exacting reality. We cannot read his greatest words, whether of command or promise, without feeling,
as it has been put, that "He not only said these things to people
in Palestine, but is saying them to ourselves now." He gets
home to our conscience in so direct a fashion ... that we feel
and touch him as a present fact.[37]

Mackintosh has in mind a moral (including volitional)
rather than a sensory kind of "feel and touch," in keeping
with the moral character of Jesus. It would be a volitional
confrontation between my will and the will of Jesus.

Since the main purpose of Jesus was or is morally
redemptive on behalf of God, we do well to consider the
option that he aimed to be known for who he truly was or is

---

[37] H. R. Mackintosh, *The Person of Jesus Christ* (London: SCM Press, 1912), p. 33. See
also Mackintosh, *The Doctrine of the Person of Jesus Christ*, pp. 312–20, and James
S. Stewart, "Who Is This Jesus?," in Stewart, *The Strong Name* (Edinburgh: T&T
Clark, 1940), pp. 87–8. Cf. Edwyn Hoskyns and Noel Davey, *The Riddle of the New
Testament* (London: Faber, 1931), pp. 181–2.

via our *moral* experience, discernment, and practice suited
to redemption reflective of God's moral character. If we
omit this moral purpose, we may omit who Jesus truly was
or is, even if we identify a range of historical facts about
him. In that case, we would suffer from a misleading bias in
our inquiry.

We lack evidence of coercion in the intervention of Jesus
in our moral experience. Instead, we have evidence of our
being able to block such intervention. Mackintosh adds:

Like any other fact, he can of course be kept out of our mind
by the withdrawal of attention. But once he has obtained
entrance, and, having entered, has shown us all things that
ever we did, he moves imperiously out of the distant years
into the commanding place in consciousness now and here.
We cross the watershed, in fact, between a merely past and
a present Christ, when we have courage to ask, not only what
we think of Him, but what he thinks of us. For that is to bring
the question under the light of conscience, with the result that
his actual moral supremacy, his piercing judgement of our
lives, now becomes the one absorbing fact. His eyes seem to
follow us, like those of a great portrait. When people accept or
reject him, they do so to his face.[38]

The metaphors of "eyes," "portrait," and "face" are to be
understood in moral terms, with special attention to
a direct volitional challenge to our wills as they go against
the moral will of Jesus and God. We will miss the main
purpose of Jesus if we leave the metaphors in sensory
terms. His redemptive aim goes beyond what is sensory
to what is inherently moral, in keeping with God's moral
character.[39]

[38] Mackintosh, *The Person of Jesus Christ*, p. 34. See also Mackintosh, *The Doctrine of the Person of Jesus Christ*, pp. 318–19.
[39] For discussion, see W. R. Maltby, *The Meaning of the Resurrection* (London: Epworth Press, 1921).

Jesus could be morally demanding not just as a moral inquirer for God but also as a moral *advocate* for God. The role of moral advocacy would be central to his function as the "life-giving spirit" for God. A decisive question about Jesus is thus about his current moral access to an inquirer: Am I willing to let him in to my moral conscience in a way that enables him to be the *Lord* of my moral life? His self-referential question for inquirers leads to that question about my acknowledged authority for moral decision-making.

Is Jesus the personal authority for me, or does something else serve this role? In deciding, on the basis of my overall evidence, I take responsibility and ownership regarding what has moral authority for me. So, coercion of my decision would be out of place. My ability and evidence allow me to turn away from the divine challenge, just as the rich man turned away from Jesus. Otherwise, we would have a morally inadequate story of coercion rather than genuine moral responsibility and responsiveness.

The stakes may be high, but my own decision has an ineliminable role, and my unwilling disposition may prompt divine hiding of self-revelation to me until I become cooperative. (Such hiding would be motivated by divine love and would not be a withdrawal of it.) So, the final question becomes: Who do *I* decide to be in the presence of moral challenge? My answer can come from my response to the self-referential question from Jesus: Who do I say that he is? We thus go beyond mere history to our own current decisions and lives, without neglecting historical evidence. In that case, the historical Jesus could emerge as no longer merely historical.

If we are willing to consider Jesus with due moral sincerity, he could loom large in our moral lives, at least as one who inquires of us on behalf of God while advocating for God. Apart from our allowing his redemptive role in our moral experience, he may become hidden from us, to save us from harmful distortion of him and premature opposition to him. In any case, each inquirer is responsible for examining his or her own relevant evidence in moral experience. We also need to consider our historical evidence regarding who Jesus understood himself to be in relation to God. The following chapters will examine such evidence in connection with our broader moral experience relevant to divine goodness. They thus will take a "both–and" approach to the importance of historical evidence and moral experience in our inquiry.

We are left with the issue of whether we are willing sincerely to consider and to cooperate with a divine intervention in our moral experience. Each of us has a self-referential question to answer here, courtesy of Jesus the inquirer of us. Moral experience is a suitable ground because it could directly reveal *God*, including God's unique moral character, and thus offer God as our ultimate authority underlying any such dependent authority as scripture, tradition, or reason. We have no better authority on offer, but our appropriation of such divine value calls for our moral cooperation, in the manner exemplified by Jesus, in his actions, teachings, and questions. We need to explore the role of God in our moral experience as a context for making sense of Jesus. That context will enable us to illuminate the distinctiveness of Jesus in relation to divine goodness.

2

~

God through Divine Goodness

Our view of God tends to color our view of Jesus – in particular, our understanding of who he was or is. If, for instance, we have doubts about God's existence or providence, we will tend to find Jesus misguided on his main teachings regarding God. If, however, we share Jesus's general view of God, we will tend to find Jesus credible in his main teachings, and we may even acknowledge a special status for him in relation to God. We should ask, then, if there is a compelling basis for sharing his general view of God. Such a basis is arguably available in moral experience of a distinctive kind. Our examination of this kind of moral experience will supply a context for understanding who Jesus was or is. It will illuminate the kind of God he promoted and followed as the center of his life. Inadequate attention to his God will leave serious misunderstanding about Jesus in its wake.

2.1 ACCOUNTABLE KNOWING

Theologians, philosophers, and others have explored how humans could have knowledge of God, and the results have been mixed at best. A more fruitful topic concerns how God could have knowledge of humans that is morally beneficial to them in a way that yields human knowledge of God. In this alternative, redemptive human knowledge of God stems from God's knowledge of humans that is morally beneficial to them as they willingly become *accountable responders* to God's interventions in their moral experience. This chapter explores this widely neglected option. It contends that being known by God in a morally beneficial way is uniquely viable for having redemptive human knowledge of God, and that such knowledge is grounded in evidence central to a person's moral identity and status before God. This kind of knowledge, we shall see, differs from mere factual knowledge that something is the case.

This chapter's perspective gains credibility if God seeks the *moral redemption* of humans as their being responsible, responsive, and reconciled to God in their agreeably cooperating with God in divine goodness. In that case, we should expect God to self-reveal to humans in ways that are morally beneficial to them and even morally searching of them as they become responsive, in an accountable manner, to God's moral challenges. Even so, humans could refrain from cooperating with God and even oppose it.

Being responsive in an accountable manner to God includes being responsive if God calls one either to give account for or to justify one's response to moral challenges in experience that manifest divine goodness. God would seek to attract a person to sympathetic cooperation with divine–human reconciliation on the basis of this goodness, and the attracting would avoid coercing a human will. The resulting accountability applies primarily to *persons* in a moral relationship but it can apply derivatively to actions and attitudes. We shall develop and assess the *theistic accountableism* introduced in Chapter 1 regarding redemptive human knowledge of God: the view that such knowledge can, and often does, arise from accountable human responses to God's intervening in human experience. We also shall identify a unique cognitive role for interpersonal conscience and for Jesus as revealer in such knowledge.

Accountableism about knowledge of God stems from a broader biblical theme about the importance of

accountable human *living to God* and not just to some lesser
reality, such as a moral law. This theme was represented
by Paul: "Through the law I died to the law, so that I might
live to God" (Gal. 2:19). He put the theme more broadly:
"We do not live to ourselves, and we do not die to ourselves. If we live, we live to the Lord, and if we die, we die
to the Lord; so then, whether we live or whether we die, we
are the Lord's" (Rom. 14:7–8; cf. 1 Cor. 6:20, 7:23). Paul thus
remarked: "I do not even judge myself. It is the Lord who
judges me" (1 Cor. 4:3–4). Leander Keck has captured
Paul's position: "For the accountable self, loyalty to God
is the non-negotiable starting point and guiding factor
in deciding what is to be done or not done, because – for
Paul at least – the One to whom one is accountable has
already realigned the self's God-relation."[1] Paul thus put
his emphasis for ethical decision-making on a person's
moral relationship with God, and not on autonomous
decision-making apart from God.

Accountableism about human living assumes that
ultimate value resides in pleasing God in an accountable
relationship with God, and not merely in obeying a
moral law or in satisfying some other value or principle
apart from pleasing God. According to such accountableism, God has the prerogative to deepen divine moral
expectations of humans by superseding previous divine
commands and laws given to them. God would have the
right to try to work with people at the level of their
moral understanding, and this could include God starting with expressed expectations that fall short of God's
perfect moral character and will. In the latter case, God
would be in a position later to raise the moral bar for
humans, seeking to bring them closer to agreement with
the divine goodness in God's perfect moral character
and will.

[1] Leander Keck, "The Accountable Self," in Keck, *Christ's First Theologian: The Shape of Paul's Thought* (Waco, TX: Baylor University Press, 2015), p. 144.

Progressive revelation arises when God self-reveals to humans while expecting them to move beyond a previous command or law to a more profound moral position that better represents God's perfect moral character. We should consider whether Jesus manifests such progressive revelation in the Sermon on the Mount and elsewhere. For example:

You have heard that it was said, "An eye for an eye and a tooth for a tooth." But I say to you, Do not resist an evildoer. But if anyone strikes you on the right cheek, turn the other also ... You have heard that it was said, "You shall love your neighbor and hate your enemy." But I say to you, Love your enemies and pray for those who persecute you, so that you may be children of your Father in heaven; for he makes his sun rise on the evil and on the good, and sends rain on the righteous and on the unrighteous ... Be perfect, therefore, as your heavenly Father is perfect. (Matt. 5:38–9, 43–5, 48)

Jesus began with a citation from the Jewish Bible but then offered a contrasting moral standard after "But I say to you." His basis for the contrast was being "children of your Father in heaven," with the accompanying standard set by sharing in God's perfect moral character: "Be perfect ... as your heavenly Father is perfect" (cf. Luke 6:36).

We may understand Jesus as commending our accountably living to God, as God's children, in order to please God by receiving and reflecting God's perfect moral character. Accountableism about human living implies that humans are accountable to God in that way, above all else. Some of the parables of Jesus highlight such human accountability to God (see, e.g., Matt. 24:45–51, 25:14–30, Luke 16:1–9). (Chapter 5 returns to the purpose of his parables.)

As suggested, a person's being responsive to God in an accountable manner includes that person's being responsive if God demands an account or a justification from that person for a response. An *approved* accountable response has an account or a justification for itself approved by God. If, for instance, God calls a person to undertake a particular mission, that person could respond cooperatively, with the motive of putting God's will first in the mission. That motive could yield an account or a justification for the person's response that is approved by God. In that case, the human response would be approvedly accountable before God, because it would be pleasing to God. In contrast, an *unapproved* accountable response has an account or a justification for itself not approved by God. Cases of intentionally disobeying God would serve as typical examples.

An exemplary case of approved accountability is the filial response of Jesus to God in Gethsemane. After initial hesitation, he responded cooperatively to God's call to lay down his life for others, and he was motivated by the expressed intention and plan (or account) to put God's will, rather than his own will, first in his life: "He said, 'Abba, Father, for you all things are possible; remove this cup from me; yet, not what I want, but what you want'" (Mark 14:36; cf. Matt. 26:39, Luke 22:42). Gethsemane thus shows Jesus living accountably to God in a way approved by God, and this offers a model for other humans.[2] We turn to the bearing of accountableism on human knowledge of God.

2.2 SOME BIBLICAL DATA

Some biblical materials enable us to elucidate accountableism about redemptive human knowledge of God. Part of Psalm 139 is illuminating for our topic, because it acknowledges a cognitive role for God in human moral experience.

---

[2] Chapter 3 clarifies the filial responsiveness of Jesus to God as his Father, proposing that it serves as the center of his self-understanding and redemptive mission.

O Lord, you have searched me and known [וַתֵּדָע] me.
You know when I sit down and when I rise up;
you discern my thoughts from far away.
You search out my path and my lying down,
and are acquainted with all my ways.
Search me, O God, and know [וְדַע] my heart;
test me and know [וְדַע] my thoughts.
See if there is any wicked way in me,
and lead me in the way everlasting.

(Psalm 139:1–3, 23–4)

God's knowing the psalmist in this context is not abstract
or merely theoretical. It is, instead, experience-oriented and
morally practical, with the focus on God searching and
knowing *the psalmist,* and not just truths about the psalmist.
This focus includes God searching and knowing the psalmist interpersonally in the psalmist's moral character and
attitudes relative to God's presented righteous character.
Such knowing is *morally searching* in its arising from God
seeking to know interpersonally, through interacting and
testing in human experience, the moral condition and
inclination of the psalmist. (On divine moral testing of
humans, see also Job 7:17–19.)[3]
    The divine searching aims to reveal, at least to the psalm-
ist, his chosen response to God manifesting divine goodness and what accounts for his response to that goodness.
If he is not attracted to agreeable cooperation with God by
the manifested goodness, he should explore why that is so.
A key issue is whether the account or justification for his
response involves a motive approved by God, and that
issue includes the question of whether his motive puts
God's will first in his life. So, as suggested, the morally

---

[3] Theological writers have used the phrase "known by God" with various senses, but
our focus will be guided by the morally relevant theological sense of Psalm 139. For
some other senses, see Brian S. Rosner, "Known by God," *Tyndale Bulletin* 59 (2008),
207–30. With influence from the apostle Paul, P. T. Forsyth used the idea in his
theistic epistemology; see Forsyth, *The Principle of Authority* (London: Hodder and
Stoughton, 1913), pp. 99–101.

searching knowing in question is not just factual knowledge that something is the case; it is intended to reveal
human accountability before God, in particular, to reveal
that the psalmist is being held accountable *by God*. It also
aims to reveal whether the psalmist's motive for his
response is approved by God. The knowledge stemming
from such revealing directs the psalmist to consider and to
value God's moral character for the sake of a morally beneficial, redemptive relationship with God.

The psalmist requests of God: "Search me, O God, and
know my heart; test me and know my thoughts." The fact
of this request suggests that God's interpersonal knowledge of the psalmist depends on the *willingness* of the
psalmist to be known by God. So, the knowledge does not
emerge without the psalmist's intention to have it arise and
thus without his cooperating with its arising. Otherwise,
the request by the psalmist would be dispensable, and the
key personally interactive feature would be omitted. In this
regard, the knowledge is cooperative and interpersonal
rather than one-sided and unilateral. It has an *interpersonal
mutuality* in being desired and valued both by a human
known by God and by God. Matthew's Gospel evidently
attributes an accountableist understanding of knowledge
to Jesus when he says to some uncooperative people:
"I never knew you" (Matt. 7:23).

Humans known by God, in the relevant sense, must
value the knowledge enough to welcome it from God,
even if it brings some turbulence to their lives. So, the
interpersonal knowledge in question is mutually voluntary, on the part of humans and God. God does not force
the matter by proceeding unilaterally, but instead allows
the knowledge to arise as freely interactive with humans.
This allows for the genuine accountability of humans, free
of coercion of their wills, in their response to divine interventions in human experience. It thus allows for their
genuine agency as potential responders to God who can
either choose, reject, or ignore cooperation with God in

manifesting divine goodness, including divine love for humans.

An aim of God in intervening and searching in the moral experience of humans, according to the psalmist, is to "lead [them] in the way everlasting" – that is, in God's way of divine goodness (Psalm 139:24). The same idea emerges in Psalm 23:3: "He leads me in paths of righteousness for his name's sake." Such divine leading has a special role, too, in the teaching of Jesus about prayer: "Lead us not into temptation" (Matt. 6:13, RSV). It also figures centrally in the theology of Paul: "All who are led by the Spirit of God are children of God" (Rom. 8:14). This divine leading, as suggested, is not coercive of humans; they can resist it, and sometimes they do.

Divine leading relies on manifested divine goodness, including divine love, to *attract* people voluntarily to be led, and it aims for human moral improvement in leading people to cooperate willingly with God toward their moral righteousness, in a right relationship with God and others. This divine effort toward the good of all concerned would seek to advance a community, society, or kingdom of people flourishing in God's characteristic moral goodness. C. H. Dodd thus identifies the following intention of Jesus: "His aim was to constitute a community worthy of the name of a people of God, a divine commonwealth, through individual response to God coming in his kingdom."[4]

A morally good God would aim for a moral kingdom offering righteousness, in right relationships, for all willing people. A God who does not seek to lead in that way would not be the Lord worthy of worship, owing to a failure in moral leadership. As a result, God would engage in the *intended moral leading* of cooperative people toward divine righteousness on the basis of their experiencing divine goodness. This would be a main intended impact of God upon humans for their moral good. Such intended leading

---

[4] Dodd, *The Founder of Christianity*, p. 90.

would be a key component of divine self-manifestation in human experience and of morally beneficial knowledge of God for humans that arises from divine moral searching. God would hold people accountable for their responses to this kind of intended leading of them. In doing so, God would manifest the profound moral importance for humans of being led by the divine goodness of God's righteous character and will. This consideration fits well with the focus of the impact–response model of interpretation we have proposed.

Intended moral leading would be an indicator of God's *personal* character as an *intentional*, or goal-directed, moral agent. It would indicate a personal agent irreducible to mere processes, events, or things. It would *aim* to attract a voluntary moral response from humans that fits with God's moral character, for the benefit of the responders. Even so, it could fail, given human opposition or indifference; people could fail to value manifested divine goodness, including divine love. God, then, would have no guarantee of success in the intended moral leading. Such is the price of interacting with free moral agents, and we should expect a redemptive God to pay that price in an effort to build a community of morally responsible agents committed to divine goodness. (Chapter 8 returns to this topic as God's gambit.)

God could bring turbulence to human experience in various ways for the moral benefit of people. Paul identified one way God brings anti-God human ways to frustration and futility: "The creation was subjected to futility, not of its own will but by the will of the one who subjected it, in hope that the creation itself will be set free from its bondage to decay and will obtain the freedom of the glory of the children of God" (Rom. 8:20–1). God thus would frustrate the achievement of various human goals opposed to God in order to challenge people to embrace divine ways as better alternatives. Psalm 139:5 suggests the limiting part of such a divine strategy: "You hem me in, behind and before, and lay your hand upon me." The parameters set by God, however frustrating, would have a redemptive purpose: to lead people, with their cooperation, in the righteous ways of God for their own moral benefit.

A morally searching challenge from God could come by way of a troubled conscience in a person. Paul acknowledged this in his role for conscience as bearing witness to the law of God and thereby to the moral character of God (Rom. 2:15; cf. Rom. 9:1, 1 Cor. 4:3–4, 2 Cor. 1:12).[5] Suppose, for example, that I intend to take advantage of a friend for my own financial gain. As I make my plan, however, I face a guilty conscience about my intention to exploit my friend. My conscience presents me with a morally better alternative. It shows me a good moral character that benefits rather than exploits him, cares for him rather than steals from him. This moral character stands in sharp contrast to my own moral character, particularly in connection with my intention to exploit my friend. My conscience did not necessarily present me with such a good moral character, but, as it happens, it does, even though I did not ask for it or seek it. This was an intrusion in my moral experience, for my good. It was an impact on me of genuine good, and it calls for a response from me.

The moral contrast in my experience puts me in a morally challenging situation. It prompts me to decide between my dubious moral character and the morally good alternative presented in my conscience. This alternative, in Paul's thinking, would be *God's* moral character, perhaps shown in the divine law, that challenges my covetousness and other unrighteousness. It would include God using divine moral presence and action, rather than mere propositional information, to attract and to guide me, without coercing me, toward righteousness and away from greed. Paul characterized such a divine intervention as including

---

[5] For discussion of Paul on conscience, see Paul Lehmann, *Ethics in a Christian Context* (New York: Harper and Row, 1963), pp. 352–67, and C. A. Pierce, *Conscience in the New Testament* (London: SCM Press, 1955), pp. 60–90.

God pouring out divine love in a willing human "heart" as a basis for hope in God (Rom. 5:5). (Romans 2:15 indicates the close connection between the "heart" and conscience in Paul's thinking.) This divine intervention, according to Paul, is morally experiential, and it yields a representation of God's moral character in a human conscience. It thus serves as moral evidence of God's reality and presence.

We may understand divine intervention in moral conscience as part of what Paul meant by "being known by God." Paul talked of being known by God as having a kind of priority in human knowledge of God. He remarked: "Formerly, when you did not know God, you were enslaved to beings that by nature are not gods. Now, however, that you have come to know God, or rather to be known by God, how can you turn back again to the weak and beggarly elemental spirits? How can you want to be enslaved to them again?" (Gal. 4:8–9). Paul's question for the Galatian Christians assumes that being known by God is *morally* significant, bearing on what one values in life. In another context, he suggested that a human motive of love figures in being known by God: "Anyone who loves God is known by him" (1 Cor. 8:3). In this regard, being known by God is morally beneficial for humans – at least given its role for human love of God and its benefits.

The relevant function of conscience, in keeping with etymology, suggests that it is human knowing with God, a *co-knowing* in moral experience with God. It suggests a human knowing of something in agreement with God, at the prompting of divine intervention in moral experience. The deliverances of human conscience are fallible, being susceptible to error. So, they are not to be identified wholesale with the voice or the will of God. They are candidates for divine intervention only when they fit with a perfect moral character suitable to a being worthy of worship. A test question is thus: Does this particular deliverance of conscience represent the moral goodness, including righteousness, characteristic of God? A negative answer recommends a source other than God, lacking in divine authority. In any case, we do not reject a means of receiving data, such as in vision or hearing, just because it is fallible in its deliverances. This policy should apply to conscience, too. In general, humans can reject or suppress a deliverance of conscience, and this allows for our typically being responsible as genuine agents in our decisions regarding conscience.

If our conscience delivers a moral challenge from God to us, it delivers a good gift as well as a serious challenge. The gift would be the self-revealing to us of God's good moral character and will for our moral benefit. It would not be earned by us, because God would take the initiative in self-revealing to us, and we would lack the moral perfection needed to earn divine approval on moral grounds. God would intend the good gift to attract our trust and sympathetic cooperation, rather than our earning, toward God. Even so, what we value could lead us in a different direction – away from God and divine goodness.

An important challenge would be for us to conform, cooperatively, to the good moral character and will self-revealed to us. This conforming would benefit our own moral character, including in relation to others. We would be challenged to acknowledge our own moral deficiency relative to God's presented moral character and will, and to turn away from that deficiency by repenting of it. The redemptive focus, however, would be on our turning *to God*, in sympathetic cooperation with God's character and will. Even if our cooperation is morally imperfect, it still could be cooperation as our primary motive overall toward God.

Jesus gave the parable of the prodigal son to illustrate redemptive turning to God for reconciliation. The striking feature, however, is the response of the son's father in representing God:

[The wayward son] set off and went to his father. But while he was still far off, his father saw him and was filled with compassion; he ran and put his arms around him and kissed him. Then the son said to him, "Father, I have sinned against heaven and before you; I am no longer worthy to be called your son." But the father said to his slaves, "Quickly, bring out a robe – the best one – and put it on him; put a ring on his finger and sandals on his feet. And get the fatted calf and kill it, and let us eat and celebrate; for this son of mine was dead and is alive again; he was lost and is found!" And they began to celebrate. (Luke 15:20–3)[6]

The running father illustrates the eagerness of the divine Father of Jesus for reconciliation with wayward humans. The God portrayed by Jesus takes the initiative in setting up the opportunity for redemption as the cooperative reconciliation of humans to God. We may understand this to be prevenient grace, a divine gift prior to any human effort or merit.

When prompted by dire circumstances (perhaps they, too, include a divine gift, if with subtlety), the wayward son begins to return to his father. His father then expedites the process by running to his son and embracing him. Jesus used this parable to highlight God's gracious and compassionate intervention aimed at reconciling humans to God. Even so, a role for a human moral response is central to the divine redemption of humans as reconciliation to God.

2.3 MORAL RESPONSES

When a moral challenge arises in our conscience, we face three main options: cooperate with it; oppose or suppress it; or be indifferent to it, perhaps by ignoring it. Opposition and indifference amount to the same thing from the standpoint of cooperation; they both block cooperation. If

---

[6] On the historical authenticity of the parable of the prodigal son, see Joseph A. Fitzmyer, *The Gospel According to Luke*, AB (New York: Doubleday, 1985), vol. 1, pp. 1084–5, and Arland J. Hultgren, *The Parables of Jesus* (Grand Rapids, MI: Eerdmans, 2000), pp. 82–4.

indifference is more common than opposition, this may result from its requiring less effort than does opposition. In any case, we typically have genuine options in how we respond to challenges of conscience (assuming that a psychological disorder is not present), and, if God seeks our redemption, we would be accountable to God for how we respond. We then would be expected to be available to give an account or a justification to God for our response.

The aim of divine challenges in conscience would be to reveal to us our moral inferiority relative to God's superior moral character. They also could expose our lack of moral authority in comparison with God, and thereby they could challenge the replacement of God with something inferior in the moral domain. As a result, they would enable us to identify our moral weakness and inadequacy by contrast with the divine goodness of God's impeccable moral character. This could attract us to cooperate with the goodness manifested by God in our experience.

H. Richard Niebuhr comments:

Revelation [from God] is the moment in which we find our judging selves to be judged not by ourselves or our neighbours but by one who knows the final secrets of the heart; revelation means the self-disclosure of the judge. Revelation means that we find ourselves to be valued rather than valuing and that all our values are transvaluated by the activity of a universal valuer ... What this means for us cannot be expressed in the impersonal ways of creeds or other propositions but only in responsive acts of a personal character. We acknowledge revelation by no third person proposition, such as that there is a God, but only in the direct confession of the heart, "Thou are my God."[7]

---

[7] H. Richard Niebuhr, *The Meaning of Revelation* (New York: Macmillan, 1941), pp. 153–4. Similarly, see John Baillie, *Our Knowledge of God* (London: Oxford University Press, 1939), pp. 159–62, 220–4.

Niebuhr's comment should be restricted to *direct* meaning, expression, and acknowledgment of divine revelation, apart from the indirect analogs involving an intermediary of some sort.

People often use creeds and other propositions to try to express or acknowledge indirectly what they experience directly, in direct response to God's personal character. The direct I–Thou nature of the interaction indicates, however, that personal characters are directly interacting, and there may or may not be propositional descriptions, or at least theological descriptions, formulated in the process. The interacting could include God's presented moral character or will setting a standard in human experience, such as in the moral experience of conscience, for the benefit of a human moral character.

If the ultimate source of a moral challenge for a human comes from the self-presentation of God's moral character or will, the challenge would include a clash of interacting moral characters or wills. God's perfect character or will would clash with an imperfect human character or will. We should not expect, however, a *coercive* clash from God's character or will that forces a human will to conform to God's will. Such coercion would be depersonalizing manipulation rather than the benevolent challenge of a good God. The clash would be an opportunity for us to come to our moral senses, responsibly and responsively, and thereby to be attracted to cooperate voluntarily with God's moral character and will.

God would want our motive to be cooperative and welcoming toward God's own perfect character and will. Grudging obedience from us would fall short because it would lack our motivational agreement with God's glad motive in redemption (see, e.g., Luke 12:32). In the absence of our sympathetic agreement, God could hide from us until we are ready to cooperate sympathetically. In that case, more self-revelation from God to us would be premature and ineffective. Our motive in response to divine intervention would matter, and it could call for divine patience and withdrawal of divine presence until an opportune time. God thus would have the ongoing redemptive problem of attracting suitable human motivation for uncoerced cooperation with God.[8]

In embracing sympathetic cooperation with God's redemptive motive, humans would allow God to know them as coworkers in redemption. Being thus known by God, people would welcome God's intervention in their experience with its moral searching, examining, and testing. An important result of human cooperation would be the rearrangement of their priorities to agree (better) with God's self-revealed priorities. As valuers, these people would learn to value as God values, at least in certain respects, and they would value what God values, at least in certain areas. Their direct experience of divine intervention could be accompanied by the indirectness of some moral challenges to them, via contributions from some other humans. It would be unduly restrictive, however, to assume that all moral challenges must be thus indirect. Divine intervention in human moral experience may or may not be indirect, depending on God's purpose and on whether a human relies in the relevant experience on the experience of another human.

2.4 JESUS IN RECONCILIATION

Jesus contributes to accountableism in the New Testament teachings about his mission, and we can identify some relevant features. One traditional approach to Jesus focuses on his metaphysical relation to his divine Father. For instance, the Nicene Creed of 325 CE describes Jesus as "the only Son of God, eternally begotten of the Father, God from God, Light from Light, true God from true

---

[8] On the importance of audience motive for the teaching of Jesus, including his parables, see Chapter 5. On the relevance of divine hiding to the teaching of Jesus, see Chapter 4.

God, begotten, not made, of one Being [*homoousion*] with the Father." The New Testament writings tend to have a different kind of focus on Jesus. They emphasize his functional relation to God and humans. For instance, they portray him as the unique and authoritative filial revealer of God, as one who serves God and others in the redemption of humans, and as the one who will judge others for God. The talk of Jesus as "the Son of Man" in the synoptic Gospels likewise has a functional emphasis regarding his representing God and humans in the divine kingdom, in suffering and in exaltation.[9]

The following distinction adds some clarity: A characterization of Jesus is *mainly functional* if its main focus is on *how Jesus serves* as an agent of God; in contrast, a characterization of Jesus is *mainly metaphysical* if its main focus is on *the constitution or make-up*, rather than the function, of Jesus in relation to God. The New Testament writings are thin on mainly metaphysical characterizations of Jesus, but they offer a range of mainly functional characterizations. A mainly functional characterization of Jesus can, and typically will, have some metaphysical implications regarding him. For instance, talk of Jesus as God's unique filial revealer entails that Jesus is an intentional agent with a will that can be used to reveal God in various intentional ways. A mainly functional characterization of Jesus, however, does not have the constitution or makeup of Jesus in relation to God as its *main* focus. We shall focus on a mainly functional characterization in order to highlight the role of Jesus in divine–human reconciliation.[10]

---

[9] For explanation of the self-understanding of Jesus in connection with his role as "the son of man" and as the gatekeeper for God's kingdom, see Chapters 6 and 7.

[10] In this regard, I share the general approach to understanding Jesus found in such twentieth-century philosophical theologians as P. T. Forsyth, H. R. Mackintosh, John Baillie, and H. H. Farmer. See Forsyth, *God of Holy Love*, eds. Paul K. Moser and Benjamin Nasmith (Eugene, OR: Pickwick/Wipf & Stock Publications, 2019), Mackintosh, *God in Experience*, eds. Paul K. Moser and Benjamin Nasmith (Eugene, OR: Pickwick/Wipf & Stock Publications, 2018), Baillie, *The Place of Jesus Christ in Modern Christianity* (New York: Charles Scribner's Sons, 1929), and Farmer, *The Word of Reconciliation* (New York: Abingdon, 1966). For a mainly functional

The following passage bears on characterizing Jesus in relation to accountableism:

At that time Jesus said, "I thank you, Father, Lord of heaven and earth, because you have hidden these things from the wise and the intelligent and have revealed them to infants; yes, Father, for such was your gracious will. All things have been handed over to me by my Father; and no one knows the Son except the Father, and no one knows the Father except the Son and anyone to whom the Son chooses to reveal him." (Matt. 11:25–7; cf. Luke 10:21–2)

Jesus assumes that God is related to him as his Father, but he does not offer a mainly metaphysical characterization of this relation. Instead, his characterization is mainly functional, here in terms of his being the unique filial revealer of his Father for humans: "No one knows the Father except the Son and anyone to whom the Son chooses to reveal him." Jesus has this functional role given that "all things have been handed over to [him] by [his] Father."[11]

An important issue concerns how Jesus reveals his Father. A related issue concerns what, if anything, indicates that his revealing his Father is actually present, rather than merely apparent, to a person. These questions matter because there are many ways to be wrong about whether a person experiences Jesus revealing his Father. In the perspective of Paul, as Chapter 1 noted, Jesus reveals God beyond his mission as a merely historical human. This role,

---

approach to Christological titles, see Cullmann, *The Christology of the New Testament*. For an illustration of how a mainly metaphysical approach to Christology raises problems, see Mackintosh, *The Doctrine of the Person of Jesus Christ*, pp. 209–15, and Baillie, *The Place of Jesus Christ in Modern Christianity*, pp. 123–36. Cf. Morna D. Hooker, "Chalcedon and the New Testament," in *The Making and Remaking of Christian Doctrine*, eds. Sarah Coakley and David A. Pailin (Oxford: Clarendon Press, 1993), pp. 73–93.

[11] On the historical authenticity of Matthew 11:25–7 and its parallel in Luke's Gospel, see Davies and Allison, *A Critical and Exegetical Commentary on the Gospel According to Saint Matthew*, vol. 2, pp. 271–97, and Fitzmyer, *The Gospel According to Luke*, vol. 2, pp. 868–70.

according to Paul, is clarified in what Jesus became after his resurrection, and it bears on an understanding of who Jesus is. Paul says of Jesus: "The last Adam became a life-giving spirit" (1 Cor. 15:45), and he reports that "God has sent the Spirit of his Son into our hearts, crying, 'Abba! Father!'" (Gal. 4:6; cf. Rom. 8:15–16), thus suggesting that a filial relationship with God is significant. Paul does not offer a mainly metaphysical characterization, but he does give us an idea of the functional role of the life-giving spirit identified with Jesus.

Paul comments on the kind of life-giving Jesus offers:

The love of Christ urges us on, because we are convinced that one has died for all; therefore, all have died. And he died for all, so that those who live might live no longer for themselves, but for him who died and was raised for them. From now on, therefore, we regard no one from a human point of view [κατὰ σάρκα]; even though we once knew Christ from a human point of view, we know him no longer in that way. So, if anyone is in Christ, there is a new creation: everything old has passed away; see, everything has become new! (2 Cor. 5:14–17)

Three points stand out here, in relation to the accountable-ism on offer. First, Paul identifies the importance of Jesus giving his life "so that those who live might live no longer for themselves, but *for him* who died and was raised for them" (italics added). The primary importance of living for Christ requires, in Paul's thought, human accountability to him as God's representative, rather than living just for some principle or law. This agrees with the accountableism about human life we have identified.

Second, Paul sees Christ's life-giving work in terms of the motivational power of Christ's love for some people: "The love of [that is, from] Christ urges us on," or attracts and moves us, toward cooperation with God's self-giving moral character. As suggested previously, Paul expresses a closely related idea: "Hope [in God] does not disappoint us, because

God's love has been poured into our hearts through the Holy Spirit that has been given to us" (Rom. 5:5). Love from God, according to Paul, can emerge in human experience in a way that worthily attracts, motivates, or empowers a person to live for God. It thereby can save that person from disappointment about the value or the purpose of human life and about the evidence of divine reality in human life. It can be the kind of evidence that enables one to give an account of one's conduct to God, an account approved by God. It also can be combined with considerable mystery and with the absence of a theodicy as a comprehensive explanation of divine purposes in allowing evil or in divine hiding.[12]

The relevant evidence, according to Paul, is in the divine love attracting, convicting, and guiding a person in life, and such love can yield a human experience of forgiveness and reconciliation from God.[13] This is not a mechanical or coercive process in Paul's understanding. It demands a cooperative human response, and Paul thinks of this response as part of faith in God or Christ. He thus portrays the relevant faith as being "energized [ἐνεργουμένη] by love" – that is divine love (Gal. 5:6, my translation). Such a faith response to God figures in what Paul calls "the obedience of faith" (Rom. 1:5, 16:26). It includes agreeable human resolve to cooperate with the divine goodness of God's character and will as manifested in Christ and in human experience. Paul understands the divine manifestation in Jesus, who relinquished his prior existence with God, as follows: "You know the generous act of our Lord Jesus Christ, that though he was rich, yet for your sakes he

---

[12] For an explanation of how New Testament Christology bears on theodicy, see Paul K. Moser, "Theodicy, Christology, and Divine Hiding," *Expository Times* 129 (2018), 191–200. See also Chapter 8.

[13] For discussion of the role of divine love as evidence, see Moser, *Understanding Religious Experience*, chap. 7. On the human experience of divine forgiveness and reconciliation, see H. R. Mackintosh, *The Christian Experience of Forgiveness* (New York: Harper, 1927), Vincent Taylor, *Forgiveness and Reconciliation* (London: Macmillan, 1941), and Moule, "The Energy of God," pp. 99–103.

became poor, so that by his poverty you might become rich" (2 Cor. 8:9; cf. Phil. 2:5–7).[14]

Third, Paul regards Christ's life-giving work as leading to some humans knowing Christ, but not from "a human point of view," or "according to flesh" as antithetical to God. Knowing from a human point of view, in Paul's perspective, contrasts with knowing from *God's* point of view, that is, the unique perspective of divine redemptive power as exemplified in Christ (1 Cor. 1:26–30, 2:6–13).[15] Knowing Christ from a divine point of view acknowledges him as God's agent of divine–human reconciliation, in a manner suited to such reconciliation in Christ. Paul thus says: "In Christ God was reconciling the world to himself, not counting their trespasses against them, and entrusting the message of reconciliation to us. So, we are ambassadors for Christ, since God is making his appeal through us; we entreat you on behalf of Christ, be reconciled to God" (2 Cor. 5:10–20).[16]

Paul thinks of redemption as entailing reconciliation to God, and he thinks of knowing Christ from God's point of view as effective for reconciliation to God. Going beyond merely factual knowledge that something is so, such knowing is *reconciliatory* knowing, and it entails accountability to God for one's response to divine intervention in one's experience. So, Paul's epistemological approach involving the risen Christ fits with the accountableism

---

[14] See Victor Paul Furnish, *II Corinthians*, AB (New York: Doubleday, 1984), pp. 416–18, and Ralph P. Martin, *2 Corinthians*, WBC (Waco, TX: Word Books, 1986), pp. 262–4.

[15] For a proposal to understand Paul on knowing from a human point of view in terms of self-seeking knowledge at odds with the character of Christ and God, see Margaret E. Thrall, "Christ Crucified or Second Adam? A Christological Debate between Paul and the Corinthians," in *Christ and Spirit in the New Testament*, eds. Barnabas Lindars and Stephen S. Smalley (Cambridge: Cambridge University Press, 1973), pp. 152–6.

[16] On the role of Jesus in reconciliation in the New Testament, see Peter Stuhlmacher, "Jesus as Reconciler," in *Reconciliation, Law, and Righteousness*, trans. E. R. Kalin (Philadelphia: Fortress Press, 1986), pp. 1–15, Ralph P. Martin, *Reconciliation: A Study of Paul's Theology* (Atlanta: John Knox Press, 1981), pp. 201–33, and I. Howard Marshall, *Aspects of the Atonement* (Milton Keynes: Paternoster, 2007), chap. 4. See also Farmer, *The Word of Reconciliation*. Chapter 4 returns to this topic.

about knowledge under consideration. By means of self-manifestation, climactically (but not exclusively) through Christ, God seeks to reveal to a person that person's moral standing before God and thereby to encourage turning to God cooperatively. This kind of moral challenge reveals God's reality and presence to a person, supremely through Christ, thereby leaving that person with evidence and accountability regarding God. Reconciliatory evidence and knowledge regarding God are thus irreducibly interpersonal and morally challenging.

Accountableism about human knowledge of God makes sense if God, as perfectly redemptive, aims for us to learn to love as God loves, including to love our enemies. In that case, God's self-revelation typically would be morally challenging for us to that end. In addition, we would be accountable for our response to God in the process. For an approved response, we would need to avoid opposition and indifference toward divine interventions in our moral experience, including in moral conscience. We would need to opt for due cooperation.

The fitting way of knowing Christ suggested by Paul entails a "new creation" that includes our moral renewal on the basis of divine love manifested to us.[17] Such renewal comes by way of what Paul calls "being known by God." In being thus known, we cooperate with God's renewal of us, by allowing God to show us our inferior moral character relative to God's perfect moral character. We also allow God to empower us to conform to God's moral character, often through considerable struggle against our selfishness. In doing so, we can benefit from social influences as others cooperate with us toward God's redemptive will, but the ultimate power would be in divine goodness. We would appropriate that morally significant power as we cooperate with it.

---

[17] On the role of new creation in Paul's thought, see Moyer V. Hubbard, *New Creation in Paul's Letters and Thought*, SNTSMS (Cambridge: Cambridge University Press, 2002).

When we find ourselves being attracted and *led* increasingly toward moral renewal (cf. Rom. 8:14), we rightly deem the leading to be *intentional*, and, given fitting evidence in our moral experience, to be something intended by God as a *personal* agent. Suitable moral experience representative of God's character and will can provide basic, foundational evidence for God's reality and presence, and it therefore can figure in knowing God as our redemptive Lord. Divine lordship thus includes moral leadership toward God's moral character and will. This is a key feature of the perfect divine goodness central to God's being worthy of worship. Indeed, we may use the term "God" as a perfectionist title requiring worthiness of worship and hence moral perfection in a redemptive effort. The question then becomes whether our experience includes definite evidence of such a redemptive God, and the answer can vary among humans, owing at least to human differences in response to initial divine interventions in experience.

2.5 GOD SELF-AUTHENTICATED

According to accountableism about knowing, God self-authenticates God's reality and presence to a human by knowing that human in a morally challenging and beneficial way. One might argue that this is the only way to get redemptive, reconciliatory knowledge of God's reality and presence. In addition, one might contend that this is the only way to get *any* enduring knowledge of God's reality and presence, given God's unique moral character and purpose. Both positions, I find, are defensible, but their defense would exceed the space of a single chapter. It is more to the point now, for purposes of this book, to consider how God self-authenticates divine reality to some humans in their moral experience in a way that leaves them accountable to God.

Paul offers an injunction for human moral renewal: "Be transformed by the renewing of your minds, so that you may discern what is the will of God – what is good and acceptable and perfect" (Rom. 12:2). He understands such renewal to include profound moral renewal by God as humans yield to God's self-manifestations of divine love in human experience. (Romans 5:5 and 2 Corinthians 5:14, we noted, illustrate Paul's overall position.) More generally, we may speak of intrusions of creative divine goodness in human experience without the coercion of human wills toward God. Such intrusions come with a creative divine intention to attract a person morally to God. They aim, creatively, for one's disclosing oneself morally to God relative to the standard set by divine self-manifestation in one's moral experience. They aim also for our willingly conforming to that self-manifestation and thus our sympathetically cooperating with God's will in our experience. In thus cooperating, we would be in a position to have further moral leading toward God's character and will and thereby to receive further, and more salient, evidence of God's reality and presence.

If accountableism is on the right track, human moral experience matters, and it matters profoundly. Such experience can offer an area of divine evidence in experience for humans that may be overlooked by them as such evidence. God, then, could be trying to self-reveal to some humans who may or may not properly value the kind of divine self-revelation on offer. The question becomes whether humans responsibly value the intrusions of creative divine goodness in their moral experience. If we do not, we could obstruct divine self-authentication (and its evidence) of God's reality and presence in our experience. Given that God's goodness aims for us to cooperate with it, our failing to cooperate would hinder it coming to fruition as what it is intended to be in our experience: something cooperatively received. Our hindering it with such failing could prompt God to hide divine self-manifestation to us until a more opportune time for our responding appropriately. Chapter 4 will indicate that Jesus acknowledged divine hiding of that kind.

The challenge we face, at least as responsible inquirers of Jesus, is to be duly attentive and accountable regarding our moral experience, in a way that safeguards its actual moral character and its potential theological significance. A key issue is whether our experience includes our being challenged to conform to what is morally good, sometimes in conflict with our own preferences and our peers. If so, a related key issue is whether this challenge comes from a moral agent characterized by impeccable moral goodness and by an aim to lead us to cooperate with and to conform to such goodness. The moral experience of different humans can vary in the answers supported, and this fits with a God who can distribute divine self-manifestation variably to humans, as God deems suitably redemptive. God could wait patiently in some cases for people to become willing to respond appropriately, in keeping with God's redemptive intention for self-manifestation and cooperative reconciliation.

Given the accountableism proposed, knowing God is not a spectator sport or an academic pastime; instead, it is a life-defining moral challenge. It focuses on our moral experience in order to make room for God's unique moral reality and presence to be found there. We should expect God to be found there if God is worthy of worship and thus morally perfect. In that case, God will have a quest for our moral renewal that extends to our moral experience. We then will not be left with only abstract or speculative arguments for God's existence. Instead, we will have an evidential basis in our moral experience that forms, with our cooperation, who we are as moral agents. Our evidence and knowledge of God then will be as secure as our moral identity and status in relation to God.

A remaining issue is whether we have the moral courage to face the challenging evidence of a God who holds us accountable, for our own good. Here are left with a human decision that will form a life, for better or worse. Our decision will be a response to God's moral impact on us, in our moral experience, and it will extend to our future. In deciding to cooperate or not with creative divine goodness in our experience, we decide the moral status of our future: in particular, whether our future will be guided by divine goodness aimed at a cooperative redemptive community.

We need to consider how Jesus fits with the kind of redemptive God just portrayed. This God is probing and seeking toward humans for their redemptive good in a community of morally responsible agents. We will consider whether Jesus reflects this kind of God in his teaching and conduct. We also will examine the relation Jesus presumed to have with God. In doing so, we will benefit from understanding who Jesus was or is in his theological context. The issue of his ongoing existence, in relation to God's existence, will get our attention in due course.

3

~

Divine Goodness from *Abba*

Given our historical evidence, Jesus is rightly known for his probing and challenging teachings about God, but he has left us with a difficult question: What, according to the synoptic Gospels, motivated and empowered him to go, willingly, to Jerusalem to undergo suffering and death? So far as we know, he could have chosen to avoid the fatal confrontation in Jerusalem, but he resolved to endure it, despite its tragic end. This situation calls for an explanation in terms of what empowered him to carry out his intention while facing suffering and death. Our explanation will take us to the center of Jesus's self-understanding in relation to God and of his redemptive mission. Jesus understood God as "*Abba*, Father" in the light of the Jewish Bible, but, as we shall see, he factored in his own distinctive experience of God as *Abba*.

3.1 JESUS, AGAPĒ, AND GETHSEMANE

We shall use the Gethsemane narrative of the Gospel of Mark to identify Jesus's *Abba* relationship to God, asking whether Jesus's obedience in Gethsemane was just a means to a more basic end rather than an end in itself. Some New Testament writers suggest a more basic end, in terms of his ultimate *filial relationship* with God, and we shall examine this end. We shall see that obedience is necessary but not sufficient for this relationship, because obedient actions fall short of a cooperatively responsive filial relationship with God.

We cannot understand Jesus adequately in Gethsemane without attention to his experience of God at his baptism. Mark's Gospel reports:

In those days Jesus came from Nazareth of Galilee and was baptized by John in the Jordan. And just as he was coming up out of the water, he saw the heavens torn apart and the Spirit descending like a dove on him. And a voice came from heaven, "You are my Son, the Beloved; with you I am well pleased." (Mark 1:9–11; cf. Matt. 3:13–17, Luke 3:21–2)

The report of the baptism of Jesus occurs in all four canonical Gospels, and it comes as a surprise, because John the Baptist called for "a baptism of repentance for the forgiveness of sins" (Mark 1:4).[1] Matthew's Gospel senses the problem, and portrays Jesus as having a purpose not to repent but "to fulfill all righteousness" (Matt. 3:15). Whatever that purpose involves, Jesus did identify, in his undergoing baptism, with John's audience called to repentance, but it does not follow that Jesus himself repented at his baptism. We have no evidence that he expressed a need for repentance from disobeying God.

A central feature of Jesus's baptism is his being proclaimed as God's *beloved* (ἀγαπητός) son. This feature recurs in the parable of the wicked tenants, where Jesus represents himself as God's "beloved son" (υἱὸν ἀγαπητόν) (Mark 12:6; cf. Luke 20:13). We find a similar expression of God's caring attitude toward humans in Jesus's teachings in the Gospels of Matthew and Luke (Matt. 6:26–32, Luke 12:24–30). The theme of being loved, or cared for, by God is not abstract or speculative in the perspective of Jesus. Instead, it has an experiential component as a counter to anxiety, worry, and

---

[1] On the historicity of the gospel reports of the baptism of Jesus by John, see John P. Meier, *A Marginal Jew, vol. 2: Mentor, Message, and Miracles*, ABRL (New York: Doubleday, 1994), pp. 100–16.

fear, and this grounds his injunctions to his disciples not to be anxious, worried, or afraid. Abstract or speculative ideas of divine love would not motivate his injunctions here.

Our best available explanation of Jesus's attitude toward God's love is that he *experienced* this love for himself directly as God's son, and he did not just represent it in a concept or a theory regarding God.[2] His experience of God's love for him included an experience of God's merciful will (cf. Luke 6:36), and this attracted and motivated him to try to please God, in prayer to God and in broader action on behalf of God and others. His experience of divine love thus related him to an attractive personal reality that is volitional, and not merely sentimental or intellectual. It thus could guide his action beyond matters of mere feeling or thinking. We thus find congruence between the overall portrait of him in the New Testament Gospels and his teachings about God's love toward humans.

Jesus's experience of divine love motivated him to seek other people to share in his experience and to benefit them in relating to God as a caring Father. The synoptic Gospels confirm this effort in unison, at many places. Jesus's good news of divine redemption would ring hollow if the motivational experience of divine love valued by him could not be shared by others. It then would reflect poorly on God's moral character in a way that challenges moral perfection and thus worthiness of worship.

Jesus's parable of the lost sheep portrays God as a caring shepherd who rejoices in seeking and finding lost people and bringing them to God:

Which one of you, having a hundred sheep and losing one of them, does not leave the ninety-nine in the wilderness and go

---

[2] For a similar claim about Jesus's experience of sonship under God as Father, see Vincent Taylor, *The Person of Christ in New Testament Teaching* (London: Macmillan, 1958), p. 174, James D. G. Dunn, *Jesus and the Spirit* (London: SCM Press, 1975), pp. 38–9, and Bernard Cooke, *God's Beloved: Jesus' Experience of the Transcendent* (Philadelphia: Trinity Press International, 1992), pp. 13–15.

after the one that is lost until he finds it? When he has found it, he lays it on his shoulders and rejoices. And when he comes home, he calls together his friends and neighbors, saying to them, "Rejoice with me, for I have found my sheep that was lost." (Luke 15:4–6; cf. Matt. 18:10–14)[3]

Jesus added that there is, likewise, "joy in heaven" over a person who turns to God (Luke 15:7). He embraced and practiced the same kind of caring search for others in his mission (Luke 19:10), on the basis of his experience of God's self-giving love for himself and others.

Jesus's experience of divine love left him *feeling indebted* to God for the goodness in his life and the world. Such indebtedness motivated his gratitude and sense of obligation toward God, and it was expressed in his actions, including verbal actions, toward God and others. We get a sense of the indebtedness from his blunt advice to his apostles: "When you have done all that you were ordered to do, say, 'We are worthless slaves; we have done only what we ought to have done!'" (Luke 17:10). Humans, in Jesus's perspective, are not candidates for earning divine love, and they are in no position to begrudge God for divine mercy or generosity, as the parable of the laborers in the vineyard illustrates (Matt. 20:1–15).

An experience-based perspective of a loving God anchored Jesus's responses and relationship to God as his Father. Omitting this perspective would rob Jesus of the center of his self-understanding in relation to God and his mission. Scholarly attention to Jesus often neglects this perspective despite its firm basis in all layers of our literary evidence. We shall clarify how this important perspective figured in his decisive response to God as *Abba* in Gethsemane. His experience of God's love for him and others attracted and grounded his conviction that God is

---

[3] On the historical integrity of the parable of the lost sheep and its variations, including in the Gospel of Thomas, see Hultgren, *The Parables of Jesus*, pp. 46–63.

worthy of, and deserves, cooperative trust and love from humans.

Cooperative filial responsiveness to God, of a sort to be clarified, is central to Jesus's self-understanding in relation to God and hence to his demanding mission. So, religious experience of a distinctive filial sort plays a key role in the identity of Jesus in relation to God. In neglecting this experience and the accompanying filial relationship, we would fail to understand Jesus and his mission. We shall see how this consideration figures importantly in our impact–response model for interpreting Jesus in relation to God. In doing so, we shall find considerable evidence to resist the sweeping skepticism about the self-understanding of Jesus, contrary to some New Testament scholars.

The relevant evidence, we shall see, includes some repeating patterns of literary evidence in the synoptic Gospels. Chapter 1 noted that the evidence is best understood in terms of the *intentional impact* of Jesus on his disciples, given that Jesus himself did not produce writings for posterity. These "impressions," we noted, include "Jesus remembered" by his first disciples, but the impact of Jesus can extend to readers of the synoptic Gospels. We shall see how this impact calls for filial responsiveness to God in a manner reflective of Jesus's relation to God and of his redemptive mission.

In Mark's Gospel, Jesus prays to God in awareness of his impending suffering and death: "*Abba*, Father, for you all things are possible; remove this cup from me; yet, not what I want, but what you want" (Mark 14:36; cf. Matt. 26:39, Luke 22:42). The use of the Aramaic term "*Abba*" in a Greek gospel suggests that the gospel's author aimed to capture an actual expression by Jesus of a filial relationship with God. In addition, Paul offers some confirmation of this term's historical value in relation to Jesus by using it for divinely inspired prayer in two of his Greek epistles (Gal. 4:6, Rom. 8:15–16). Use of this Aramaic term would be odd if the writers did not regard the term as used by Jesus in praying to God as his Father. Our concern, however, is not with how rare Jesus's linguistic use of "*Abba*" for God was for his time, but instead it is with the key features of his relationship with God as *Abba*. His understanding of the *Abba* relationship was distinctive, even though others, too, called God "Father."[4]

According to the author of Mark's Gospel, Jesus was not *just* performing obedient actions in Gethsemane; he was *relating interpersonally and cooperatively to God as his Father*. The difference is important: Jesus could have performed obedient *action* by God's standard but without *relating* interpersonally and cooperatively *to God*. Obedient action does not require a cooperative motive in relating interpersonally to God. For instance, it could be performed grudgingly and without an aim to please God. Jesus, however, did not fit that prospect in his cooperative relating to God.

A key action of Jesus in Gethsemane was his submission of his own will to God's will in his direct response to God, despite his initial preference for an alternative plan. His settled will submitted to God's will even at the expense of his continued earthly life. Paul identified this kind of obedience, rather than physical suffering, as the center of Jesus's submitting himself to God for human redemption (Phil. 2:5–8). The obedience of Jesus in Gethsemane was obedience directly *to God*, in a context of life-directing prayer to God. It thus was directly interpersonal, and no mere submission to a law or a principle. Such Gethsemane prayer to God, according to the synoptic Gospels, was an identifiable feature of Jesus's interpersonal life with God, and it set the personal context for his obedience as willing cooperation in relating to God.

---

[4] For duly cautious discussion of the historical context of Jesus's use of "*Abba*" for God, see Joseph A. Fitzmyer, "*Abba* and Jesus' Relation to God," in *À cause de l'évangile: études sur les synoptiques et les Actes*, LD (Paris: Cerf, 1985), pp. 15–38, James Barr, "*Abba* Isn't 'Daddy'," *Journal of Theological Studies* 39 (1988), 28–47, and Raymond E. Brown, *The Death of the Messiah*, ABRL (New York: Doubleday, 1994), vol. 1, pp. 172–5. These discussions correct some sweeping claims in the literature about the uniqueness of Jesus's linguistic use of the term.

The crisis of Jesus in Gethsemane was a struggle for cooperation with moral power from the presence of God's redemptive will. (We have characterized that will in terms of God's uncoerced directedness toward divine goodness in interpersonal relationships.) The disciples fell asleep, and Jesus responded: "Watch and pray [in order; ἵνα] that you may not enter into temptation; the spirit indeed is willing, but the flesh is weak [ἀσθενής]" (RSV, Mark 14:38; cf. Mark 13:35–7, Matt. 26:41, Luke 22:46). The RSV and the NRSV in its wake translate "ἵνα" in Mark 14:38 (and in Matthew 26:41 and Luke 22:46) as if it indicates *mere content* for the prayer rather than either *a purpose* or *an intended result* for the prayer. This is arguably misleading.

Despite some complexities in translating "ἵνα" in the Greek New Testament,[5] a translation should not foreclose or obscure a natural interpretation of the Greek terms being used. Specifically, a translation should not foreclose or obscure the natural reference of "ἵνα" to a *purpose*, a *goal*, or an *intended result* of Jesus's advised watching and praying by indicating *mere content* of the praying. (The NAB, NEB, REB, and ESV share the defect of the RSV and NRSV.) This is a defect because it obscures the consideration that the relevant *content* for Jesus's advised praying should include, at its center, the content expressed by Jesus: "*Abba*, Father, ... not what I want, but what you want."

A prayer of submission to God, rather than a request to avoid a trial, was central to the Gethsemane response of Jesus. The KJV (AV) is more plausible here; it adds a comma after "watch ye and pray" and inserts "lest ye enter into temptation," thus indicating a purpose or an intended result for the watching and praying, without settling the matter of content.[6] The NIV also indicates

---

[5] See C. F. D. Moule, *An Idiom Book of New Testament Greek*, 2nd ed. (Cambridge: Cambridge University Press, 1959), pp. 142–6.

[6] A similar recommendation occurs in Max Zerwick and Mary Grosvenor, *A Grammatical Analysis of the Greek New Testament*, rev. ed. (Rome: Biblical Institute Press, 1981), p. 157.

a purpose or an intended result, with "so that you will not fall into temptation," without settling the matter of content.

Commenting on the parallel to Mark 14:38 in Matthew 26:41, W. D. Davies and Dale C. Allison remark:

It is unclear whether ἵνα depends solely upon προσεύχεσθε and so gives the content of the prayer or whether – the option to which we incline – it depends upon both verbs. In the latter case ἵνα introduces the goal of watching and praying ... We give the phrase eschatological content: the disciples are to watch and pray so as not to be overcome by the last trial.[7]

This suggestion is plausible, given the context of Jesus's advice and the Greek terms used. In contrast to what the RSV, NRSV, NAB, NEB, REB, and ESV suggest, Mark, Matthew, and Luke arguably used "ἵνα" to indicate the purpose, goal, or intended result of the watching and praying advised by Jesus. They thus are not specifying the content of the praying.

The questionable translations obscure an important lesson: Gethsemane prayer of the kind exemplified by Jesus, with its practical, life-guiding endorsement of the supremacy of God's will, was central to Jesus's appropriating divine power as the antidote to human weakness. The weakness is relative to the human prospect of one's obeying God's difficult will. The struggle to appropriate the divine power should not culminate in a prayer simply that one be spared a test, as the dubious translations suggest. Instead, the expected culmination is in one's yielding, obediently, to the supremacy of God's will, *as Jesus yielded and prayed*: "*Abba*, Father, ... not what I want, but what you want." With that sincere prayer of yielding, Jesus made himself *volitionally available* to God, to be conformed, cooperatively, to God's will.

---

[7] Davies and Allison, *A Critical and Exegetical Commentary on the Gospel According to Saint Matthew*, vol. 3, p. 499.

Human *appropriation* of the needed divine power, as an antidote to human weakness, comes in Jesus-modeled submission in Gethsemane, for the sake of personifying God's will in human action. The needed power is not *in* the prayer's content but is in divine intentional power sensitive to human volitional availability to God. The latter availability, being under human control (at least typically), is needed for willing cooperation with God, but it need not come easily, as Jesus himself showed. (Luke's version of Gethsemane (22:44) has Jesus's sweat becoming like drops of blood, in his anguish of prayer.)

The volitional submission guided by the content expressing Jesus-modeled submission would include one's being *attracted* and *willingly receptive* to that power in and from God. This kind of practical, life-directing submission is part of what it is for God to be *one's* God and Lord, including *my* God and Lord, and not just *a* God or Lord or a hypothesis about God. Actual divine lordship *in human action* requires human submission of the Gethsemane sort found in Jesus. Such lordship leaves room, however, for its rejection by humans as responsible agents, thus maintaining genuine human agency.

John's Gospel plausibly interprets Jesus's struggle in Gethsemane as a struggle for power for obedience, divine or anti-divine. It represents Jesus as saying: "I will no longer talk much with you, for the ruler of this world is coming. He has no power over me [ἐν ἐμοὶ οὐκ ἔχει οὐδέν]; but I do as the Father has commanded me, so that the world may know that I love the Father. Rise, let us be on our way" (John 14:30–1; cf. Mark 14:42). Gethsemane thus becomes the context of resolving whether, by one's cooperation or the lack thereof, God has actual moral power over one, and this power is for the sake of cooperative obedience, for "do[ing] as the Father has commanded." In the synoptic Gospels, Jesus recommends Gethsemane prayer of volitional submission to God as the way to appropriate the divine power for obedience – thus giving God power over oneself in volitional cooperation. In this regard, the process is directly interpersonal and not mechanical. It calls for human cooperation.

The Last Supper narratives indicate that Jesus thought of his yielding to God's will in his death as self-giving for the redemptive good of others (Mark 14:24, Matt. 26:28). He was not valuing dying in itself; instead, he was valuing God's redemptive love for others manifested in his self-giving death. He was attracted to cooperate with divine love in a way that led him to give up his life for the manifestation of that love for others. So, it would be misleading to suggest that Paul was the first to think that "God proves his love for us in that while we still were sinners Christ died for us" (Rom. 5:8). In Gethsemane, Jesus showed his being attracted to, and his cooperating with, his Father's love for others that would be manifested in his obedience in self-giving death. Omitting the role of divine love would leave out the theological depth of Jesus's self-understanding and mission. It would hinder our best available explanation here.

Regarding the historicity of the main contours of the synoptic Gethsemane story, Eduard Schweizer comments:

There is no reason to question the historicity of Jesus's struggle in prayer in Gethsemane. The essence of it has been handed down also in John 12:27 (cf. 18:11b) and Hebrews 4:15, 5:7 f. Moreover, it does not fit the picture of the Servant of God and is even less appropriate for the glorious miracle-worker and divine Lord.[8]

Davies and Allison also avoid excessive historical skepticism here, proposing that "the different texts preserve

---

[8] Eduard Schweizer, *The Good News According to Mark*, trans. D. H. Madvig (London: SPCK, 1970), p. 310. Similarly, see Dunn, *Jesus and the Spirit*, pp. 18–20, Brown, *The Death of the Messiah*, vol. 1, pp. 218–27, and Morna D. Hooker, *The Gospel According to St Mark*, BNTC (London: A&C Black, 1991), pp. 346–7. Cf. Joel Marcus, *Mark*, AYB (New Haven, CT: Yale University Press, 2009), vol. 2, pp. 976–7.

at least some historical memory." They add that Jesus's "surprising grief in the face of death, a potential embarrassment, contrasts sharply with Jewish and Christian martyrdom ... So, it is plausible that shortly before his arrest, Jesus, in a place called Gethsemane, prayed for death to pass him by."[9] Such considerations do not yield the exact words of Mark's Gethsemane story, but we should not expect them to do so.

Jesus evidently proceeded toward his death without seeking an alternative, and this suggests that he resolved his initial hesitation in favor of God's redemptive will through his death. At least this is the consensus impact Jesus left on his disciples, according to the synoptic Gospels. So, the content of his Gethsemane prayer, regarding obeying God above his own will, is favorable given our overall historical evidence about him, as well as our literary evidence from Matthew's version of the Lord's Prayer assigned to him: "Thy will be done."[10]

3.2 ABBA AND FILIAL RESPONSIVENESS

Jesus's use of "*Abba*" for God indicates a filial relationship between God as a parent and himself as a child responsively attracted and led or guided by God. God intervened first, to attract Jesus to cooperate, if only by setting up a situation as an opportunity for Jesus to respond to God.[11] This is unearned divine *grace* (to borrow a notion from Paul) aimed at having Jesus cooperate with God, and it called for his careful response guided by God's moral

---

[9] Davies and Allison, *A Critical and Exegetical Commentary on the Gospel According to Saint Matthew*, vol. 3, pp. 492–3.

[10] On some historical background to the Lord's Prayer, and how the Gethsemane prayer of Jesus "harmonises easily" with the Lord's prayer, see David Catchpole, *Jesus People: The Historical Jesus and the Beginnings of Community* (London: Darton, 2006), pp. 121–68.

[11] John's Gospel credits God with setting up the situation calling for Jesus's decision in Gethsemane, with Jesus asking: "Am I not to drink the cup that the Father has given me?" (John 18:11).

character and will.[12] Jesus as a child of God responded cooperatively to the Gethsemane challenge from God's will, and thereby he showed his agreeable attitude toward God's gracious opportunity for his cooperation.

Jesus's response had some main options: It could have included (a) resisting or opposing, (b) cooperating or conforming, or (c) ignoring or disregarding. For practical purposes, any such potential response could have yielded his (potential) response *to God*. In addition, responses (a) and (c) would have been equally inadequate from the standpoint of his expected cooperation with God. Those two responses do not entail or even allow for his volitional coordination with God's will.

We shall introduce some straightforward distinctions, grounded in the literary evidence of the synoptic Gospels, to elucidate the filial responsiveness of Jesus to God in Gethsemane. In doing so, we shall clarify Jesus's interpersonal response to the impact of God on his moral experience. His predicament in Gethsemane can be seen as a challenge and a gift from God. The divine challenge for him was to submit his will to God's disturbing but morally perfect will, even in the face of suffering and death. The divine gift to him included available and actual divine guidance and power for his submission expected by God. Even if many people would not consider such guidance and power a divine gift, the case was different with Jesus, who valued God's perfect will above all else, with his full commitment.

Jesus understood cooperative filial responsiveness to God to include filial *watchfulness* for God. In Gethsemane, he instructed Peter, James, and John: "Remain here, and watch [γρηγορεῖτε]" (Mark 14:34, RSV; cf. Mark 14:37, 38,

---

[12] I am not suggesting that we reduce divine self-manifestation or guidance to *moral* considerations, as if the category of the theological is just the category of the moral. The category of the theological is arguably more involved with mystery, for instance, than is the category of the moral. For current purposes, this chapter focuses on moral guidance and hence on the moral character and will of God in such guidance.

Matt. 26:38, 41). Mark 13 identifies a similar command from Jesus for his disciples to "watch," with regard to God's intervening in human affairs (Mark 13:35, 37; cf. Matt. 24:42, 25:13). Human watchfulness as attentiveness or alertness to the prospect of divine intervention is, according to Mark's and Matthew's Jesus, part of cooperative filial responsiveness to God.

Watchfulness as attentiveness to potential divine intervention matters because it provides a fitting context for filial *discovery* of God at work in human experience – that is, for suitably apprehending God's presence in a person's experience. It is attentiveness to the option of God's intervening in human experience, including in conscience, by the self-manifestation of divine goodness, including God's moral character and will. Without such attentiveness, a person could fail to apprehend such a manifestation and thereby miss out on important evidence of God's reality and presence. One then could lose an important opportunity to discover God at work in human experience, including one's own moral experience.

Discovering God's presence would include a distinctive qualitative experience or awareness of, or attention-attraction by, an intervening will morally superior to one's own (see, for Paul's indication of this: Rom. 5:5, 2 Cor. 5:14). It thus would differ from mere thought or reflection, but we should not expect God's will to coerce a human will to comply and thereby to depersonalize a human agent in this area. Seeking reconciliation in volitional agreement, God would use divine power to attract, rather than to control, human cooperation. In Gethsemane, Jesus discovered God at work through his attraction and conviction by God, in his moral experience, to give up his life as part of the divine redemptive plan.[13]

---

[13] Being thus convicted does not presuppose disobeying God. It can amount to being convicted *toward deeper righteousness* in relation to God; this is a defensible way of interpreting the kind of conviction regarding righteousness mentioned in John 16:8, 10. Chapter 5 returns to the latter topic.

As noted, the Gospels of Mark and Matthew suggest Jesus's prior awareness of this plan at the Last Supper, even if his awareness there was less vivid than in Gethsemane (Mark 14:22–5, Matt. 26:26–9).[14]

Jesus's filial responsiveness to God went beyond watchfulness and discovery to what we have called *volitional availability* to God. Such availability includes a *readiness of one's will* to cooperate with God under the guidance of divine self-manifestation of goodness. We see this kind of availability in Jesus in Gethsemane, particularly in his taking time to pray to God repeatedly, thus seeking God's will for him. Luke's Gospel suggests that he would regularly "withdraw to deserted places and pray" (Luke 5:16), and the synoptic Gospels illustrate this habitual practice of his.

After his initial request for an alternative plan ("remove this cup from me"), Jesus expressed his readiness to cooperate with God's will ("not what I want, but what you want"), despite the deadly result. He thus was prepared to trust and to obey God, come what may. This was not blind trust and obedience, however, because he was familiar in his firsthand experience with God's moral character and will, in particular, with their unsurpassed goodness in their impact on him and others. He was attracted and moved by that divine goodness in his experience, as many of his teachings illustrate (see, e.g., Matt. 6:28–32, Luke 12:27–32). So, "come what may" implies "come what good God will bring out of a situation, however bad the situation." (Chapter 8 returns to the latter kind of redeeming evil, in relation to explaining evil.)

Jesus's responsiveness in volitional availability to God developed into his agreeable *cooperation* with God, in putting God's will first in his decision and action in

---

[14] See C. F. D. Moule, "The Sacrifice of Christ," in Moule, *Forgiveness and Reconciliation*, pp. 135–76, Joachim Jeremias, *The Eucharistic Words of Jesus*, trans. Norman Perrin (Philadelphia: Fortress Press, 1977), pp. 138–203, John Koenig, *The Feast of the World's Redemption: Eucharistic Origins and Christian Mission* (Harrisburg, PA: Trinity Press International, 2000), pp. 3–44.

Gethsemane. This cooperation included the kind of good response to God's self-revelation attributed to the good soil in his parable of the sower: "hold it fast in an honest and good heart, and bear fruit with patient endurance" (Luke 8:15).[15] Such a response enabled Jesus to be led cooperatively by God to do God's will, in keeping with God's moral character. It thus included his cooperative trust in God as one who leads toward divine goodness to be shared, beyond beliefs regarding God. His experience of God's goodness attracted him to cooperate with God as trustworthy for redemptive goodness.

3.3 MOTIVE AND BEING LED

As indicated, we find a corollary to Jesus's Gethsemane prayer in the Lord's Prayer in Matthew's Gospel: "Thy will be done." We also find there the important idea of being led by God: "Lead [εἰσενέγκῃς] us not into temptation, but deliver us from evil" (Matt. 6:13, RSV; cf. Luke 11:4). As Chapter 2 noted, this idea of divine leading emerges also, with crucial importance, in Paul's letter to the Romans: "All who are led [ἄγονται] by the Spirit of God are children of God" (8:14). The idea of divine leading, as similarly noted, goes back at least to the Psalms: "He leads me in paths of righteousness for his name's sake" (23:3, RSV). Such divine leading seeks to bring people to conform, cooperatively, to God's moral character and will, and it can advance deepening of this conforming over time. It led to Jesus going to Jerusalem to please God, in filial cooperation with God's will, despite the resulting tragedy.

The filial responsiveness of Jesus came from a motive indicated by his primary love command regarding God: "The first [commandment] is, 'Hear, O Israel: the Lord our God, the Lord is one; you shall love the Lord your God with all your heart, and with all your soul, and with all your

---

[15] On the importance of audience motive in Jesus's use of parables, see Chapter 5.

mind, and with all your strength'" (Mark 12:30; cf. Matt. 22:36–40, Deut. 6:4–5).[16] In putting this command first, Jesus assumed that it should be satisfied in one's motivation for cooperating with God. He did not assume, however, that a human can self-manufacture the required love.

In one of his most difficult statements, Jesus reported that "no one is good but God alone" (Mark 10:18), even though he attributed goodness to some people (as "good soil") in his parable of the sower (Mark 4:20; cf. Matt. 7:17). So, he evidently had in mind God as the *ultimate* source of goodness for humans, including their good motivating love. As a result, he evidently held that one's motivation for cooperating with God should stem from a source in *God's* powerful love. This fits with his view that God loves humans first, before they love God. We are exploring how Jesus appropriated such love for his own motivation to cooperate with God. It would be misleading to suggest that he thought of himself as manufacturing the needed love on his own, apart from divine power.

Jesus's primary love command gains a motivational ground and corresponding motivational power in the context of his aforementioned experience of God's love. That experience, as suggested, conveyed to him the worthiness of *God's* being loved, given God's caring love toward him. It left him, as noted, with felt indebtedness to God for the divine goodness, including the divine love, in his life. So, his primary love command was not abstract or speculative for him. Instead, it had a motivational base in his experienced divine love, in his attraction to it, and he pointed to a similar base for others. The self-understanding and mission of Jesus acquire plausibility when grounded in his experience of divine goodness in the manner suggested.

---

[16] On the historicity of this command, see John P. Meier, *A Marginal Jew, vol. 4: Law and Love*, AYBRL (New Haven, CT: Yale University Press, 2009), pp. 499–527. See also Victor Paul Furnish, *The Love Command in the New Testament* (Nashville, TN: Abingdon Press, 1972), pp. 62–9.

Jesus offered a striking example of divine love and filial responsiveness in his parable of the prodigal son. The core response, as Chapter 2 noted, is as follows:

[The wayward son] set off and went to his father. But while he was still far off, his father saw him and was filled with compassion; he ran and put his arms around him and kissed him. Then the son said to him, "Father, I have sinned against heaven and before you; I am no longer worthy to be called your son." But the father said to his slaves, "Quickly, bring out a robe – the best one – and put it on him; put a ring on his finger and sandals on his feet. And get the fatted calf and kill it, and let us eat and celebrate; for this son of mine was dead and is alive again; he was lost and is found!" And they began to celebrate. (Luke 15:20–4)

Prior to the wayward son's departure and return, his father had shown love to him, but the son chose his own alternative life apart from his father, in "a distant country" (Luke 15:13). The father was left waiting for his son's return, after the son comes "to himself" in his self-imposed alienation. Upon seeing his returning son, the father was "filled with compassion," and "he ran and put his arms around him and kissed him" (Luke 15:20).

Jesus portrayed God as a father running, full of compassion, to bring reconciliation to a wayward child. So, his understanding of filial responsiveness to God included a divine father who eagerly takes the initiative to attract and restore children to a good relationship with God. The final celebration shows divine joy in redeeming humans in reconciliation to God. Unfortunately, talk of divine "fatherhood" can be, and sometimes is, grudging, sexist, and otherwise harmful, but the standard assumed by Jesus is free of such hostilities. This parable sets the tone for his perspective on a filial relationship with his Father, and that tone stems from the moral character of a compassionate, perfectly good God whose divine goodness has an impact on human experience.

The Gethsemane narratives of Mark's and Matthew's Gospels portray the relationship of Jesus to God as his Father to include his being *God's child who gives himself supremely for God's redemptive will*. This suggestion does not rest just on linguistic considerations, such as Jesus's uses of *"Abba"* or "the Son," but it can accommodate the latter uses.[17] The basis is a broader pattern of material about Jesus in the Gospels, and it can find support from the New Testament letters that point in a similar direction. The relevant literary evidence indicates that Jesus considered himself to have a special filial relationship to God, and that this relationship included unique authority, responsibility, and communion from God.[18] For instance, the enacted parable of the Last Supper highlights the distinctiveness of Jesus's relationship to his covenantal God, in giving his life for God's new redemptive covenant (Mark 14:23–5, Matt. 26:27–9, Luke 22:19–20).

The disciples of Jesus could share in his child–parent relationship with God, and, as indicated by his primary love command in the Gospels, Jesus instructed them to do so, with unqualified love toward God. The relationship in question, however, does not reduce to an episodic experience of God; an awareness of God need not be constant in an ongoing relationship with God. In fact, Jesus's final cry of dereliction in the Gospels of Mark and Matthew suggested that his relationship with God, *as his God*, could persist in the absence of present awareness of God (Mark 15:34, Matt. 27:46).[19] An important lesson is that neither

---

[17] On Jesus's use of "the Son," including in relation to his use of *"Abba,"* see Dunn, *Christianity in the Making, vol. 1*, pp. 709–24, Ben Witherington, III, *The Christology of Jesus* (Minneapolis: Fortress Press, 1990), pp. 221–8, and Richard Bauckham, "The Sonship of the Historical Jesus in Christology," *Scottish Journal of Theology* 31 (1978), 245–60.

[18] See Manson, *Jesus the Messiah*, pp. 71–6, 152–6.

[19] For an interpretation of Jesus's cry of dereliction agreeable to this approach, see Gérard Rossé, *The Cry of Jesus on the Cross*, trans. S. W. Arndt (New York: Paulist Press, 1987). See also Brown, *The Death of the Messiah*, vol. 2, pp. 1043–58, 1083–8,

God nor God's supervision is reducible to an experience or awareness available to humans.

We have characterized Gethsemane as a decisive inter-personal moral episode for Jesus, with two prominent features in his filial responsiveness to God. First, Jesus willingly faced God as Father directly in life-guiding prayer, and, second, he finally yielded his will to God's superior will, even at the cost of his own life. Such Gethsemane prayer, according to our literary evidence, was empowering for Jesus, because it subjected his will to God's will in a way that made room for and embraced God's volitional power in his life.

Jesus focused on divine power to attract and sustain him in obedience toward his redemptive death, and this obedi-ence, according to Paul, led to God's vindication of Jesus with the resurrection (Phil. 2:8–9; cf. Rom. 1:4). Gethsemane prayer, then, was the avenue for Jesus to moral empower-ment by God. This empowerment supported his agreeable obedience in submission to God's will, but it was not *mere* obedience. It relied on his interaction *with God* directly for guidance through moral conviction from God. At its core, Gethsemane prayer is volitional union as *willing cooperation* with God in interpersonal communion with God. It was the signature, the center, of Jesus as God's obedient son, seen in his decisive actions, beyond any disputes about specific titles for Jesus. In addition, the Gethsemane empowerment of Jesus had significance beyond Jesus alone; it extends, at least in the intentional impact of Jesus, to his disciples. We turn to that impact.

3.4 GETHSEMANE BEYOND JESUS

Jesus showed no illusion about the difficulty of cooperative filial responsiveness to God for humans. He faced such

and Richard Bauckham, "God's Self-Identification with the Godforsaken: Exegesis and Theology," in Bauckham, *Jesus and the God of Israel* (Grand Rapids, MI: Eerdmans, 2009), pp. 254–68.

difficulty not only for himself but also for his disciples in
Gethsemane, according to Mark's narrative (Mark 14:37,
40, 41; cf. Matt. 26:40, 43, 45). He also faced it in his disciples
outside Gethsemane, as Mark's Gospel reports at various
places (Mark 9:19; cf. Matt. 17:17, Luke 9:41). When people
are not responsive in the cooperative filial manner suggested, according to Jesus, God rightfully can withdraw
divine presence from their experience until an opportune
time. In fact, as Chapter 2 noted, he thanked his Father for
such divine hiding:

At that time Jesus said, "I thank you, Father, Lord of heaven
and earth, because you have hidden these things from the
wise and the intelligent and have revealed them to infants;
yes, Father, for such was your gracious will. All things have
been handed over to me by my Father; and no one knows the
Son except the Father, and no one knows the Father except
the Son and anyone to whom the Son chooses to reveal him."
(Matt. 11:25–7; cf. Luke 10:21–2)

The "infants" are cooperative in their response to God as
Father, in contrast with the response of "the wise and the
intelligent." The difference results in divine hiding from
"the wise and the intelligent" and in divine self-revealing
to the "infants."

The model for the response of "infants" to divine impact
was set by Jesus in Gethsemane, in his attentiveness, volitional availability, discovery, and willing cooperation
toward God as Father. In contrast, "the wise and the intelligent" lack such cooperative responsiveness to God, given
their own "wisdom" and "intelligence." They see no need
to respond cooperatively to God because they have their
own resources for being "wise" and "intelligent."

The attitude of "the wise and the intelligent" corresponds to an attitude of resistance identified by Jesus:
"Those who are well have no need of a physician, but
those who are sick; I have come to call not the righteous

but sinners" (Mark 2:17; cf. Matt. 9:13, Luke 5:32). Unlike "the righteous," the "sinners" see their need to be reconciled to God as Father. In this respect, they are akin to the prodigal son. In contrast, "the wise and the intelligent" resist or at least ignore the divine–human reconciliation on offer, and their attitude invites divine hiding until a better, more cooperative attitude toward God arises from them.

According to Matthew's Gospel, Jesus promoted cooperative filial responsiveness by making the obeying of the will of God a requirement for entering the kingdom of God: "Not everyone who says to me 'Lord, Lord' will enter the kingdom of heaven, but only the one who does the will of my Father in heaven" (Matt. 7:21; cf. Luke 6:46, Mark 3:35). In this perspective, just as Jesus focused responsively in Gethsemane on doing the will of God as his Father, so also his disciples are to focus their lives in a cooperative filial relationship with God. Jesus thereby set an interpersonal standard for a filial relationship with God (Mark 3:33–5, Matt. 12:48–50, Luke 8:20–1; cf. Matt. 5:20). Moral accountability *to God* becomes inherently interpersonal by his standard, and it thus goes beyond satisfying a moral rule or law. The focus becomes a divine impact of moral challenge from divine goodness to humans that calls for their filial response.

The standard for discipleship set by Jesus, as Chapter 1 suggested, agreed with his own decision in Gethsemane: "[Jesus] called the crowd with his disciples, and said to them, 'If any want to become my followers, let them deny themselves and take up their cross and follow me'" (Mark 8:34; cf. Matt. 10:38, 16:24, Luke 9:23, 14:27). So, Jesus's filial response in Gethsemane is to be normative for his disciples, just as his understanding of God as Father is to be shared by them. In addition, according to Matthew's Gospel (and the Q tradition), following Jesus depends on receiving and reflecting God's moral character as Father in the wake of Jesus: "Be perfect as your heavenly Father is perfect" (Matt. 5:48). Luke's

Jesus has a variation on the same filial theme: "Be merciful, just as your Father is merciful" (Luke 6:36). We thus find an emphasis on imitating God as benevolent Father, in keeping with the standard set by Jesus.

A recurring feature of the synoptic Gospels is the afore-mentioned command of Jesus to deny oneself, take up one's cross, and follow him. The denial of oneself is *Gethsemane denial* – that is, the denial and death of one's will at odds with God's will, after the model of Jesus. We have noted the same demand in the Lord's Prayer in Matthew's Gospel, "Thy will be done."

The cross required by Jesus, at its center, is not about crucifixion or physical suffering in itself but is about something more deeply interpersonal. Its center is cooperative obedience to God for the sake of receiving, enacting, and manifesting the power of divine redemptive love for people (Mark 14:22–4; cf. Rom. 5:5–8). This kind of obedience can give meaning to the talk of "the Holy Spirit whom God has given to those who obey him" (Acts 5:32). Such obedience is presented not as a condition for earning divine approval but as a cooperative means for receiving God's empowering Spirit, understood as God in active divine goodness.

The Gospels portray Jesus as guided by the Spirit of God, beginning with his baptism by John and leading to his temptation in the wilderness (Mark 1:10–12, Matt. 3:16–4:1, Luke 3:21–2, 4:1; cf. John 1:28–32). The Gospels of Matthew and Luke cite the book of Isaiah to identify the Spirit of God as being "upon" Jesus in a distinctive way for his mission (Matt. 12:18, Luke 4:18). In addition, according to Matthew's Gospel, Jesus attributed his exorcisms to the Spirit of God as an indication of God's present kingdom: "If it is by the Spirit of God that I cast out demons, then the kingdom of God has come to you" (Matt. 12:28; cf. Luke 11:20). So, as an exemplar for discipleship toward God, Jesus prompted his audience to ask about the bearing of God's empowering Spirit on his disciples.

Some commentators have noted restraint in Jesus's talk of God's Spirit, perhaps akin to his guarded talk of the Messiah.[20] Arguably, he wanted to characterize God's Spirit in his distinctive way, in keeping with his own character and mission, and thus he needed to wait for readiness to understand and cooperate on the part of his audience. John's Jesus gives an indication of his likely pedagogical problem: "I still have many things to say to you, but you cannot bear them now" (John 16:12). We should acknowledge, in any case, the more abundant talk in the New Testament of God's Spirit in relation to (the risen) Jesus after Pentecost.

Some of the post-resurrection talk of God's Spirit in the New Testament calls for "being led" by God's Spirit, in the wake of Jesus's being led by God. It includes, in particular, a demand to oppose and "kill" anti-God tendencies in oneself by the power of that Spirit (Rom. 8:13). Gethsemane bears directly, because it shows Jesus calling on God for the power needed to put God's will first, over his initial preference for an alternative plan. Paul invoked the importance of being "led by the Spirit" in a similar context of conflict between "the flesh" (including natural human willing) and what *God* wills or desires (Gal. 5:17–18; cf. Rom. 7:15–25).

Paul's acknowledged role for leading by God's Spirit coheres with the interpersonal Gethsemane perspective outlined here. Both perspectives go beyond obeying a rule or a law to an interpersonal *meeting* for cooperation with God's will as a means of divine empowerment. Paul would characterize the meeting in terms of the presence of the "spirit of God" or the "spirit of Christ" (Rom. 8:9–11). In either case, the focus is on (the impact of) the available power of God as a basis for attracting and

---

[20] See C. K. Barrett, *The Holy Spirit and the Gospel Tradition*, 2nd ed. (London: SPCK, 1966), pp. 140–62, and Anthony Thiselton, *The Holy Spirit* (Grand Rapids, MI: Eerdmans, 2013), pp. 38–40.

sustaining (a response of) human cooperation with God's will. So, we can see the basis of our impact–response model of interpretation at work.

The obedience of Jesus to God, according to the Gospels, is impeccable, but the same does not hold for his disciples, who falter at times in their commitment. Even so, according to a common New Testament perspective, a typical human can resolve, at least as a primary if imperfect commitment, to obey as Jesus did, while trusting God to show mercy in failures of obedience. Such resolving, under guidance from moral conscience, can position a person to receive divine motivational power for cooperating with God's will. God's redemptive purpose, according to this perspective, can include the divine empowerment of Gethsemane-style resolve by humans in response to divine goodness, such as divine volitional impact. The expansion of God's kingdom thus would benefit from the kind of empowered obedience, modeled after Jesus in Gethsemane, that honors God's moral authority as *Abba*.

The Lord's Prayer in Matthew's Gospel suggests that God's kingdom comes in the satisfaction of God's will, and that the coming of this kingdom can empower one's conforming to God's will. In this perspective, God moves first toward humans, with an attractive impact of divine goodness in human experience. As a response, their cooperation in a Gethsemane mode is a means to the cooperative realization of God's kingdom. In the coming of God's kingdom, God comes near to people with the goodness of divine presence, taking the initiative in doing so and bringing power for attracting and sustaining human cooperation with God's will. Because the kingdom represents *God's moral character*, God's presence favors cooperative obedience reflective of that moral character. So, God's empowering such obedience makes sense given the kingdom's goal to represent and to enact the divine goodness of God's moral character, including its self-giving nature in *agapē* for a community, a shared kingdom.[21]

We now can understand to some extent how Jesus in Gethsemane ultimately found his crucifixion at Calvary to be a live option for him, in keeping with God's supreme will. He evidently came to recognize, if with increasing vividness, that God's goodness and redemptive power would not preclude his suffering and dying in Jerusalem, but would instead vindicate him *through* his suffering and dying.[22] God would not "remove the cup" from him, but God's goodness and power were not thereby defective. In fact, divine goodness and power would emerge as uniquely redemptive *in suffering* rather than in being directed only at avoiding suffering. This can explain Jesus dropping his initial request for an alternative plan ("remove this cup from me"). Even so, we should not expect to have a full theodicy for God allowing the relevant suffering. Mark's Gospel leaves us with that lesson about a theodicy, and none of the other Gospels undermines it.[23]

We gain perspective on the center of Jesus's self-understanding and mission when we look to his interpersonal relationship to God manifested in his distinctive experiences and actions. Gethsemane is a revealing context for such experiences and actions. It reveals, we have noted, a priority for Jesus in cooperatively interacting with *God*: his meeting God through his experience of God's good, attractive intervention and his volitional cooperation with God, come what may, even at the expense of his earthly life. Such cooperative meeting, according to the gospel narratives of Gethsemane, is the way to receive divine moral

---

[21] Chapter 7 explains the unique role assumed by Jesus in the arrival and expansion of God's kingdom, with emphasis on his neglected role as a distinctive kind of moral kingmaker and gatekeeper for God.

[22] On this theme in Mark's Gospel, including in connection with Gethsemane, see Sharyn Echols Dowd, *Prayer, Power, and the Problem of Suffering: Mark 11:22–25 in the Context of Markan Theology*, SBLDS (Atlanta: Scholars Press, 1988), pp. 151–62. See also John R. Donahue, "A Neglected Factor in the Theology of Mark," *Journal of Biblical Literature* 101 (1982), pp. 586–7.

[23] Chapter 8 returns to the topic of theodicy and redeeming evil.

power and thus to endure in obeying God, even in suffering and death. So, a cooperative Gethsemane resolution is central to appropriating the divine power needed for righteous motivation before God.

Human motivation for cooperation with God need not amount to perfect righteousness, because it can be tainted by selfishness, for instance, and it can have an outcome in a morally imperfect action. (The actions of the disciples of Jesus often illustrate this in the New Testament Gospels.) An overall righteous motivation can be linked to a mixed result in action, especially if consequences of actions are *a* factor in the rightness of actions.

A Gethsemane context can be fallible in accompanying moral decision-making, but it still can aid the divine empowerment of a cooperative human. Paul's assessment fits even in a Gethsemane context: "We have this treasure in clay jars, so that it may be made clear that this extraordinary power belongs to God and does not come from us" (2 Cor 4:7). The divine power received is no less divine for being combined or even tainted with morally imperfect human power. Instead, it shows its distinctiveness by way of *contrast* with a morally imperfect human contribution. We see this, for instance, when enemy-love is tainted by human selfishness or some other abuse of human power.

According to the Gospels, Jesus endorsed God's morally perfect character as the norm grounding moral power, authority, and duty. This motivated his aforementioned injunction to his disciples: "Be perfect as your heavenly Father is perfect" (Matt. 5:48; cf. Luke 6:36). This injunction of Matthew's Jesus followed on the heels of his command to love one's enemies, thus indicating that *agapē* is to reflect, and to be guided by, God's morally perfect character, and hence is not to condone any abuse toward its practitioners or audience. The relevant *agapē*, then, is not *merely* "other-regarding"; instead, it reflects *God's perfect righteousness* that does no harm and condones no abuse, even self-abuse. On the basis of this divine moral character, Jesus rejected approaches to moral authority and obedience, implying that a powerful human sets the terms for what is morally good or commendable (Matt. 20:25–7, Luke 22:25–7).

Human cooperation matters in Gethsemane, and not just for moral empowerment. It also can serve as a test for the reality and integrity of divine moral power. The test relies on cooperative participation in a Gethsemane context, as an avenue to being directly acquainted, or presented, with the unique power of divine righteousness. Since that power, by divine intention, aims for fruition in divine–human cooperation, salient experience of what it is intended to be depends on human cooperation. In such cooperation, one would get firsthand evidence of God's unique reality and moral character, and this character opposes harmful abuses of moral power and authority.

A main concern of this chapter has been the motivational basis for Jesus and his disciples, and we now have a promising basis: divine empowerment in Gethsemane, after the model of Jesus in his prayer-oriented cooperation with a morally impeccable God of righteous *agapē*. Jesus instructed his disciples to pray in his wake, including in the case of the Lord's prayer, thus suggesting that his Gethsemane model for relating to God was to be shared by them. In doing so, he revealed to them not only how he related to God as his Father but also how *they* are to relate to God as their Father.

Translating Mark 14:38 aright, we see that a purpose behind the prayer advised by Jesus was to save his disciples from a power deficit in obeying God's will. We also see that, given the model of Jesus in Gethsemane, the attitude and content of one's ultimate prayer to God should echo Jesus: "*Abba*, Father, ... not what I want, but what you want." This would be to identify volitionally with Jesus as the model for filial responsiveness toward God as Father. We have noted that Jesus had an anchor for his responsiveness in the attractive divine love he experienced, and that this love was for him and others. This love, we saw, also gave motivational power to his primary love command, at least for cooperative recipients.

Thought or reflection alone will not serve the purpose of Gethsemane, given the central role of volition, including human decision, in appropriating the moral power of divine righteous *agapē*. In Gethsemane, Jesus offered such cooperative volition as his priority and thereby showed his volitional responsiveness to God's impact as the center of his relating to God as his "*Abba*, Father." He expected his disciples to follow suit, if with imperfection. We need to consider how our impact–response approach to Jesus and God bears on Jesus's distinctive message of good news from God and on its varied reception among humans.

4

℘

Good News of Divine Goodness

Jesus preached a gospel of the kingdom of God but its reception by his audience was mixed at best. Even when welcomed by some people, it was ignored by some people and rejected by others. As a result, we need an account of its *means of appropriation* by people who welcome it. This calls for an explanation of how the gospel is "hidden," "secret," or "mysterious" in the ways suggested by the Gospels and Paul's undisputed letters. This chapter provides the needed explanation while distinguishing the following: the gospel as mere *informational content* and the gospel as the *redemptive power* of God.[1]

Some parts of the New Testament distinguish between the earthly Jesus as the historical proclaimer of the gospel and the risen Jesus as "a life-giving Spirit" who became part of the proclaimed gospel message. In both stages, the gospel is "hidden" from some people for redemptive purposes, and its intended appropriation depends on "the

---

[1] The present distinction does not challenge the importance of the informational content of the gospel; it simply resists a suggestion that this is the only source of its importance. On the relevant informational content, see C. H. Dodd, *The Apostolic Preaching and Its Developments* (New York: Harper & Row, 1937), and Eugene E. Lemcio, "The Unifying Kerygma of the New Testament," in Lemcio, *The Past of Jesus in the Gospels*, SNTSMS (Cambridge: Cambridge University Press, 1991), pp. 115–31. For some historical background for the New Testament use of the term "gospel," see Graham Stanton, *Jesus and Gospel* (Cambridge: Cambridge University Press, 2004), pp. 9–62, and William Horbury, "'Gospel' in Herodian Judaea," in *The Written Gospel*, eds. Markus Bockmuehl and Donald A. Hagner (Cambridge: Cambridge University Press, 2005), pp. 7–30.

obedience of faith." This chapter finds such obedience exemplified by the obedience of Jesus in Gethsemane and based in a distinctive kind of divine power. It explains how such obedience and power figure in the "hiddenness" of Jesus's gospel as the power of God for salvation. In doing so, it illuminates how the good news from Jesus is indeed good, being anchored in divine goodness.

4.1 GOSPEL POWER

The gospel presented in the New Testament comes in two stages, and both involve Jesus centrally. The first stage involves Jesus before his resurrection, the second, Jesus after his resurrection. The two stages differ in specific content for the gospel, given a change in the status of Jesus, from pre-resurrection to post-resurrection. They share, nonetheless, a practical core in terms of what they demand of responsive, and responsible, inquirers. In order to understand the redemptive mission of Jesus, we need to clarify that core and to identify its significance for the hiddenness of the gospel relative to some people.

The talk of the gospel "of Jesus" could mean at least the gospel "about Jesus," the gospel that "is Jesus," and the gospel that either "belongs to" or "comes from" Jesus. We shall begin with the gospel that comes *from* Jesus, and then see that the gospel becomes a message *about* him. In due course, we will be in a position to see the redemptive purpose behind this transition.

Jesus began his mission with a focus on national Israel, but his message eventually attracted a larger audience. We see his distinctive role toward Israel overall in his calling twelve apostles, corresponding to the twelve tribes of Israel, and in his regarding himself as their leader in relation to God's kingdom (Mark 3:14–19, Matt. 10:1–4, Luke 6:13–16). We shall see that his redemptive focus expanded over time.

The synoptic Gospels present Jesus as bringing good news *from God*. (See, for instance, Mark 1:14–15, 8:35, 13:10; Matt. 4:23, 9:35, 10:7, 11:4–5, 24:14; Luke 4:17–18, 43, 7:22, 8:1, 9:6, 16:16, 20:1.) Mark's Gospel introduces Jesus, after his baptism by John and his temptation in the wilderness: "Now after John was arrested, Jesus came to Galilee, proclaiming the good news of God, and saying, 'The time is fulfilled, and the kingdom of God has come near; repent, and believe in the good news'" (Mark 1:14–15; cf. Matt. 4:17). Mark's introduction assumes an important connection between (the coming of) the kingdom of God and (the proclaiming of) the good news. We need to clarify this connection to understand a key motivational feature in the self-understanding and the mission of Jesus.

The good news, according to Mark's Jesus, is connected to the kingdom of God *having come near*. The book of Isaiah, in the explicit background of Mark's Gospel, relates the good news to the kingdom of God, in terms of *God's reigning*, or being king, as follows: "How beautiful upon the mountains are the feet of the messenger who announces peace [שָׁלוֹם], who brings good news [מְבַשֵּׂר], who announces salvation [יְשׁוּעָה], who says to Zion, 'Your God reigns [מָלַךְ]'" (Isa. 52:7). Perhaps this passage helped Jesus to formulate the good news of God's kingdom having come near, although we do not find him citing it. It is striking, in any case, how this passage anticipates four key emphases of the mission of Jesus: God's reigning as king, peace or reconciliation with God, salvation from God, and the bringing of such good news (from God). No part of the Jewish Bible offers a better summary of the overall mission of Jesus.[2]

Luke's Gospel portrays Jesus as relating his message of good news to the Spirit of God, as anticipated in the book of Isaiah (61:1–2):

---

[2] For the influence of the book of Isaiah on Mark's Gospel, see Rikki Watts, *Isaiah's New Exodus in Mark*, WUNT (Tübingen: Mohr Siebeck, 1997).

When he came to Nazareth, where he had been brought up, he went to the synagogue on the sabbath day, as was his custom. He stood up to read, and the scroll of the prophet Isaiah was given to him. He unrolled the scroll and found the place where it was written: "The Spirit of the Lord is upon me, because he has anointed me to bring good news to the poor. He has sent me to proclaim release to the captives and recovery of sight to the blind, to let the oppressed go free, to proclaim the year of the Lord's favor." Then he began to say to them, "Today this scripture has been fulfilled in your hearing." (Luke 4:16–19, 21)

The appeal to "the Spirit of the Lord" is important in indicating that the power of God is at work in the good news, or gospel, from Jesus. So, this news is not just information conveyed; it comes with divine power from the Spirit of God. James D. G. Dunn thus remarks: "Jesus believed himself to be the one in whom Isaiah 61:1 found fulfillment; his sense of being inspired was such that he could believe himself to be the end-time prophet of Isaiah 61:1: he had been anointed with the Spirit of the Lord."[3]

The good news announced by Jesus involves the kingdom of God, but it does not assume that this kingdom of God has arrived *in full*. We should ask, then, *how* it has come near to humans, and then attend to its relevant claims. In particular, we should ask how Jesus himself relates to the drawing near of God's kingdom, particularly in his distinctive actions for his mission. Those actions can signal the motivational power for his mission, and perhaps they can reveal similar power available to his disciples.

Chapter 3 suggested that a signature focus of Jesus's redemptive mission was on the divine power to attract, via an impact of divine goodness, receptive people to

[3] Dunn, *Jesus and the Spirit*, p. 61. Similarly, see Stanton, *Jesus and Gospel*, pp. 13–20. Jesus's assumed unique filial relation to God (see Chapter 3) recommends against using the category of "prophet" for the main, let alone exclusive, categorization of him.

reconciliation with God. Such power differs from the power to coerce people to yield, but some of Jesus's audience evidently neglected the difference. For instance, John's Gospel represents some of Jesus's audience as planning to force what they deemed good (that is, making Jesus king), but he withdrew to escape this effort (John 6:15). In addition, Luke's Gospel has James and John of Zebedee ask to call down fire from heaven to destroy the Samaritans, but Jesus rebuked them (Luke 9:54–5). If God has the prerogative to coerce events in some cases (such as in divine judgment), this option does not apply to forcing a particular human response to an offer of divine–human reconciliation. Such coercion would remove the key *interpersonal* component of reconciliation.

According to the Gospel of Luke, Jesus presented "the good news of the kingdom of God" as something new relative to the Jewish Bible: "The law and the prophets were in effect until John came; since then the good news of the kingdom of God is proclaimed" (Luke 16:16; cf. Matt. 11:13–14). This newness fits with Jesus's following comment on himself as the bridegroom and his disciples as wedding guests who do not fast in his company: "No one puts new wine into old wineskins; otherwise, the wine will burst the skins, and the wine is lost, and so are the skins; but one puts new wine into fresh wineskins" (Mark 2:22; cf. Matt. 9:14–17, Luke 5:33–9). Jesus thus thought of himself as having a special role in the good news of the coming near of God's kingdom, including in the initial arrival of that kingdom.

Jesus's parable of the wicked tenants confirms his idea of something new in his mission from God.

A man planted a vineyard, put a fence around it, dug a pit for the wine press, and built a watchtower; then he leased it to tenants and went to another country. When the season came, he sent a slave to the tenants to collect from them his share of the produce of the vineyard. But they seized him, and beat him, and sent him away empty-handed. And again he sent another slave to them; this one they beat over the head and insulted. Then he sent another, and that one they killed. And so it was with many others; some they beat, and others they killed. He had still one other, a beloved son. Finally, he sent him to them, saying, "They will respect my son." But those tenants said to one another, "This is the heir; come, let us kill him, and the inheritance will be ours." So they seized him, killed him, and threw him out of the vineyard. What then will the owner of the vineyard do? He will come and destroy the tenants and give the vineyard to others. Have you not read this scripture: "The stone that the builders rejected has become the cornerstone; this was the Lord's doing, and it is amazing in our eyes"? (Mark 12:1–11; cf. Matt. 21:33–42, Luke 20:9–17)[4]

The newness identified by this parable is in *the person* finally sent by the planter of the vineyard: his "beloved son" rather than a "slave." Chapter 3 identified this filial role for Jesus exemplified in Gethsemane, and this role, according to the parable, marks a new redemptive effort by the vineyard planter.

The parable points to God as seeking a fruitful, obedient response from the tenants of the vineyard planted by God – in this case, the leaders of Israel. God thus seeks a cooperative response from the leaders of Israel that is pleasing to God: in particular, their doing God's will with their fruitful response to the goodness offered by God. God's efforts to elicit such a response have been many and persistent, with the sending of various prophets to Israel, but the response of the tenants has been inadequate overall. So, a new line of challenge emerges, with the coming of God's "beloved son" as the special emissary to Israel.

---

[4] On the historical integrity of the parable of the wicked tenants, see Hultgren, *The Parables of Jesus*, pp. 351–82, and Klyne Snodgrass, *Stories with Intent* (Grand Rapids, MI: Eerdmans, 2008), pp. 286–99.

Mark's Gospel, as noted, named Jesus as God's beloved Son at his baptism by John.

Jesus served, according to the parable, as the new filial emissary from God to Israel. He thus came with a new kind of authority in representing and manifesting God's character and will in human form, and the latter included, as suggested, God's love as the caring shepherd of Israel. The tenants of the vineyard were not the ordinary people of Israel; they were its leaders, and they (at least many of them) opposed the mission of Jesus, at least for the social turbulence it created relative to their preferred status of power. The result was a sharp, deadly conflict between the power of the leaders of Israel and the power offered by Jesus on behalf of God, as God's "beloved son."

The good news, according to Jesus, is that God has come near to his audience with redemptive, life-giving power needed by humans, and this power calls for "new wineskins" for it to be received by them. Previous human ways of portraying and apprehending God are not up to the new standard, now set in human form by Jesus in his own responding to and representing God. The latter responding and representing, in the perspective of Jesus, capture God's character and will, in a manner superior to the past prophets and the temple establishment (Matt. 12:6, 41–2, Luke 11:31–2). So, the challenge from Jesus, in his good news, was and is new and unsettling for its audience.

Jesus regarded human alienation from God to stem from an internal human problem involving "the human heart":

It is what comes out of a person that defiles. For it is from within, from the human heart, that evil intentions come: fornication, theft, murder, adultery, avarice, wickedness, deceit, licentiousness, envy, slander, pride, folly. All these evil things come from within, and they defile a person. (Mark 7:20–3; cf. Matt. 15:18–20)

This is defiling of a person *in relation to God*, in a way that separates a person from reconciliation with God. The resulting separation yields the problem of needed human redemption, according to Jesus, and he called for a profound response and solution to it.

Jesus called for a special kind of interpersonal divine power, *given* as an antidote to human alienation from God. Luke's Gospel points to this unearned power in Jesus's remarks that it is his Father's good pleasure to *give* his disciples the kingdom (Luke 12:32), and that his Father will *give* the Holy Spirit to those who ask him (Luke 11:13), with Jesus promised by John the Baptist to be the giver of this Spirit (Luke 3:16; cf. Luke 24:49, Acts 1:4–8). What the Father of Jesus gives in these cases amounts to the same thing: a special redemptive relationship with God, courtesy of divine power to attract people to reconciliation with God on the basis of experienced divine goodness.[5]

The power of God's Spirit does the redemptive, reconciling work that humans could not accomplish on their own. This uncoercive interpersonal work is internal in a way that bears on motives and attitudes, and not just observable behavior. The Sermon on the Mount stresses the latter point (Matt. 5:22, 28), thus confirming the need for special redemptive power. It also assumes that recipients who cooperate are willingly cooperative with the power on offer and thus agreeably responsive to it. (Matt. 5:13–16).

Arland J. Hultgren has observed how the new standard of needed power set by Jesus emerges in its fullness in Mark's Gospel:

The vindication of the Son, his resurrection, is borne witness to by means of the psalm quotation [in Mark 12:10–11]. Even though the Son was killed by his adversaries, he was raised from death by God. The good news of Easter cries out as

---

[5] James D. G. Dunn has suggested the interchangeable uses of "kingdom" and "Spirit" in the two passages from Luke's Gospel. See Dunn, "Spirit and Kingdom" in Dunn, *The Christ and the Spirit*, pp. 137–8.

a [divine] response to the treachery of the crucifixion. A new creation is inaugurated by which God has a new future in store for his people.[6]

Jesus predicted his resurrection by God three times in Mark's Gospel (8:31, 9:31, 10:34), and this kind of life-giving power goes beyond mere information. It is the divine power to attract and sustain God's people, and thus God's kingdom, come what may, without forcing human cooperation. According to the synoptic Gospels, it vindicated Jesus, even through death, as God's beloved obedient son and as the unfailing representative of God's people.

The redemptive power exhibited by Jesus is *filial* power for the arrival of God's kingdom among humans, relying on the sympathetic cooperation of a child with a divine parent. It is power from God that worthily attracts an unworthy person, by acquaintance with divine goodness, to be an obedient child in God's kingdom. The Lord's Prayer in Matthew's Gospel thus connects filial obedience and kingdom arrival: "Our Father, ... Thy kingdom come, Thy will be done" (Matt. 6:9–10, NASB). Such obedience depends on divine power to attract receptive people to cooperation with God on the basis of their unearned experience of divine goodness, including divine love.

Divine power, according to the parable of the wicked tenants, can include the power of divine judgment, and such judgment can end human lives. It would be an odd predicament if God were in a position to bring about human life responsibly but not ever to take human life responsibly. The suggested asymmetry would be an implausible limitation on divine moral authority. In any case, we cannot exclude a motive for divine judgment in many cases: a responsible use of force to make room among humans for God's uncoercive power to attract people to divine–human reconciliation. Certainly, Jesus

---

[6] Hultgren, *The Parables of Jesus*, p. 370.

acknowledged a role for divine judgment, but he thought of this role as somehow serving God's redemptive effort toward divine–human reconciliation.[7]

As Chapter 1 suggested, Jesus sought to clarify for his disciples his special role in God's redemptive plan with a question for them, "Who do you say that I am?" (Mark 8:27–30; cf. Matt. 16:13–20, Luke 9:18–21). Peter's answer, "You are the Messiah," was dangerous, because it misrepresented the kind of divine power advocated by Jesus for his followers and God's kingdom. It risked misunderstanding Jesus with a use of a title connoting a triumphant Davidic Messiah-king with familiar political ambitions.[8] So, Jesus enjoined silence regarding public use of the title "Messiah" for him.

Jesus tended to characterize himself in terms of his distinctive actions. When in jail, John the Baptist sent Jesus a question regarding who he is, in relation to "the one who is to come." Luke's version is:

John summoned two of his disciples and sent them to the Lord to ask, "Are you the one who is to come, or are we to wait for another?" When the men had come to him, they said, "John the Baptist has sent us to you to ask, 'Are you the one who is to come, or are we to wait for another?'" Jesus had just then cured many people of diseases, plagues, and evil spirits, and had given sight to many who were blind. And he answered them, "Go and tell John what you have seen and heard: the blind receive their sight, the lame walk, the lepers are cleansed, the deaf hear, the dead are raised, the poor have good news brought to them. And blessed is anyone who takes no offense at me." (Luke 7:18–23; cf. Matt. 11:2–6)

Jesus's response to John echoed some passages from the book of Isaiah and its message of good news (for instance,

[7] Chapter 7 returns to the topic of Jesus and divine judgment.
[8] For relevant discussion, see Bruce Chilton, "Jesus *ben David*: Reflections on the *Davidssohnfrage*," *Journal for the Study of the New Testament* 14 (1982), 88–112.

Isa. 29:18–19, 35:5–6, 61:1).[9] When applied to Jesus, the passages from Isaiah give him a distinctive role in God's redemptive plan. We need to clarify this role if we are to understand his gospel from God.

4.2 ROYAL POWER RECONCEIVED

As Chapter 1 noted, the special role assumed by Jesus is, according to E. P. Sanders, that of the viceroy for God. Citing Matthew 19:27–9, where Jesus claimed the role of appointing judges over God's kingdom, Sanders comments: "This makes him, presumably, viceroy: at the head of the judges of Israel, subordinate only to God himself . . . God was king, but Jesus represented him and would represent him in the coming kingdom."[10] Even so, Luke's Jesus acknowledged his own kingly status to his disciples, courtesy of God: "I confer on you, just as my Father has conferred on me, a kingdom, so that you may eat and drink at my table in my kingdom, and you will sit on thrones judging the twelve tribes of Israel" (Luke 22:29–30). Just as God gave Jesus a kingdom, Jesus gave a kingdom to his disciples. (Chapter 7 returns to the latter theme.)

Jesus claimed a key role for himself, as "the Son of Man," in God's final judgment and resolution of this world: "Those who are ashamed of me and of my words in this adulterous and sinful generation, of them the Son of Man will also be ashamed when he comes in the glory of his Father with the holy angels" (Mark 8:38; cf. Luke 9:26, Matt. 16:27). A person's response to Jesus thus figures in Jesus's response to that person in the final divine resolution of things. We thus can say that, in one sense, a person's

---

[9] See the parallel in "the Messiah Apocalypse" of the Dead Sea Scrolls, 4Q521, and the corresponding parallel between Luke 4:16–21 and Isaiah 61:1. For comment on 4Q521, see Stanton, *Jesus and Gospel*, pp. 16–17, and Joseph A. Fitzmyer, *The One Who Is to Come* (Grand Rapids, MI: Eerdmans, 2007), pp. 96–7.

[10] Sanders, *The Historical Figure of Jesus* (London: Penguin, 1993), pp. 239, 248. See also Sanders, *Jesus and Judaism* (Philadelphia: Fortress Press, 1985), pp. 306–8. Similarly, see Barrett, *The Holy Spirit and the Gospel Tradition*, p. 156.

response to Jesus will decide whether his message of good news is actually good *for that person*. A negative response to Jesus could make his news negative for a person.

Jesus presented himself as having a unique role from God in relation to his disciples as well as others. He reported to James and John of Zebedee, "The cup that I drink you will drink; and with the baptism with which I am baptized, you will be baptized; but to sit at my right hand or at my left is not mine to grant, but it is for those for whom it has been prepared" (Mark 10:39–40; cf. Matt. 20:23). Jesus thus suggested that in his "glory," he will have a special throne from God, with a unique authority from God in the final resolution of the world.

An important case reported by all four New Testament Gospels indicates an *atypical* kingly role for Jesus, corresponding to an unusual kind of royal power from God. The Gospel of Matthew reports:

When they had come near Jerusalem and had reached Bethphage, at the Mount of Olives, Jesus sent two disciples, saying to them, "Go into the village ahead of you, and immediately you will find a donkey tied, and a colt with her; untie them and bring them to me. If anyone says anything to you, just say this, 'The Lord needs them.' And he will send them immediately." This took place to fulfill what had been spoken through the prophet, saying, "Tell the daughter of Zion, Look, your king is coming to you, humble, and mounted on a donkey, and on a colt, the foal of a donkey." (Matt. 21:1–5; cf. Mark 11:1–3, Luke 19:33–8, John 12:12–15; see Zech. 9:9)

Jesus's atypical understanding of kingship is illustrated by the donkey as a sign of humility and peace instead of domination and war. We have an enacted parable, then, indicating that Jesus redefined what it is to be God's appointed king and thus what it is to be God's kingdom. His redefining set him apart, sharply, from King David and any Davidic Messiah. The core of the good news, according to Jesus, is that God's kingdom comes with the primary aim to reconcile humans to God in peace, and not to condemn them or to manipulate them.

Sanders remarks: "The entry [into Jerusalem] was probably deliberately managed by Jesus to symbolize the coming kingdom and his own role in it. I account for the fact that Jesus was not executed until after the demonstration against the temple by proposing that it was an intentionally symbolic action, performed because Jesus regarded it to be true (he would be king, but a humble one) and for the sake of the disciples."[11] Jesus's combining being king with being humble leads to a distinctive image, status, and understanding of power for him. To clarify that image, status, and understanding, we need to explore Jesus's perspective on being humble before God and humans. Matthew's Jesus relates the general topic to God's kingdom: "Blessed are the poor in spirit, for theirs is the kingdom of heaven" (Matt. 5:3). We shall see that the relevant humility is anchored in a particular kind of agreeable obedience to God.

A helpful hint arises from the New Testament portrait of Jesus as referring to himself as "the Son of Man."[12] The most plausible account of this portrait, as Chapter 6 explains, is that Jesus sought to describe himself in a distinctive manner via his use of an Aramaic phrase in Daniel 7 (כְּבַר אֱנָשׁ), translated as "one like a son of man." The mysterious figure of Daniel 7 has two distinctive features. He receives a lasting kingdom from God, and he shares this kingdom with the persecuted people of God (Dan. 7:13–14, 18, 27). Daniel has a vision suggesting that a kingdom opposed to God and God's people "shall devour the whole earth, and trample it down, and break it to pieces" (Dan. 7:23; cf. 7:19). His vision thus suggests that the recipients of God's kingdom, including "one like a son of man,"

---

[11] Sanders, *Jesus and Judaism*, p. 308. Similarly, see Davies and Allison, *A Critical and Exegetical Commentary on the Gospel According to Saint Matthew*, vol. 3, p. 114.
[12] As Chapter 6 documents, the literature on the topic is extensive, representing a wide range of approaches.

undergo persecution and suffering for a while, on behalf of God's kingdom, from someone or some group opposed to God.

Daniel's vision can make some sense of the acknowledged suffering in the ministry of Jesus: "[Jesus] began to teach them that the Son of Man must undergo great suffering, and be rejected by the elders, the chief priests, and the scribes, and be killed" (Mark 8:31; cf. Luke 9:22, Matt. 16:21). Similarly: "[Jesus] said to them, 'Elijah is indeed coming first to restore all things. How then is it written about the Son of Man that he is to go through many sufferings and be treated with contempt?'" (Mark 9:12; cf. Matt. 17:10–12). The mention of what is "written" suggests a textual biblical source for the idea of the suffering Son of Man. Daniel 7 is the most plausible basis for this key idea for Jesus in the Gospels, even though it does not mention God's "Messiah."[13] His understanding of it would have prepared him for the suffering of the Son of Man and even his being "devoured" or killed on behalf of God's kingdom. It thus would have left him ready for the challenge of Gethsemane and its aftermath.

In referring to himself, Jesus evidently preferred "the Son of Man" to "Messiah" and "Son of David." The following consideration may have contributed to a lesser role for him for talk of "Son of David" and perhaps even of "Messiah":

While Jesus was teaching in the temple, he said, "How can the scribes say that the Messiah is the son of David? David himself, by the Holy Spirit, declared, 'The Lord said to my Lord, "Sit at my right hand, until I put your enemies under your feet."' David himself calls him Lord; so how can he be his son?" (Mark 12:35–7; cf. Psalm 110:1)

Jesus evidently thought of the awaited Messiah as having a status higher than that of the Son of David assumed by the

---

[13] Here I agree with C. F. D. Moule, *The Origin of Christology* (Cambridge: Cambridge University Press, 1977), p. 14, regarding a role for Daniel 7. Chapter 6 returns to this topic.

scribes. In any case, Jesus thought of himself as central to the coming near of God's kingdom, with power that liberates but includes suffering: "If it is by the finger of God that I cast out the demons, then the kingdom of God has come to you" (Luke 11:20; cf. Matt. 12:28, using "the Spirit of God"). This coming includes the coming near of God to humans in the distinctive power of God that is to be received in agreeable human obedience, despite accompanying suffering. It demands, according to Jesus, one's repentance as turning to God in obedience. Such repenting cannot be reduced to one's feeling guilty, ashamed, or sorry for one's shortcomings relative to God's commands. Something more profound occurs in the turning to God demanded by Jesus.

4.3 SIGNS FOR RECONCILIATION

The best illustration of Jesus's understanding of turning to God in repentance occurs in the parable of the prodigal son. A runaway son, as Chapter 2 noted, responds to his father:

"Father, I have sinned against heaven and before you; I am no longer worthy to be called your son." But the father said to his slaves, "Quickly, bring out a robe – the best one – and put it on him; put a ring on his finger and sandals on his feet. And get the fatted calf and kill it, and let us eat and celebrate; for this son of mine was dead and is alive again; he was lost and is found! And they began to celebrate." (Luke 15:21–4)

Repentance is thus a turning away from one's alienation from God for the sake of a reconciled relationship with God. The runaway son is reconciled to God, courtesy of divine forgiveness, despite the son's previous alienating ways. The emphasis is on repentance *for reconciliation with God*, and not on human sorrow or shame.[14]

---

[14] E. P. Sanders has proposed that Jesus did not give an important role to repentance in relation to God's kingdom. See his *Jesus and Judaism*, pp. 206–7, 227. Our evidence in the synoptic Gospels does not support this proposal. For critical

The ministry of Jesus exemplified in various ways the role of divine–human reconciliation in the good news. For instance, Jesus announced forgiveness in response to inquiring humans, and he claimed to have authority from God to do so (Mark 2:5–12, Matt. 9:2–7, Luke 5:20–5). He assumed that his authority as the "Son of Man" is from God, and he held that the forgiveness is for the sake of divine–human reconciliation.

Jesus suggested that the power of divine forgiveness and reconciliation is more profound and difficult in manifesting God's power than is his power of physical healing (Mark 2:9–11, Matt. 9:5–6, Luke 5:23–4).[15] This suggestion went against some familiar conceptions of divine power, but it pointed to the center of the good news from Jesus: God seeks reconciliation with humans through forgiveness. Whether humans received the forgiveness on offer was up to them, but the offer undercut any assumption of human earning of divine approval. It put them at the mercy of God, without divine condoning of human wrongdoing.

We should not confuse Jesus's healings or other miraculous signs with his goal of divine–human reconciliation; they were intended to be pointers or attention-getters for his goal. Luke's Jesus does not refuse to give miraculous signs altogether but instead acknowledges a "sign" provided by Jesus himself: "Just as Jonah became a sign to the people of Nineveh, so the Son of Man will be to this generation ... The people of Nineveh will rise up at the judgment with this generation and condemn it, because they repented at the proclamation of Jonah, and see, something greater than Jonah is here!" (Luke 11:30, 32). Jesus is thus a sign to his generation in a manner analogous to Jonah's being a sign to the people of Nineveh.

discussion, see Bruce Chilton, "Jesus and the Repentance of E.P. Sanders," *Tyndale Bulletin* 39 (1988), 1–18.

[15] On the historicity of Jesus's healing miracles and related miracles, see Meier, *A Marginal Jew*, vol. 2, chaps. 19–22.

The key point is that the people of Nineveh "repented at the preaching of Jonah, and behold, something greater than Jonah is here" in the person of Jesus. The sign of Jonah thus includes the repentance of Nineveh at his preaching, and this sign has an analog in the sign of Jesus to his generation. Just as Jonah was a sign from God to Nineveh, in virtue of Nineveh's repentance at his preaching, Jesus presents himself as a sign from God to his generation.

John's Gospel takes up the theme of Jesus as a sign from God: "They said to [Jesus], 'What sign are you going to give us then, so that we may see it and believe you? What work are you performing? Our ancestors ate the manna in the wilderness; as it is written, "He gave them bread from heaven to eat."' Then Jesus said to them, ... 'the bread of God is that which comes down from heaven and gives life to the world'" (John 6:30–3). Many people did not acknowledge Jesus as such a sign, and this prompted the following explanation from John's Jesus: "Everyone who has heard and learned from the Father comes to me" (John 6:45). Being receptive to (learning from) God, then, is central to recognizing Jesus as a sign from God. This fits with the claim of John's Gospel that "anyone who resolves to do the will of God's will know whether the teaching [of Jesus] is from God" (John 7:17).

Jonah's role as a sign from God included his role in the repentance of the people of Nineveh. Given Jonah's message of judgment on Nineveh, the king of Nineveh announced to his people: "Human beings and animals shall be covered with sackcloth, and they shall cry mightily to God. All shall turn from their evil ways and from the violence that is in their hands. Who knows? God may relent and change his mind; he may turn from his fierce anger, so that we do not perish" (Jonah 3:8–9). Jonah thus became, with the unintended aid of the king, an agent of repentance toward God for the people of Nineveh. Seeing the repentance of the people of Nineveh, God had mercy on them in "steadfast love" and called off the judgment announced by

Jonah (Jonah 3:10, 4:2). Jonah, then, was a living sign of God's merciful love that calls for human repentance for the sake of divine–human reconciliation.

Jesus, like Jonah, presented himself as a living sign of divine love that seeks human repentance for the sake of a reconciled relationship with God. There was, nonetheless, an important difference: Jesus *agreeably* delivered the divine message for humans, whereas Jonah delivered it with a disagreeable attitude. Jonah thus was a disobedient prophet used by God, whereas Jesus was the perfectly obedient prophet and son who carried out God's mission to humans. Both prophets, however, took their divine message beyond the Jewish people to gentile outsiders. Jesus focused his mission on the people of Israel (Matt. 15:24), but he extended his mission to gentiles too (Mark 7:29, Matt. 15:28, Luke 7:1–10). His extended mission for reconciliation became a matter of controversy among some Jews early in his ministry (Luke 4:23–8), but that mission did not cease.

All of the Gospels report that Jesus performed remarkable signs of various sorts. According to Matthew's Gospel, some critics of Jesus attributed some of his powerful signs, particularly his exorcisms, to the power of Satan (Matt. 9:34, 12:24–7, Luke 11:15; cf. John 7:20–1, 8:48–54, 11:47–8). Jesus claimed a contrary source: "If it is by the finger of God that I cast out the demons, then the kingdom of God has come to you" (Luke 11:20; cf. Matt. 12:28). According to all strata of the gospel traditions, Jesus performed remarkable signs, and these signs attracted the attention of critics and supporters. We can dispute the source of these signs, but the reports of them call for some explanation.

On occasion, Jesus refused a sign to people seeking a sign (Mark 8:12), but he reportedly included a range of signs in his ministry. He suggested at times that he had come as the divinely anointed one promised in the Jewish Bible, including the book of Isaiah (61:1–2), as God's redeeming representative (Matt. 11:4–6, Luke 4:18–19).

Jesus suggested that his miracles are signs not only of God's power but also of his own unique role in the coming of God's kingdom on earth. This fits with his preaching that inaugurated his ministry (Mark 1:15, Matt. 4:17), indicating that the kingdom of God was drawing near through him.

Jesus's signs were not impartial "proofs" of his unique status relative to God or of God's reality. Instead, they were elusive and subtle indicators of the power of God in his life. This raises the question of what God or Jesus aimed to accomplish with such elusive signs. We can approach this question by considering human failure to recognize God's signs for what they seek.

In denying that Jesus is a sign from God, many people demand a preferred different sign to indicate that Jesus is a genuine sign from God. In doing so, they suggest that Jesus himself was and is an inadequate sign from God, if he was a sign at all. In response, Alan Richardson has remarked:

It is possible for us to fail to see Christ as the manifestation of the power and the purpose of God; then we shall be content with an explanation of the miracle-stories in terms of modern psychology or folk-mythology. The miracle-stories, as an essential part of the preaching of apostolic Christianity, confront us with the question whether the power of God was or was not revealed in the person and work of Jesus Christ. They compel us to say Yes or No.[16]

This perspective fits with the discussion in Chapter 1 regarding Jesus's question for us about his status.

We are left to question whether Jesus himself is a sign of the unique power and purpose of God. A negative answer would be premature without clarification of the talk of "the power and the purpose of God." It would be akin to

---

[16] Alan Richardson, *The Miracle-Stories of the Gospels* (London: SCM Press, 1941), p. 126.

denying God's existence without a clarification of what the exalted title "God" connotes – a problem among many inquirers.

Richardson has proposed that "to understand the meaning of the miracle-stories of the gospel tradition it is first necessary to have penetrated the incognito of Jesus, and to have seen behind the Jesus of Galilee the Christ of New Testament faith."[17] This may be so, but we still need clarification of the relevant talk of the power and the purpose (or meaning) of God in the signs of Jesus. We also need clarification of what is included in the talk of "the Christ of New Testament faith."

Richardson adds:

[Jesus] was not concerned to impress his contemporaries with his marvelous power; but rather he asked them by the same token to believe that he had authority upon earth to forgive sins. He not merely opened the eyes of blind men, but claimed by that sign the power to make men see the truth of God ... He not merely raised a child or a man from the dead, but claimed in doing so to be the resurrection and the life ... In the last resort it was the sign of the resurrection which authenticated all Jesus's other signs and the claims which they involved. (cf. John 2:18–22)[18]

Richardson points in a plausible direction, a direction arguably suggested by Jesus himself (Mark 2:9–11, Luke 5:22–4). It seems odd, however, to invoke the resurrection of Jesus as what "authenticated" his signs and claims. One problem is that his resurrection does not have an impartial "proof" for all concerned. In fact, invoking the resurrection of Jesus will seem question-begging to many critics.

Some crucial evidence regarding the resurrection of Jesus is arguably sensitive to an inquirer's will (regarding God's will) in a manner that challenges its use as an

---

[17] Richardson, *The Miracle-Stories of the Gospels*, p. 137.
[18] Richardson, *The Miracle-Stories of the Gospels*, pp. 131–2.

impartial authentication for all concerned. Jesus himself evidently acknowledged this in ascribing the following remark to Abraham in a parabolic story: "If they do not listen to Moses and the prophets, neither will they be convinced even if someone rises from the dead" (Luke 16:31). This remark conflicts with any simple historical empiricism as a means for confirming the resurrection of Jesus or related divine signs. A person's listening to Moses and the prophets somehow figures in being suitably convinced of the resurrection. The clarification of "somehow" is important now.

We can benefit by attending to the idea of "listening to Moses and the prophets." A natural question is: Listening to *what* in Moses and the prophets? Jesus did not have in mind *all* of the details of the Mosaic law and the prophets' teachings, because he corrected some of the teachings of the Jewish scriptures, including those about God as hating God's enemies. For instance, some of the Psalms (5:5, 11:5) teach that God hates wicked people but Jesus taught that God loves evil people, including God's enemies, and that the children of God should follow suit (Matt. 5:43–8, Luke 6:27–36). Jesus did not share the hateful attitude of the psalmists or assign that attitude to God.

Jesus thought of the main lesson of the Jewish scriptures (including "Moses and the prophets") as pointing to God's redemptive love, humanly personified in himself. This love, according to Jesus, includes definite commandments to be obeyed by humans. According to Matthew's Gospel, he portrayed "the [Mosaic] law and the prophets" as depending on two commandments: first, the commandment to love the Lord your God with all your heart, soul, and mind; and, second, the commandment to love your neighbor as yourself (Matt. 22:37–40; cf. Mark 12:29–31). Mark's Gospel portrays Jesus adding that there is no commandment greater than these two (12:31), and Luke's Gospel represents Jesus offering these two commandments in response to the question of what one can do to inherit eternal life (10:25–8).

Jesus recognized that humans do not fully obey the love commandments at the heart of his teaching and therefore are in need of forgiveness and repentance. He says of humans: "If you, who are evil, know how to give good gifts to your children, how much more will your Father who is in heaven give good gifts to those who ask him?" (Matt. 7:11). He also taught that it is impossible for humans to save themselves but that human salvation is nonetheless possible for God (Mark 10:26–7, Luke 18:26–7, Matt. 19:25–6). He offered, as Chapter 3 suggested, the parable of the laborers in the vineyard to teach that God's kingdom operates by God's gracious generosity rather than by human scales of merit or earning (Matt. 20:1–16). In addition, he offered the parable of the Pharisee and the tax collector to illustrate that justification before God stems from God's mercy rather than human self-righteousness (Luke 18:9–14). Divine love, according to Jesus, involves a life-giving merciful gift of right relationship with God as well as a command to love God and others.

The Gospel of John considers human failing to perceive Jesus as the culminating sign of God for human redemption. The brothers of Jesus say to him: "If you do these things [that is, these signs], show yourself to the world" and the author interjects an editorial remark: "Not even his brothers believed in him" (John 7:4–5). John's Gospel thus suggests that Jesus's brothers were not in a position to understand the nature of his signs, particularly that they point to a distinctive kind of divine love. Their charge to "show yourself to the world" showed their serious misunderstanding of God and Jesus regarding the divine purpose of special signs.

John's Jesus contrasted his brothers with himself: "The world cannot hate you, but it hates me because I testify of it that its works are evil" (John 7:7). In this context, we get the previously mentioned lesson that "anyone who resolves to do the will of God's will know whether the teaching [of Jesus] is from God" (John 7:17). "Resolving to do God's will" thus emerges as significant in discerning whether Jesus is genuinely a sign from God. As a self-avowed sign from God in the tradition of Jonah, Jesus sought a response of human repentance and trust in the light of God's merciful and demanding love.

We now can clarify what God wants from redemptive signs, including the personified signs of Jonah and Jesus. The case of Jonah illustrates that God seeks to show that God is "gracious ... and merciful, slow to anger, and abounding in steadfast love, and ready to relent from punishing" (Jonah 4:2). God thus assigned Jonah to call the people of Nineveh to repentance and cooperative trust toward God, and when they repented, God called off the judgment threatened by Jonah (3:4–5, 4:2, 11).

The sign of Jonah manifests God's "merciful, steadfast love" for the sake of calling wayward people into reconciliation with God. This is the concluding lesson of the book of Jonah (4:11), and Jesus found it to anticipate his own ministry on behalf of God toward wayward people. Like Jonah, Jesus regarded himself as one sent by God to manifest, in his life and his death, God's merciful, steadfast love toward wayward people. Luke thus portrays Jesus as announcing: "Do not be afraid, little flock, for it is your Father's good pleasure to give you the [divine] kingdom" (Luke 12:32). God's merciful, unearned giving of his kingdom, through Jesus, to wayward people is his "grace," in Paul's influential language (Rom. 3:21–6). Such language of "grace" is a variation on the language of divine *agapē*, or self-giving, merciful redemptive love, even toward God's enemies.

The redemptive love manifested by God in the sign of Jesus is not only offered by God but also, as suggested, commanded by God of recipients. Given the divine love included in the signs offered by Jesus, we should not expect it to coerce human acceptance but to allow for voluntary appropriation by humans with cooperative trust. The divine power of love includes the uncoercive power to attract cooperative humans to receive the forgiveness and reconciliation on offer. The attracting stems from the power of divine goodness experienced by receptive humans, but it does not find universal cooperation from humans. The ministry of Jesus met the failure of many humans to be attracted by his offer of divine forgiveness and reconciliation, despite his efforts to reach them, even through amazing signs. As genuine agents, they had the option to resist or to ignore the good news of reconciliation, and some people chose not to cooperate.

In his quest for divine–human reconciliation, Jesus ate with "tax collectors and sinners," instead of avoiding the morally impure people around him. Luke's Gospel links this practice to a call from Jesus to repentance: "The Pharisees and their scribes were complaining to his disciples, saying, 'Why do you eat and drink with tax collectors and sinners?' Jesus answered, 'Those who are well have no need of a physician, but those who are sick; I have come to call not the righteous but sinners to repentance'" (Luke 5:30–2; cf. Mark 2:16–17, Matt. 9:11–13). This repentance was intended for the kind of reconciliation illustrated by a shared meal with the "Son of Man" as God's representative. This kind of meal resembles the meal of reconciliation at the center of the parable of the prodigal son.

The reconciliation or peace sought by Jesus was guided by God's perfect moral character and hence was not an "anything-goes" prospect. Luke's Jesus thus announced: "Do you think that I have come to bring peace to the earth? No, I tell you, but rather division! From now on five in one household will be divided, three against two and two against three" (Luke 12:51–2; cf. Matt. 10:34–6). Jesus thus ruled out any kind of morally thin reconciliation or peace that condones a partnership in unrighteousness. Morally robust divine–human reconciliation brings division in the presence of uncooperative humans, even though peace in divine goodness is the ultimate goal.

God's character of morally righteous love is the standard for divine–human reconciliation because such reconciliation is reconciliation *to God*. This fits with the observation of Victor Paul Furnish that "the kingdom of God is the Rule of God's forgiving and commanding love; Jesus's call to repentance and discipleship is a call to obey God's will, to manifest the reality and meaning of his kingship in one's life."[19] In believing in God's good news and in loving God, as Jesus commanded (Mark 1:15, 12:28–31), one trusts in the God of good news, and such trust calls for obeying, or cooperating with, that God. So, Jesus commanded: "Have faith in God" (Mark 11:22), and he had in mind full sympathetic and cooperative trust in God. Jesus himself manifested the relevant kind of loving, trusting in, and cooperating with God, paradigmatically in Gethsemane. In doing so, he showed in action what it is to embrace and manifest God's kingdom as a human's priority.

The unique character of the reconciliation sought by Jesus emerged from his own obedient filial relationship to God, and, as Chapter 3 explained, that relationship had a high point in Gethsemane. If God is king, and one turns to God as king, then God's rule by God's redemptive will takes on supremacy for one. God thus becomes *one's own* God and Lord, beyond just *a* God and Lord. Jesus was the exemplar for humans in Gethsemane as he prayed to God as God's obedient child: "Abba, Father, for you all things are possible; remove this cup from me; yet, not what I want, but what you want" (Mark 14:32–6; cf. Matt. 26:36–9, Luke 22:39–42, John 12:27).

Jesus *initially* sought an alternative to his impending death in Jerusalem ("remove this cup from me"), but he settled on filial obedience to God as his Father. As Chapter 3 noted, the initial will of Jesus needed reconciliation with God's superior redemptive will. His filial obedience in Gethsemane was sincere cooperation with God's will, and

[19] Furnish, *The Love Command in the New Testament*, pp. 194–5.

he thereby set the model for human cooperating with God for the sake of God's kingdom.

Mark's version of Gethsemane, as Chapter 3 noted, gives a central role to the matter of *power* in pleasing God. Jesus raised the issue of the strength or power of his disciples: "He came and found them sleeping; and he said to Peter, 'Simon, are you asleep? Could you not [οὐκ ἴσχυσας; literally: are you not *able* or *strong* enough to] keep awake one hour?'" (Mark 14:37). The matter of power emerged also in the following advice of Jesus to his disciples in Gethsemane: "Keep awake and pray that you may not come into the time of trial; the spirit indeed is willing, but the flesh is weak" (Mark 14:38). The weakness of "the flesh" can undermine the willingness of a human spirit, and therefore a human spirit needs supporting power.

Gethsemane cooperation with God, in the example of Jesus, served God's kingdom as the means to a human's receiving the formative power of the kingdom. This is the power to receive, manifest, and share God's moral character, will, and life in a human life. It includes the intentional power of divine righteous love expressed to a human, and agreeable cooperation with this interpersonal power includes trust in it and conformity to it. We have noted the connection between God's kingdom and God's will in the Lord's Prayer in Matthew's Gospel: "Thy kingdom come; Thy will be done" (Matt. 6:10; cf. Luke 11:2). This prayer makes the volitional cooperation of Gethsemane central to the coming of God's kingdom on earth.

Jesus acknowledged his Father's call for him to give up his life for others, as seen at the Last Supper (Mark 14:23–5, Matt. 26:27–9) and Gethsemane. He needed, however, divine power to cooperate with this severe call, and therefore he needed to call on God as follows: "Not what I want, but what you want." The needed power is in God's morally perfect will, and a human agreeably receives this power by sharing in God's will, by agreeably cooperating with it above all else. The good news from Jesus applies here, because it includes the news of God's powerful moral life coming to a cooperative human life and giving it new value, purpose, and motivation, grounded in divine goodness, including righteous love. The new life comes to humans via the model of Jesus in Gethsemane, and its center is a reconciled, peaceful relationship with God.

A key requirement, suited to Gethsemane, is that one yield, or die to, one's anti-God will and ways, to make room for God's will and ways. As Chapter 3 noted in part, Jesus stated: "If any want to become my followers, let them deny themselves and take up their cross and follow me. For those who want to save their life will lose it, and those who lose their life for my sake, and for the sake of the gospel, will save it" (Mark 8:34–5; cf. Matt. 16:24–5, Luke 9:23–4; see also Matt. 10:38–9, Luke 14:27). Just as Jesus obediently took up his cross for others, his disciples must follow suit, in keeping with God's character of self-giving love.

According to Matthew's Gospel, Jesus related worship of God to needed reconciliation to offended humans: "When you are offering your gift at the altar, if you remember that your brother or sister has something against you, leave your gift there before the altar and go; first be reconciled to your brother or sister, and then come and offer your gift" (Matt. 5:23–4; cf. Mark 11:25). One's deepening reconciliation to God thus can depend on one's reconciliation to offended humans. So, divine–human reconciliation has an important social component among humans, as Chapter 7 will consider.

4.4 SECRET KINGDOM, HIDDEN GOSPEL

The good news announced by Jesus is candid about our own bad news, regarding our anti-God wills and ways. It promises divine power to counter and replace our bad wills and ways with the perfect will and way of God. Jesus thus presented the kingdom of God as coming with conflict between good and evil, including the "demonic." He presented himself as overcoming the world's demonic evil that obstructs God's kingdom: "No one can enter a strong man's house and plunder his property without first tying up the strong man; then indeed the house can be plundered" (Mark 3:27; cf. Matt. 12:29, Luke 8:21–2). However one understands the demonic, such talk indicated a clash of wills, divine versus anti-divine, and Jesus exemplified in Gethsemane God's intended priority for human wills in God's perfect will.

Many people opt for an anti-God priority and thus reject the good news of God's kingdom offered by Jesus. His parable of the sower identified various human motives for rejecting the message of good news from God (Mark 4:13–20, Matt. 13:18–23, Luke 8:11–15). Those motives run afoul, in one way or another, of Jesus's command to "strive first for the kingdom of God and his righteousness" (Matt. 6:36; cf. Luke 12:31). The reception of God's kingdom anchored in God's will should come as a top priority, according to Jesus, and not as a backup insurance policy. As a result, Jesus identified the standard for entering God's kingdom: "Not everyone who says to me, 'Lord, Lord,' will enter the kingdom of heaven, but only the one who does the will of my Father in heaven" (Matt. 7:21; cf. Luke 6:46). By this standard, the Gethsemane cooperation of Jesus exemplified the criterion for entering God's kingdom.

In the face of human resistance to God and himself, Jesus taught in parables: "When he was alone, those who were around him along with the twelve asked him about the parables. And he said to them, 'To you has been given the secret [or, mystery; μυστήριον] of the kingdom of God, but for those outside, everything comes in parables'" (Mark 4:10–11). The Gospels of Matthew and Luke put the point in terms of knowledge: "To you it has been given to know the secrets of the kingdom of heaven, but to them it has not been given" (Matt. 13:11; cf. Luke 8:10). If we combine the two statements, we have a secret, or mystery, about not only the kingdom of God but also human knowledge of

God's kingdom. The parables of Jesus somehow protect such a secret. Matthew's Jesus adds: "The reason I speak to them in parables is that 'seeing they do not perceive, and hearing they do not listen, nor do they understand'" (Matt. 13:13). Mark's parallel statement is sometimes interpreted to imply that the parables seek to exclude some people from repentance and forgiveness, but we can follow Matthew's Gospel in avoiding such an unduly harsh reading.[20]

The secret in question involves a kind of divine redemptive elusiveness or hiddenness. It is intended to avoid the deepening of the alienation of resistant humans from God. Given the redemptive purpose of the gospel of Jesus, we should expect this purpose not to be satisfied just by human intellectual assent to information about God. Such assent would not bring a person to interpersonal reconciliation with God; in fact, it is compatible with one's hating God. The gospel from Jesus thus sought a deeper kind of human commitment to God, including sincere *volitional* cooperation with God's will. Such cooperation is central to interpersonal reconciliation with God, and it can enable a person to receive and to manifest God's moral character, if imperfectly.

Matthew's Jesus offered a blessing: "Blessed are the pure in heart, for they will see God" (Matt. 5:8). He did not say anything similar about mere purity of mind, such as mere doctrinal correctness, because he wanted to name the deepest center of a person, including one's volitional center. His concern was for what one values in cooperative commitment, not just what one thinks or believes. The reason: "For where your treasure is, there your heart will be also" (Matt. 6:21). Luke's Jesus expressed the same concern in his parable of the sower (Luke 8:15). So, we should not expect

---

[20] See Davies and Allison, *A Critical and Exegetical Commentary on the Gospel According to Saint Matthew*, vol. 2, p. 392. Cf. T. W. Manson, *The Teaching of Jesus*, 2nd ed. (Cambridge: Cambridge University Press, 1935), pp. 75–80. Chapter 5 returns to this topic.

a merely intellectual means of appropriating the gospel of Jesus. We should expect instead a demand on the whole person relative to cooperating with God's will.

Purity of heart, according to Jesus, centers on singleness of cooperative commitment to God and the primacy of God's will. It requires one to will what God wills regarding various matters, above all else and with full commitment. Jesus manifested that practice in Gethsemane, in the face of tragic consequences. Lack of purity of heart will obstruct one's apprehension of God aright, because it will include one's failing to apprehend God's signature moral will *in sympathetic cooperation* where it reaches its intended fruition for the sake of divine goodness among humans.

God's moral will can lack salience in human experience in the absence of its intended fruition in human cooperation. In that case, its distinctive power is not apprehended for what it is intended to be in human experience: a power worthily attracting human cooperation, owing to the divine goodness of that power. God thus may hide the divine moral will, in its salience, in the purity of a cooperative heart, courtesy of God's redemptive intention for humans. This intention includes God's aim to self-reveal in ways that are *morally beneficial* to humans, in keeping with God's moral character. This aim seeks to attract humans to cooperate agreeably with God on the basis of their experienced goodness of God's will, without coercion of a human will.

The gospel of Jesus, including the volitional power of God's redemptive moral character, can elude us in its distinctive power when we choose not to cooperate with God's will. In that case, God can hide the divine moral character, power, and presence from us for our moral and redemptive benefit. This would be by divine redemptive intent, because God typically seeks *willing* human conformity to God's perfect will when it is apprehended in experience. God thus seeks not to trivialize or to discredit this will among humans by letting it

routinely be a morally ineffective phenomenon of experience. So, divine hiding on occasion is a live option for
a morally perfect God aiming for the redemption of
humans.

God's redemptive aim is to challenge and attract humans
to turn cooperatively, with full commitment, to the divine
will, for the sake of their reconciliation to God. When we
neglect or resist an experienced Gethsemane challenge to
put God's will first in our lives, we distance ourselves from
God's will and thereby make it distant from us as a vital
moral power from God. We then contribute to divine elusiveness in our experience, and God can comply with divine
hiding, in order to allow prodigal humans to come, responsibly and without coercion, to their senses when they are
ready. So, God can hide for a good redemptive reason, and
human resistance can contribute to God's hiding.

As Chapter 2 noted, Jesus expressed the redemptive
hiddenness of God's ways, in commenting on the mixed
human response to him, his ministry, and his gospel. He
did so, as indicated, by giving thanks to God: "I thank you,
Father, Lord of heaven and earth, because you have hidden
these things from the wise and the intelligent and have
revealed them to infants" (Matt. 11:25; cf. Luke 10:21). His
thanksgiving prayer to God captured a familiar attitude of
God in the Jewish Bible toward people who exalt their own
understanding over God's wisdom (Isa. 29:14, Job 28:28; cf.
1 Cor. 1:19). God typically hides from them for their own
redemptive good, to give them the room needed to learn
their own folly (as in the case of the prodigal son). Jesus
thanked God for such redemptive hiding, and he showed
no misgiving about it.

W. D. Davies and Dale C. Allison have commented on
the kind of knowledge of God pertinent to Jesus's prayer of
Matthew 11:25:

Religious knowledge ... has a moral dimension. Such knowledge cannot be grasped either by dispassionate, neutral

observers or by those who have no thirst for "the things above." Spiritual things are only discerned by the spiritual (1 Cor. 2:14–15) and only those who love God can know him (1 John 4:8). Revelation, it follows, is necessarily hid from self-seeking savants and the vain exemplars of worldly reason, of however a devout demeanour. The doors to true wisdom remain closed to them … Divine truths are, therefore, revealed only to "babes," that is, to the truly meek and humble.[21]

This consideration about knowing God results from God's redemptive purpose in self-revealing and self-hiding, and it need not come from anything more abstract or metaphysical. So, we need caution in use of "necessarily" here. The focus should be instead on God's good purpose in relating to humans.

Jesus did not condemn intellectual or theoretical work in general by humans. He was, rather, countering an intellectual attitude that is presumptuous before God about divine ways of redemption, particularly ways involving Jesus and his mission. Even so, we need a more specific account of the hiddenness of divine revelation in the gospel; we cannot leave the matter in the general terms offered.

The thanksgiving prayer of Jesus has a unifying role in Matthew's Gospel. Davies and Allison explain: "[Matthew] 11:25–30 is a capsule summary of the message of the entire Gospel. In this passage, Jesus reveals that he is the revealer. That is, he reveals that, as the meek and humble Son of the Father, he fulfills the calling of Israel, embodying in his own person Torah and Wisdom and thus making known the perfect will of God."[22] He thus made known God's will

[21] Davies and Allison, *A Critical and Exegetical Commentary on the Gospel According to Saint Matthew*, vol. 2, pp. 275–6. See page 278 for their comment in favor of the historical authenticity of Matthew 11:25–6, with their conclusion that "the arguments could hardly be stronger." See also A. M. Hunter, "Crux Criticorum – Matt. 11:25–30 – A Re-appraisal," *New Testament Studies* 8 (1962), 241–9. On the parallel passage in Luke and its authenticity, see Fitzmyer, *The Gospel According to Luke* (New York: Doubleday, 1985), vol. 2, pp. 864–76.
[22] Davies and Allison, *A Critical and Exegetical Commentary on the Gospel According to Saint Matthew*, vol. 2, p. 296.

in word and action, paradigmatically in Gethsemane, but overall in a way unmatched by other humans. His mission as "the Son" is directed not to himself but to "the Father" who is his God.

Leonhard Goppelt has observed the pivotal role of Jesus in God's kingdom: "'The secret of God's kingdom' was the manner of the kingdom's eschatological coming. For the Jesus tradition, the secret was not the kingdom's imminent coming (cf. Mark 1:14 f.), but its present coming in the ministry of Jesus ... Recognition of this secret was, in fact, 'given' by God only to the disciples (Matt. 13:11 f.)."[23] Jesus, then, became the one to whom people should look for knowing his divine Father and God's perfect will for his kingdom. Jesus's crisis in Gethsemane enabled others to share in his "secret" kingdom of God so long as they share his cooperative attitude in Gethsemane toward the primacy of God's will. We need to follow this lesson into the post-resurrection gospel of Jesus, in order to understand his hidden gospel.

4.5 EXPANDED GOSPEL

The good news from Jesus regarding God's coming kingdom expanded when the crucified and risen messenger became part of the Christian message. The foundational proclaimer himself became a figure in the proclaimed good news.[24] Even so, a kind of divine hiddenness persists for the gospel from Jesus, and we need to explain it.

Goppelt remarks: The "concealment [of Jesus's role in God's kingdom] ended with Easter; from that point on, Jesus was openly proclaimed as the promised One. The hiddenness of the eschatological revelation of salvation

---

[23] Goppelt, *Theology of the New Testament*, trans. J. E Alsup (Grand Rapids, MI: Eerdmans, 1981), vol. 1, pp. 174–5.

[24] See Rudolf Bultmann, *Theology of the New Testament*, trans. Kendrick Grobel (New York: Charles Scribner's Sons, 1951), vol. 1, p. 33.

remained, however."[25] Similarly, Markus Bockmuehl remarks on Paul's understanding of the concealment of God's plan of salvation: "This hiddenness continues in the present era: contrary to the opinion of some critics, the 'wisdom in a mystery' is not simply 'a divine secret, hitherto concealed, but now revealed.'"[26] Such hiddenness is widely neglected among interpreters of Jesus, and it is rarely explained. We need to explain how it continues in the present era.

Paul remarks to the Corinthians:

Among the mature we do speak wisdom, though it is not a wisdom of this age or of the rulers of this age, who are doomed to perish. But we speak God's wisdom, secret and hidden, which God decreed before the ages for our glory. None of the rulers of this age understood this; for if they had, they would not have crucified the Lord of glory. (1 Cor. 2:6–8)

The NRSV translates a Greek word for "mystery" (μυστηρίῳ) as "secret," and that helps somewhat to capture Paul's thinking. Paul had in mind the elusive way God worked in the crucified Jesus to bring the good news of salvation for humans.[27]

Paul understood the mystery of God's wisdom and gospel in terms of the working of God's Spirit. He remarks:

Now we have received not the spirit of the world, but the Spirit that is from God, so that we may understand the gifts bestowed on us by God. And we speak of these things in words not taught by human wisdom but taught by the Spirit, interpreting spiritual things to those who are spiritual.

---

[25] Goppelt, *Theology of the New Testament*, vol. 1, p. 176.

[26] Markus Bockmuehl, *Revelation and Mystery in Ancient Judaism and Pauline Christianity*, WUNT (Tübingen: Mohr Siebeck, 1990), p. 165.

[27] For discussion of Paul's talk of "mystery," see Bockmuehl, *Revelation and Mystery in Ancient Judaism and Pauline Christianity*, pp. 157–77.

Those who are unspiritual do not receive the gifts of God's Spirit, for they are foolishness to them, and they are unable to understand them because they are spiritually discerned. (1 Cor. 2:12–14)

Paul thought of receiving the gospel as receiving a gift from God's Spirit, because he thought of the gospel as the redemptive power of God given to humans by God's Spirit. He commented on the divine power in the gospel: "I am not ashamed of the gospel; it is the power [δύναμις] of God for salvation to everyone who has faith, to the Jew first and also to the Greek" (Rom. 1:16).

Paul named the Spirit of God as crucial to receiving aright the gospel message of Jesus as Lord: "No one can say 'Jesus is Lord' except by the Holy Spirit" (1 Cor. 12:3). He meant "say with a proper basis in God's power," and not just the enunciation of words. Paul also linked "the Spirit of God's Son" to human reception of (the good news of) divine redemption as reconciled adoption into God's family: "When the fullness of time had come, God sent his Son, born of a woman, born under the law, in order to redeem those who were under the law, so that we might receive adoption as children. And because you are children, God has sent the Spirit of his Son into our hearts, crying, 'Abba! Father!'" (Gal. 4:4–6; cf. Rom. 8:15–16). Paul offered a clear summary of the relation of the gospel to God's Spirit: "Our message of the gospel came to you not in word only, but also in power and in the Holy Spirit and with full conviction" (1 Thess. 1:5; cf. 1 Cor. 1:18, 2:4, Rom. 15:19). So, Paul's gospel is pneumatic, courtesy of the empowering Spirit of God and of God's Son.

We need to distinguish between a gospel as mere good *information* and Paul's gospel as good news accompanied by *the power of God's Spirit* for redemption. In speaking of the gospel as mere good information, we miss out on what Paul had in mind, including how the gospel can be hidden from humans even after the proclaimed resurrection of Jesus. The gospel *as divine power* of a morally relevant sort can be hidden in the elusive working of God's Spirit for redemption. Even if the gospel as mere good information is explicit to a person, the same need not be true of the gospel as God's power for salvation. This distinction emerges from the fact that the redemptive power of God's gospel is the intentional power of God for attracting and reconciling cooperative humans to God.

The divine power for reconciliation includes the needed power for humans cooperatively to obey God's moral will, after the model of Gethsemane. Humans need to yield willingly to God for that moral power, because, in their moral weakness, they do not have it on their own. Like Jesus in Gethsemane, they need to depend on divine power by yielding to it, even against any initial opposing inclinations. (One could argue that Romans 7:21–5 represents Paul's view in this regard, but we cannot digress.[28])

If we decide not to cooperate with God's will, we will lack direct acquaintance with the redemptive divine power in its intended fruition in human cooperation with it. We then will lack direct awareness of that divine power in its intended culmination in divine–human reconciliation. Our own will thus can obstruct our apprehension of God's will in its intended fruition, as we suppress it in denying it due primacy in our lives. In that case, we will fail to have direct experience of the gospel as God's power for salvation in actual divine–human reconciliation. The gospel, in that regard, will be hidden from us regarding what it is intended to be, owing to our failure to cooperate with God's will. God can hide from humans for various redemptive purposes (not all of which we should expect to know), but the present kind of case leaves the redemptive power of the gospel in actual reconciliation hidden from a recalcitrant human.[29]

---

[28] For relevant discussion, see Will N. Timmins, *Romans 7 and Christian Identity: A Study of the "I" in Its Literary Context*, SNTSMS (Cambridge: Cambridge University Press, 2017), pp. 137–99.

[29] On the broader role for divine hiddenness in human redemption, see Paul Moser, *The God Relationship* (Cambridge: Cambridge University Press, 2017), chap. 3, and Moser, *The Elusive God* (Cambridge: Cambridge University Press, 2008). We do not

The needed power of cooperatively obeying God's will is to be received by humans in a Gethsemane context of decision regarding God's will, after the model of Jesus. This context reveals the signature power of Jesus – in obedience to God through prayer in Gethsemane. As Chapter 3 noted, Paul identified such power with the definitive power of obedience, rather than suffering, exercised by Jesus in his crucifixion (Phil. 2:8). This power of cooperating with God enables the uncoercive power of the primacy of God's intentional redemptive will over a morally inferior human will, and this primacy manifests God *as God and Lord* relative to cooperative humans.

Paul spoke of the message of the cross of Jesus as the power of God to those "who are being saved," while it is foolishness to those who ignore or resist its self-giving power (1 Cor. 1:18). This gospel message seeks to attract proper acknowledgment of God as one's God and Lord in a Gethsemane context, as one cooperatively obeys God's supreme will. Paul thought of God as working in human conscience to give some *initial* self-revelation of God's moral character to humans, but he allowed for human rejection of this initial revelation (Rom. 2:14–15). Such rejection would result in the hiddenness of the gospel in its intended fruition as divine power for divine–human reconciliation.

Paul identified a role for "the god of this world" in the hidden gospel after Easter: "Even if our gospel is veiled, it is veiled to those who are perishing. In their case the god of this world has blinded the minds of the unbelievers, to keep them from seeing the light of the gospel of the glory of Christ, who is the image of God" (2 Cor. 4:3–4; cf. Mark 4:15). The "light of the gospel," in Paul's perspective, is no mere intellectual matter; it includes the redemptive power of the gospel, courtesy of God's purposive Spirit. We need to put this power-oriented approach to the gospel in its larger context.

have, and should not expect to have, a full theodicy for divine hiding that identifies all of the underlying divine purposes. Chapter 8 returns to the topic of theodicy.

Paul offered a summary of his gospel to the Corinthian Christians:

I would remind you, brothers and sisters, of the good news that I proclaimed to you, which you in turn received, in which also you stand, through which also you are being saved, if you hold firmly to the message that I proclaimed to you – unless you have come to believe in vain. For I handed on to you as of first importance what I in turn had received: that Christ died for our sins in accordance with the scriptures, and that he was buried, and that he was raised on the third day in accordance with the scriptures. (1 Cor. 15:1–4)

Paul understood the risen Christ as having a unique redemptive status that is often neglected by interpreters. He remarked: "Thus it is written, 'The first man, Adam, became a living being'; the last Adam became a life-giving spirit" (1 Cor. 15:45).

Paul associated the Spirit of God with the Spirit of the risen Christ in some contexts, that is, the Christ who, in Paul's view, is the crucified Jesus (Rom. 8:9–11). Even so, the risen Christ is not *merely* the historical Jesus, in Paul's understanding, as he has taken on a new role for God. As G. W. H. Lampe notes: "'Christ' as a present reality always means more than the historical figure of Jesus."[30] Paul thus referred to "Christ the power of God" (1 Cor. 1:24), and not just as a past power, thus indicating that he is no *mere* historical figure.[31]

The idea of Jesus as a "life-giving Spirit" who gives God's Spirit to people did not originate with Paul. All of the Gospels, including John's Gospel, include the promise that the historical Jesus baptized by John the Baptist will

---

[30] G. W. H. Lampe, *God as Spirit* (Oxford: Clarendon Press, 1977), p. 3; cf. p. 5.

[31] For relevant discussion, see Dunn, "The Spirit of Jesus," pp. 329–42; and James D. G. Dunn, "1 Corinthians 15:45 – Last Adam, Life-giving Spirit," in *Christ and Spirit in the New Testament: Studies in Honour of C.F.D. Moule*, eds. Barnabas Lindars and Stephen S. Smalley (Cambridge: Cambridge University Press, 1973), pp. 127–41. On the relation of the risen Jesus to the Spirit of God, see Dunn, *Christology in the Making*, 2nd ed. (London: SCM Press, 1989), pp. 146–9.

baptize people with God's Spirit (Mark 1:8, Matt. 3:11, Luke 3:16, John 1:33; cf. Acts 1:4–5, John 3:34). In that regard, Jesus is predicted to be the Lord of Pentecost (Acts 2:32–3), the one responsible for sending God's Spirit to humans for their salvation as reconciliation to God. The risen Jesus thereby supplies the interpersonal power needed by humans to respond cooperatively to the gospel's accompanying charge to repent and to trust God. We need to clarify further *how* power for life is given by the life-giving Spirit associated with the risen Christ. In doing so, we shall identify a common core to appropriating aright the two-stage gospel of Jesus.

Notably, Paul did not talk much of "repentance" in his letters (cf. Rom. 2:4), but he did capture its idea of turning to God with his talk of being "reconciled" to God.[32] In fact, he issued a command to be reconciled to God, including to Christians at Corinth: "In Christ God was reconciling the world to himself, not counting their trespasses against them, and entrusting the message of reconciliation to us. So, we are ambassadors for Christ, since God is making his appeal through us; we entreat you on behalf of Christ, be reconciled to God" (2 Cor. 5:19–20). Paul thus did not limit needed reconciliation to God to people outside the Christian church. Even Christians can be in need here.

Paul assumed a difference between reconciliation and justification in relation to God, but he identified a connection: "Since we are justified by faith, we have peace with God through our Lord Jesus Christ" (Rom. 5:1). Divine justification brings the peace of reconciliation to God, but the two are not identical. As C. E. B. Cranfield notes, God "conferring the status of righteousness" on guilty humans in their justification is not the same thing as God's reconciliation of "giving Himself to us in friendship and establishing peace

---

[32] For Paul on repentance, see Eckhard J. Schnabel, "Repentance in Paul's Letters," *Novum Testamentum* 57 (2015), 159–86; cf. E. P. Sanders, *Paul and Palestinian Judaism* (London: SCM Press, 1977), pp. 499–502.

between Himself and us."[33] Even so, given who God is as a purposive reconciling redeemer, the divine justification of humans typically *leads* to their reconciliation to God.

What, then, of the Corinthian Christians whom Paul challenged to be reconciled to God? Perhaps Paul acknowledged degrees or levels of reconciliation to God, along with some people needing to deepen their reconciliation to God. This understanding of reconciliation would correspond to different levels of trust or faith in God (cf. Rom. 12:3). It is also possible that Paul identified a failure in some Corinthian Christians to look beyond the divine justification of humans to divine–human reconciliation.

Margaret Thrall has asked whether the Corinthian Christians "had fully realized their own need to be reconciled to God." She adds: "Without a keen appreciation of the depth and extent of human enmity towards God, exposed by the desperate measures God took to overcome it, the original message of reconciliation may have remained somewhat lacking in its impact upon them."[34] The important point, however, is that Paul's version of the gospel called for a kind of divine–human reconciliation that cannot be reduced to justification.

An emphasis on justification at the expense of interpersonal divine–human reconciliation is not limited to the first-century Corinthian Christians. It has marked various sectors of later Christianity as well, to the detriment of some interpersonal aspects of divine–human redemption. A result has been a misrepresentation of the interpersonal center of divine–human atonement in the New Testament.

---

[33] C. E. B. Cranfield, *A Critical and Exegetical Commentary on the Epistle to the Romans*, ICC (Edinburgh: T&T Clark, 1975), vol. 1, p. 258. See also Friedrich Büchsel, "αλλάσσω," in *Theological Dictionary of the New Testament*, ed. Gerhard Kittel, trans. Gerhard Friedrich (Grand Rapids, MI: Eerdmans, 1964), vol. 1, pp. 255–8, and, in contrast, Victor Paul Furnish, *Theology and Ethics in Paul* (Nashville, TN: Abingdon Press, 1968), pp. 148–52. For Paul on reconciliation more generally, see Martin, *Reconciliation*.

[34] Margaret Thrall, "Salvation Proclaimed: 2 Corinthians 5:18–21: Reconciliation with God," *Expository Times* 93 (1982), 230–1.

We find a similar misrepresentation when a focus on a metaphysics of Jesus's relation to God takes priority over his role in interpersonal reconciliation to God. The latter misplaced focus arises in some largely intellectual and creedal approaches to God that neglect interpersonal divine–human factors in redemption. The interpersonal factors include the matter of how the risen Christ, as a "life-giving Spirit," gives new life to humans.

Vincent Taylor has proposed: "The best New Testament word to describe the purpose of the atonement is *Reconciliation*. It is true that the word is used [in the New Testament] only by Paul, but in the teaching of Jesus its essential content is expressed in the Parable of the Prodigal Son and in the idea of a New Covenant established by the death of Christ between God and [humans]."[35] We have identified some evidence supporting this perspective on Jesus, and we have linked Jesus's aim for reconciliation with cooperative human obedience as a response to divine goodness.

Divine forgiveness and justification can serve as means to divine–human reconciliation. They thus can gain value from an interpersonal cooperative relationship that extends beyond them while relying on them. Similarly, in Paul's thought, God "justifies the ungodly" (Rom. 4:5) as "a gift in grace" (Rom. 5:15) – that is, a "gift of righteousness" (Rom. 5:17) – not simply to approve of them, but to lead them to interpersonal reconciliation to God.[36] So, neither forgiveness nor justification by God is the end of the line in Paul's account.

The reconciliation in question goes beyond an assigned legal status to the center of God's moral character:

---

[35] Vincent Taylor, *The Atonement in New Testament Teaching*, 3rd ed. (London: Epworth Press, 1958), p. 191. Cf. T. W. Manson, *On Paul and John* (London: SCM Press, 1963), pp. 50–3.

[36] On Paul's understanding of divine grace, see John M. G. Barclay, *Paul and the Gift* (Grand Rapids, MI: Eerdmans, 2015). For an explanation of how the obedience of faith poses no problem for Paul's contrast between grace and "works," see Paul K. Moser, *The Severity of God* (Cambridge: Cambridge University Press, 2013), chap. 4.

righteous *agapē*. Paul thus identified the role of divine love in God's reconciliation of humans:

God proves his love for us in that while we still were sinners Christ died for us ... For if while we were enemies, we were reconciled to God through the death of his Son, much more surely, having been reconciled, will we be saved by his life. But more than that, we even boast in God through our Lord Jesus Christ, through whom we have now received reconciliation. (Rom. 5:8, 10, 11)

God supplies a perfect moral basis of righteous forgiveness, justification, and reconciliation in the filial obedience of Jesus, thus giving historical moral robustness to divine redemption (Rom. 5:17–19). The obedient life of Jesus thus morally grounds, in a personal intentional manner, the perfect forgiveness, justification, and reconciliation on offer, in keeping with God's perfect moral character of righteous *agapē*. This is not a story about God punishing Jesus to secure "justice." Instead, it is a divine effort to attract humans to reconciliation with God in divine goodness, including self-giving love.

God's reconciliation of humans is not mechanical or coercive. It calls for voluntary appropriation, or reception, by humans for it to be the reconciliation *of them* to God. The needed appropriation is by the cooperative response of faith in God, the human embrace, in agreeable trust, of God's interpersonal offer of relational peace. Paul thus issued the aforementioned command to "be reconciled to God."

After mentioning faith in God and peace in God, Paul added: "Hope [in God] does not disappoint us, because God's love [ἀγάπη] has been poured into our hearts through the Holy Spirit that has been given to us" (Rom. 5:5). Faith and hope in God are central to a cooperative response to the divine love manifested to a person by God's Spirit. The relevant kind of faith, according to Paul, is "the obedience

of faith" (Rom. 1:5, 16:26) that includes a willing commitment to conformity to God's will. As Chapter 2 noted, Paul
thought of this as "faith energized [ἐνεργουμένη] through
love [ἀγάπη]" (Gal. 5:6, my trans.). Being thus "energized"
is to be cooperatively *empowered* by divine love. As
Friedrich Büchsel notes, the love and reconciliation from
God "are for Paul present realities which are revealed to the
conscience and which can be adduced in an answer to
opponents (2 Cor. 5:11–15)." He adds: "This is particularly
clear in Romans 5:5. In us (the reconciled), the love [from]
God has become a present and actual reality."[37] We need to
identify how the divine empowerment in question occurs if
we are to understand the human appropriation of the gospel from Jesus and Paul.

4.6 GETHSEMANE GOODNESS

Jesus announced God's coming kingdom with what
amounted to this command: Obey God with the singularity
of commitment I show – that is, do God's will with the
priority I am exemplifying. His love commands, regarding
love of God and humans, captured the singular way he was
doing God's will, including his ultimate motivation for
action. We should consider that singular way as a means
to understanding who he was.

A cooperative trusting response to God's will is the
heart of faith in God, as Jesus understood such faith.
The risen Jesus, as portrayed by Paul, continues and
expands the mission of the earthly Jesus, now as
a mission of faith's obedience beyond Israel to the larger
world. Jesus, according to Paul, is now a "life-giving
Spirit" and "the power of God" who has become the
Spirit of Gethsemane for all people – that is, the Spirit
set on the human doing of God's will regardless of ethnic
or national affiliation. In seeking faith in God from all

---

[37] Büchsel, "ἀλλάσσω," pp. 255–6.

responsive humans, Jesus thus seeks Gethsemane cooperation with God from humans of all backgrounds, even from ungodly gentiles.

Jesus's love commands as an expression of God's will demand *agapē* toward God and humans, even toward our enemies. They are accompanied by the following elaboration from the Jesus of Matthew's Gospel:

You have heard that it was said, "You shall love your neighbor and hate your enemy." But I say to you, Love your enemies and pray for those who persecute you, so that you may be children of your Father in heaven; for he makes his sun rise on the evil and on the good, and sends rain on the righteous and on the unrighteous. For if you love those who love you, what reward do you have? Do not even the tax collectors do the same? And if you greet only your brothers and sisters, what more are you doing than others? Do not even the Gentiles do the same? Be perfect, therefore, as your heavenly Father is perfect. (Matt. 5:43–8; cf. Luke 6:27–36)

God's moral character of perfect goodness and *agapē* sets the standard here, and this standard is as high as moral standards go. We have been examining the importance of understanding Jesus through this perspective, the perspective of perfect divine goodness. We must ask about the prospect of our meeting the standard of *agapē* as commanded.

It is doubtful that we can supply on our own the righteous love demanded by Jesus, without help from the ultimate source of the demand: God. Our own efforts toward loving God and humans typically waver and falter, and they are often mixed with our selfishness and indifference. This is partly an empirical matter, but our relevant evidence seems clear. Jesus exemplified Gethsemane obedience as the means to his *appropriating* divine *agapē*, in his conforming to God's redemptive will when his life was at stake. His resolve to go to his death for the sake of others exemplified the divine *agapē* that seeks what is good for others, all things considered, even at a high cost. Gethsemane obedience gains divine power by one's yielding, in direct interaction with God, to God's will rather than one's own contrary will. This is the power to receive and to manifest God's moral character, even in human weakness, for the good of all concerned.

Humans have an ongoing need for divine grace as a gift of divine moral power, and God, according to Jesus and Paul, has chosen to give such grace for moral empowerment in the human "obedience of faith" as cooperative trust. We evidently have no alternative better than faith's obedience to God. Otherwise, God's chief emissary would have come in a very different mode, without his Gethsemane lesson to obey God's will. Divine love is, however, unlike what is often deemed "love"; it is "holy" (or perfectly good) in its demand for moral righteousness, even when one's righteous obedience risks one's life. Gethsemane highlights this lesson, if painfully.

If the risen Jesus is the life-giving Spirit of Gethsemane, how is this Spirit to be received by humans? Paul held that God's Spirit is received by "faith" (Gal. 3:2–8, 14), and he had in mind the obedience of faith as cooperative trust, and not mere intellectual assent to claims about Jesus. It is "living by faith" in God and not just assenting by faith, as Paul's quotation from Habakkuk implies (Gal. 3:11). Paul thus could say that "not all have *obeyed* the good news" while citing Isaiah on *believing* God's message (Rom. 10:16). He understood the good news to offer a gift of reconciliation with God while demanding that one yield cooperatively, in self-sacrificial obedience, to God's perfect will (Rom. 12:1–2). In this regard, Paul shared with Jesus a morally robust approach to faith in God that calls for the Jesus-style obedience of Gethsemane. We thus find Paul, while using the Aramaic term *"Abba,"* echoing a theme from Jesus in Gethsemane on the struggle for obedience to God as Father against the human flesh (Rom. 8:3–15).[38]

G. W. H. Lampe has remarked on the experience of Gethsemane:

We are right in seeing a disclosure of God in Jesus's prayer in Gethsemane and in the events which were the consequence of his submission there to the Father's will; but this is a disclosure of God inspiring and moving and acting through the mind and will, the conscience and the resolution of a consecrated [person] in a human situation. It is the archetypal revelation of the manner in which God acts in and through the spirit of [a human person].[39]

Lampe adds that "Jesus became both the pattern of sonship [to God] and also the inspiration and power which can create in us a response, analogous to his own, to the Spirit of God that was in him and is in us."[40] I recommend instead talk of "attract in us a response," rather than talk of "create in us a response," because the needed interaction is interpersonal, voluntary, and not coercive. Gethsemane, then, is paradigmatic for this divine disclosure and empowerment role for Jesus, both pre- and post-resurrection. So, we should not limit the significance of a Gethsemane challenge to the historical Jesus.

The key role of Jesus as model and life-giving Spirit entails that we cannot abstract his love commands from *him* without loss – that is, we cannot reduce his role to mere ethics, a matter of principles for right and wrong, or good and bad.[41] The correct story of Jesus is *through divine*

---

[38] For discussion, see David Wenham, *Paul* (Grand Rapids, MI: Eerdmans, 1995), pp. 276–80. More broadly on Paul on faith as including obedience, see Don B. Garlington, *"The Obedience of Faith": A Pauline Phrase in Historical Context*, WUNT (Tübingen: Mohr Siebeck, 1991), and Garlington, *Faith, Obedience, and Perseverance: Aspects of Paul's Letter to the Romans*, WUNT (Tübingen: Mohr Siebeck, 1994).

[39] Lampe, *God as Spirit*, p. 138.   [40] Lampe, *God as Spirit*, p. 24.

[41] See Furnish, *The Love Command in the New Testament*, p. 196.

goodness, because it stems from *God's* perfectly good character of reconciling love. That personal and purposive moral character explains why Gethsemane obedience is required, pre- and post-resurrection, with no room for a quick and easy fix for humans. The purpose is for humans to receive and to manifest that character as they willingly cooperate with it, come what may.

Gethsemane cooperation is the way to share in God's moral life, in ways that are volitional, emotional, and intellectual. It is the way to do God's will in a manner that brings God's kingdom to earth. Thus: "Once Jesus was asked by the Pharisees when the kingdom of God was coming, and he answered, 'The kingdom of God is not coming with things that can be observed; nor will they say, "Look, here it is!" or "There it is!" For, in fact, the kingdom of God is among you'" (Luke 17:20–1). It is among us in the morally relevant power of God appropriated by humans in Gethsemane cooperation with God. This was the signature power of Jesus in his Gethsemane obedience, and it extends, according to Paul and other New Testament writers, to his post-resurrection life.

The obedience at issue is irreducibly interpersonal, stemming as it does from an interpersonal prayer of Jesus to God in Gethsemane. So, it exceeds obeying a law or satisfying a principle. In Gethsemane, Jesus obeyed *his Father* and trusted him for the consequences. After his resurrection, Jesus shared his Father's life with others on the same ground: through people being attracted and convicted to obey and trust likewise.

God's redemptive will can arise in human moral experience, if permitted, and it can convict (ἐλέγξει) cooperative people *both* against anti-God ways *and* toward God's moral character of righteousness, including righteous *agapē* (John 16:8). We thus should not portray the Spirit's "convicting" in John 16:8–11 as just negative, against anti-God ways, if the Spirit's charge is to guide the followers of Jesus "into all the truth" (John 16:13).[42] The guiding or attracting toward conviction comes from God's Spirit, according to John's Gospel, and this Spirit is the direct reflection of the risen Jesus, overlapping at times, at least in role, with the risen Jesus (John 14:16–18, 16:15).[43]

Cooperation with God is mixed among humans because the divine effort is not coercive by God. It allows for human agency that often goes its own way – against God's will. So, Jesus's parable of the sower still holds, even with the sower as God's life-giving Spirit in Christ. The reign of Jesus, then, is both hidden and revealed, owing at least to opposing human responses to Gethsemane challenges in human lives.

We now can understand *the problem of noncompliance* in Christian faith: the problem of believing that the informational content of the gospel is true while consistently failing to act in accordance with it on central matters. The problem of noncompliance is a problem of volitional incongruity. It stems from either of two sources: an *intellectual* source of failing to *understand* what Christian faith requires of a person in many cases, or a *volitional* source of failing to *will* or *resolve* what Christian faith demands in many cases. Both kinds of failing can apply to a single person. Belief *that* the Christian gospel is true does not exclude either of those sources of failing. It allows that a person can fail to understand implications *and* fail to will what is demanded for many cases, thereby leaving volitional incongruity and thus noncompliance in Christian belief.

---

[42] Raymond E. Brown, among others, makes this mistake. See his *The Gospel According to John*, AB (New York: Doubleday, 1971), vol. 2, p. 705. C. K. Barrett rightly notes the relevance of conscience to the convicting from God's Spirit in John. See Barrett, *The Gospel According to St. John*, 2nd ed. (Philadelphia: Westminster Press, 1978), pp. 486–8.

[43] The role of moral conviction in Gethsemane challenges gives specificity to what is often an unduly abstract portrait of an "I–Thou" relation between a human and God. The portrait becomes morally robust as it takes on the features of a Gethsemane challenge in moral conscience to put God's moral will first in one's life. We may think of this as a Gethsemane I–Thou relation, as exemplified by Jesus. The broader epistemological role of moral *agapē*-conviction characteristic of Gethsemane is explained in Moser, *Understanding Religious Experience*, chaps. 7–8.

An intellectual failing could arise from failing to understand that Christian faith entails, for instance, that racism is morally wrong. In addition, a volitional failing could emerge from failing to will conduct that is fair to people of different races. One also could have Christian faith that is intellectually correct on some central Christian themes but is morally deficient, even seriously so, in one's volitional stance and thus in one's intentional actions. The gospel from Jesus comes, however, with a command to be *obeyed* by its recipients.

The noncompliance at issue led to the kind of disturbing immorality in, for instance, the Corinthian church started by Paul (1 Cor. 5:1). The perspective of this book offers an available solution to the volitional side of the problem: namely, Gethsemane cooperation with God after the model of Jesus. In such cooperation, according to the proposed solution, a person is offered divine power to comply with God's perfect will and thereby to overcome volitional weakness. The test for the solution comes, as expected, in practice: in one's actual cooperation with God's will in a Gethsemane challenge to put God's will first. Mere reflection will not reveal the power that, in its intended fruition in cooperation, confirms the reality of divine goodness in a Gethsemane challenge.

A person can be mistaken about God's will and cooperation with it. In a case of such mistake, one should not expect divine support via one's supposed cooperation. The actual will of God as represented by Jesus can be difficult to discern in some cases, but it is not so in all cases. Insofar as we understand worthiness of worship in terms of moral perfection, as required by the morally perfectionist title "God," we can separate many genuine and counterfeit instances of the divine will.[44] Jesus exposed many such counterfeits by portraying the

---

[44] On the epistemological relevance of such a title, see Moser, *The God Relationship*, chaps. 2–3.

power of divine goodness in various ways. So, not all cases of Gethsemane decision are vague, even if some are.

The main point now is that we have an approach for countering volitional noncompliance. We also can use this approach to explain many cases of the hiddenness of the power of the gospel. That power is hidden in Gethsemane cooperation, for the redemptive, moral benefit of inquirers. God is, accordingly, not to be approached as a mere object of speculation or reflection. The goodness of God functions at a level of moral depth more profound than mere speculation or reflection. The gospel of divine goodness, as portrayed by Jesus, upholds divine worthiness of worship, for the sake of divine–human reconciliation, even in human inquiry about God. This, we now can see, is a key feature in appropriating the hidden gospel of Jesus. We turn to the challenging short stories Jesus told for the sake of advancing divine goodness.

5

༄

Stories for Divine Goodness

We have seen some results of understanding Jesus through divine goodness in connection with inquiry about Jesus and God, as well as with regard to God as *Abba* in relation to Jesus and the Good News of God from Jesus. Jesus did not leave any writings but he did leave short stories with his disciples: not treatises but short stories. We need to consider his purpose behind them.

5.1 RECEIVING DIVINE GOODNESS

Before turning directly to the role of Jesus's storytelling for God, we need to recall and clarify briefly the kind of divine–human reconciliation he sought to promote. According to Chapter 3, the moral power from divine goodness needed by humans comes from God's will as one submits to it, after the model of Jesus in Gethsemane. This submitting is the active way to appropriate God's power of righteous *agapē* on offer.

We are not considering power to get whatever one wants, as if God were promiscuous with divine power. Instead, it is moral power to put God's will first, even at one's initial expense. I say "initial," because Jesus's losing his life in Jerusalem was not an ultimate loss. He would be vindicated by God with resurrected, exalted life, and, as noted, he had predicted as much three times in Mark's Gospel (8:31, 9:31, 10:34). Even if Jesus alone obeyed God perfectly, other humans can share his kind of obedience in Gethsemane, if imperfectly, given their failure to cooperate at times.

According to Chapter 4, Jesus showed concern about the receptive or non-receptive attitudes of people toward the good news of his Father's arriving kingdom. The heart of this good news, in its informational content, is that God and Jesus have come to give humans, without their earning, a reconciled relationship with God and Jesus as their God and Lord. A crucial issue, however, is whether people are willing to cooperate with the intervening God who seeks divine–human reconciliation in divine goodness.

Jesus advised: "Do not give what is holy to dogs; and do not throw your pearls before swine, or they will trample them under foot and turn and maul you" (Matt. 7:6). The prospect of reconciliation would be made worse by a divine intervention that increased human hostility to God. Matthew's language attributed to Jesus seems harsh, but it fits with the seriousness of Jesus's concern for reconciliation via his good news. He thought of God's offer of reconciliation as an offer to overcome human conflict with God, volitional and otherwise, and to have a peaceful, cooperative relationship with God under divine *agapē*. God initiates the reconciliation, climactically through Jesus, but humans must respond with willing cooperation for there to be interpersonal reconciliation.

That God takes the initiative for reconciliation is a divine gift, a matter of unearned grace, in Paul's message (Rom. 3:23–4). This role for a divine gift of grace goes back to the message of Jesus himself. In his parable of the laborers in the vineyard, Jesus portrayed God as giving his kingdom, including its offered forgiveness and reconciliation, freely to humans without their earning (Matt. 20:1–16). Some people, however, prefer an option that includes human earning of divine favor in reconciliation, and thus they take exception to the role of divine grace. Jesus, in contrast, suggested that this option is begrudging toward God's perfect goodness (Matt. 20:15), as Chapter 3 noted.

Jesus's most striking illustration of divine grace, including forgiveness and reconciliation, is his parable of the prodigal son (Luke 15:11–24), as Chapter 2 indicated. The runaway son disowns and dishonors his father but comes to see the futility of his alienating behavior toward his father. He "comes to himself" (εἰς ἑαυτὸν ἐλθὼν) and decides, out of a real need, to return to his father. His return includes his expression of a need for forgiveness: "Father, I have sinned against heaven and before you; I am no longer worthy to be called your son" (Luke 15:18–19). The son acknowledges not just his sin in personal actions but also his *interpersonal* failing and unworthiness *in relation to God*. He identifies that he violated a needed filial relationship with God. His turning to God in repentance, then, is irreducible to sorrow for just personal actions. It is, at its center, a turning to God with the attitude of a child of God who needs a restored, reconciled relationship as God's child. We may think of this as *filial repentance*, given its central role for a reconciled relationship with God for a child of God.

Jesus portrayed an astonishing response by God, manifesting the grace of God in merciful, forgiving reconciliation (Luke 15:20–4). The compassionate father does not condemn the imperfect son; nor does he demand that the son somehow earn the father's acceptance. Instead, he manifests forgiveness and reconciliation, including the kind of forgiveness that pardons without condemning a person. We see this in his simple injunction "Let us eat and celebrate." Likewise, we see it in this description of the father: "Filled with compassion; he ran and put his arms around him and kissed him." Jesus thus portrayed his divine Father as running to restore people to God's kingdom family, in a reconciled relationship with God. This image, central to his good news, strikes against the portrayal of God as grudging or otherwise harsh toward returning humans (Luke 15:25–32, 12:32).

It is one thing for God to *offer* forgiveness and reconciliation to humans as an unearned gift of divine grace; it is another thing for humans to *receive* or to *accept*, with active repentance and cooperation, the divine forgiveness and reconciliation on offer. The prodigal son turning to God in repentance is the beginning of his father's offer being cooperatively received. It is the beginning of cooperation with divine–human reconciliation.

Jesus indicated the importance of cooperative receiving of forgiveness in his comment in the context of the Lord's Prayer: "If you forgive others their trespasses, your heavenly Father will also forgive you; but if you do not forgive others, neither will your Father forgive your trespasses" (Matt. 6:14–15). A plausible understanding of this comment is that if we do not forgive others, we are not properly *receiving* the forgiveness offered by God and therefore we are blocking it from being effective, universal forgiveness *from God*. We then are limiting it in a way that corrupts the redemptive gift offered by God. The problem is not that God is unforgiving regarding the offering of forgiveness; instead, it is that we are resisting, by our limitation, God's kind of universal forgiveness on offer. An important first step is to acknowledge our need of the universal forgiveness from God, given our failure to satisfy the standard set by God's perfect moral character and will (Matt. 5:48, Mark 2:17, 10:18).

We can either ignore or resist the corrective moral power in God's will for us by either neglecting it or displacing it with our own morally inferior power and will. We do this by either ignoring or opposing cooperation with God's will, thus hindering (the deepening of) reconciliation with God. God's righteous will can bother us in moral conscience, such as when we have clearly wronged another person, but we can either ignore or suppress God's desired conviction in conscience (cf. Rom. 2:14–15). In such a case, we typically meet a will other than our own in moral conscience, if we pay attention, and it can provide evidence that it is goal-directed and thus intentional toward our moral improvement in relation to God.[1]

God's corrective will, we have suggested, does not coerce our moral decisions, including in how we relate to God, and it can reasonably withdraw if neglected or opposed by us. For instance, if we divert attention to other matters, as is often the case, we typically escape its nudge in conscience. If, in addition, we neglect or block God's moral presence in our experience, God can reasonably withdraw from our experience to avoid our being alienated further from God. Paul puts this in terms of God "giving people up" to their own anti-God ways (Rom. 1:24, 26, 28), for the sake of their coming to see the error of their ways. God thus can wait for us to come to our senses, as seen from the parable of the prodigal son. This can include, as Chapter 4 indicated, divine redemptive hiding at a time for the sake of divine–human reconciliation at a later time.

We have seen the central place in repentance of relating *to God* as a counter to wayward actions that do not cooperate with God. From the standpoint of repentance for reconciliation to God, the focus is on starting and sustaining a reconciled and deepening *relationship with God*. Jesus's parable of the prodigal son makes this lesson clear. God initiates, as a gift of grace, the offer of forgiveness and reconciliation, and then gives humans room to respond as responsible moral agents. So, the process is not mechanical. Luke makes a point about the result: some people "rejected God's purpose for themselves" (τὴν βουλὴν τοῦ θεοῦ ἠθέτησαν εἰς ἑαυτούς) (Luke 7:30), and he has in mind God's redemptive purpose or will. So, a human will has the power to reject God's good will, and such an abuse of

---

[1] For discussion of goal-directedness in conscience, see Moser, *The God Relationship*, chap. 5, and Moser, *Understanding Religious Experience*, chap. 7.

power is not God's doing. We turn to what Jesus sought in his storytelling for God.

5.2 STORYTELLING FOR GOD

According to Matthew's Gospel, Jesus indicated his motive for using various short stories called "parables": "To you [his disciples] it has been given to know the secrets of the kingdom of heaven, but to them [those beyond his disciples] it has not been given ... The reason I speak to them in parables is that 'seeing they do not perceive, and hearing they do not listen, nor do they understand'" (Matt. 13:11,13; cf. Mark 4:11–12, Luke 8:10, John 12:36–40, Isa. 6:9, LXX).

"Hearing they do not listen" suggests a human decision against willing cooperation with Jesus's message from God – saying "No" to God in a Gethsemane-style decision against the priority of God's will for reconciliation. Given such an uncooperative attitude in humans, God typically would refrain from aggravating the situation with further divine intervention that increases alienation. As a result, we should expect a kind of hiding at times regarding God's self-revelation to uncooperative humans, for the sake of keeping their cooperative reconciliation a live option for the future.

The Gospels of Mark, Luke, and Matthew attribute versions of the following injunction to Jesus: "Let anyone with ears to hear listen!" Here is Luke's version: "Let anyone with ears to hear listen! ... To you it has been given to know the secrets of the kingdom of God; but to others I speak in parables, so that 'looking they may not perceive, and listening they may not understand'" (Luke 8:8–10, drawing from Isa. 6:9, LXX). The idea of having ears but not hearing or listening goes back to the prophet Jeremiah, who brought a message from God to Israel: "Hear this, O foolish and senseless people, who have eyes, but do not see, who have ears, but do not hear" (Jer. 5:21). The hearing desired by Jesus goes beyond mere hearing.

Luke's Gospel, evidently drawing from Mark's Gospel, offers the previously cited remark alluding to Isaiah 6:9: "I speak in parables, so that looking they may not perceive, and listening they may not understand." However, we do not have to read "so that" as "in order that"; it can indicate a result rather than an initial purpose and thus allow for the divine hiding to come as a result of human opposition to the message. The divine message, in that case, need not be *intended* to exclude people; instead, people can be responsible for excluding themselves and for blocking their understanding of God's word. Matthew's Gospel (13:13) clarifies the Gospel of Mark (4:12) to accommodate this point.

In Mark's Gospel, Jesus acknowledges that revealing, and not excluding, is his ultimate goal: "Is a lamp brought in to be put under the bushel basket, or under the bed, and not on the lampstand? For there is nothing hidden, except to be disclosed; nor is anything secret, except to come to light" (Mark 4:21–2; cf. Luke 8:16–17). Mark's Gospel also identifies a limitation from the audience's ability to understand: "With many such parables he spoke the word to them, as they were able to hear it [καθὼς ἠδύναντο ἀκούειν]" (Mark 4:33).[2] Such remarks count against a hypothesis that God has an independent desire to exclude some people with the parables of Jesus.

The best support for Matthew's clarification of Mark's Gospel is that none of the synoptic Gospels has *God* take the initiative to exclude some people from the divine kingdom. In particular, they do not offer a parable of the sower where God initiates human rejection of the word of God. They *might* have done so, but they do not. If, contrary to our evidence, Jesus held that God initiated the rejection of

---

[2] For discussion of the purpose of the parables, see Manson, *The Teaching of Jesus*, pp. 75–80, John Bowker, "Mystery and Parable: Mark iv. 1–20," *Journal of Theological Studies* 25 (1974), 300–17, Madeleine Boucher, *The Mysterious Parable*, CBQMS (Washington, DC: Catholic Biblical Association of America, 1977), pp 80–5, Hultgren, *The Parables of Jesus*, pp. 453–67, and Snodgrass, *Stories with Intent*, pp. 145–77.

humans, he certainly hid this view in his parable of the sower. At a minimum, he missed a good opportunity to express this view. The best available explanation of this omission is that Jesus did not hold the view of divine exclusion in question. His parable of the sower assumes that at least some humans have the available power to decide to "accept" (παραδέχονται), as a human doing (if in cooperation with divine power), the word of God (Mark 4:20).

The author of the Gospel of Luke shows a clear understanding of what Jesus aimed to accomplish with his parables. Going beyond Mark's Gospel, he represents Jesus as saying: "Nothing is hidden that will not be disclosed, nor is anything secret that will not become known and come to light. Then pay attention to how you listen [πῶς ἀκούετε]" (Luke 8:17–18). The manner of *how* people listen is, according to Luke's Gospel, central to Jesus's motive in using parables and to his understanding of hearing the word of God aright. (Mark 4:24 has: "Pay attention to *what* [τί] you hear.")

Luke portrays Jesus as explicitly linking the desired kind of hearing to *obeying* the word of God (Luke 8:21): "[Jesus] said to them, 'My mother and my brothers are those who hear the word of God and do it.'" This is hearing combined with obeying the message of God, and it is the obedient hearing required for belonging to the kingdom family of God represented by Jesus. So, occasional divine hiding is not an end in itself; it aims to be redemptive for humans. It aims to give them room to come to a recognized need to cooperate with the message from God and thereby to be reconciled to God.

The kind of hearing or listening sought by Jesus is neither merely auditory nor merely auditory and intellectual; instead, it is linked to agreeable volition, to a willingness to cooperate, in a manner favorable to obeying the message of God. A directly analogous point applies to the kind of *understanding* sought by Jesus with his parables. People

outside his receptive audience are prevented from understanding aright, in a volitionally sympathetic manner, by
their own unwillingness to cooperate with the divine
expectations of the parables. So, a kind of cooperative or
sympathetic understanding, rather than merely intellectual
understanding, was the storytelling goal of Jesus.

An absence of sympathetic understanding can leave
a person motivationally indifferent to the message of God
expressed by the parables of Jesus. Motivational indifference of that sort can prevent a person from willingly receiving, in divine–human reconciliation, the kingdom of God
announced and manifested by Jesus. It thus can prevent
one being reconciled to God, at least volitionally. It also can
block the kind of understanding of the message of God
sought by Jesus, who used the parables to test for
a hearer's sympathetic, motivated understanding of
God's message. The parables, with their various challenges, can reveal the presence as well as the absence of
such understanding in hearers.

5.3 STORIES FOR DECISIONS

The parables of Jesus invited, and invite, people to face
a *decision* on where they stand regarding God and God's
message, for or against, and the responsibility for the decision is their own. So, the parables revealed, and reveal, the
motivational effectiveness of the message of Jesus in the
lives of hearers. God supplies the needed power for
humans to cooperate with the perfect divine will, but
humans must resolve to appropriate and implement this
power in their lives. Jesus modeled the appropriation of
this power in Gethsemane, and his model bears on other
humans in relating to God as they respond to a divine
impact in their lives.

My proposed motivational reading of Jesus's intention is
confirmed by the Gospels of Mark and Luke in their
descriptions of the hearers represented by good soil in the

parable of the sower. Mark's Gospel, as suggested, portrays them as hearing and willingly receiving the word: "These are the ones sown on the good soil: they hear the word and accept [παραδέχονται] it and bear fruit, thirty and sixty and a hundredfold" (Mark 4:20). (Matthew's Gospel describes the good hearer as one who hears and understands [συνιείς] [Matt. 13:23].) Luke's Gospel is more explanatory, characterizing the good hearers as those who "when they hear the word, hold it fast in an honest and good heart" (ἐν καρδίᾳ καλῇ καὶ ἀγαθῇ ἀκούσαντες τὸν λόγον κατέχουσιν) (Luke 8:15).

"Holding the word in a good heart," in the understanding of Luke's Jesus, is not merely intellectual or reflective in nature. Instead, it is volitional, involving a person willingly "holding fast" the word of God. Such holding fast from a "good heart" includes sympathetic agreement with the word, and it thus supplies motivation to obey it, courtesy of God's power thereby being appropriated. So, Luke's Jesus supports the motivational reading of hearing and listening on offer. The same is true of Mark's Jesus, given an understanding of "acceptance" as willing sympathetic acceptance. (I would suggest a similar result for Matthew's Jesus, given a construal of "understanding" as sympathetic or agreeable understanding.)

Divine hiding of the kind acknowledged by Jesus seeks reconciliatory evidence and knowledge for humans, of the kind characterized in Chapter 2, in contrast with merely intellectual evidence and knowledge. It factors in one's *will to cooperate* (or not to cooperate) with God's will. So, in many cases, the divine hiding is reduced when one is willing to cooperate with divine–human reconciliation.[3] A person then agreeably receives God's will with the cooperation intended by God.

We may say that God and Jesus typically hide in cooperative reconciliation with humans, for the sake of

---

[3] As Chapter 2 suggested, we should not assume that we have a full theodicy as a full explanation of all cases of divine hiding or of corresponding human suffering or evil; nor should we expect to have such a theodicy. Chapter 8 returns to this topic.

advancing the promised kingdom of God in agreeable motivation as well as in narrative content. A person can experience some initial nonsalient evidence of God's will in moral conscience, but then decide either to ignore it or to suppress it (cf. Rom. 2:14–15). In such a case, a person can lack salient evidence of God's presence or power, owing to disregarding or opposing the intended fruition of the evidence in human cooperation. Salience of such evidence can arise to some extent, however, with willing human cooperation, courtesy of God's desire for redemption as divine–human reconciliation in will as well as thought.

A common factor in neglecting or resisting God's will in moral conscience is human fear of losing control or security in one's life. Perhaps God's will does not offer the protection or safety found in one's own will, at least short term. After all, Jesus was called to give up his life in following God's will, despite his initial request for an alternative (Mark 14:36). Humans typically want to avoid such a loss, and they therefore usually prefer not to give God's will an absolute demand on them. The accompanying risk can leave them in fear of dire consequences.

Humans readily look for convenient limitations on God's will (such as excluding care for an enemy), for the sake of their perceived well-being and safety. This human tendency raises a problem because if God is a person's divine *Lord*, God's will is supreme for that person, and not only in talk. Genuine lordship has *volitional leadership* in that manner. So, the challenge of Jesus in Gethsemane was ultimately one of lordship relative to humans. Jesus set the standard for obeying God, and others are challenged to follow suit, even given their moral deficits and imperfections. Divine forgiveness can, and perhaps must, help to keep alive an imperfect human struggle to receive divine reconciliation in obedience. So, human receptivity to such forgiveness figures importantly in the mission and the message of Jesus.

In Gethsemane and elsewhere, Jesus challenged a typical human concern for control and safety. As Chapter 3 noted, he offered himself as an example for people to *follow* (and not just to trust) regarding God's will: "If any want to become my followers, let them deny themselves and take up their cross and follow me. For those who want to save their life will lose it, and those who lose their life for my sake, and for the sake of the gospel, will save it" (Mark 8:34–5). We find a stronger statement in Luke's Gospel: "Whoever does not carry the cross and follow me cannot be my disciple" (14:27). These statements require that one cooperate with Jesus in the mode of Gethsemane, in putting God's will above all else, even above one's own earthly life, in full commitment. This is a tall order, but it emerges as even more demanding when we identify the motive demanded by Jesus for cooperation. We should not be surprised by a demanding standard from a God of perfect moral goodness.

Jesus, as Chapter 3 suggested, identified the primary motive for his disciples in his love commands: "The first [commandment] is, 'Hear, O Israel: the Lord our God, the Lord is one; you shall love the Lord your God with all your heart, and with all your soul, and with all your mind, and with all your strength.' The second is this, 'You shall love your neighbor as yourself.' There is no other commandment greater than these" (Mark 12:29–31; cf. Matt. 22:35–40, Luke 10:25–8). So, cooperating with God's will, after the model of Jesus in Gethsemane, is to be motivated by primary unqualified love for God and secondary love for neighbors (the latter assuming love for oneself). Such love for God and neighbors is an intentional power to will what is good in relation to them. In placing his love commands as a top priority, Jesus pointed to what should be a primary motive for his followers as they aim to follow him in Gethsemane.

As Chapter 2 noted, Jesus extended the scope of his love commands: "You have heard that it was said, 'You shall love your neighbor and hate your enemy.' I say to you, Love your enemies and pray for those who persecute you, so that you may be children of your Father in heaven; for he makes his sun rise on the evil and on the good, and sends rain on the righteous and on the unrighteous ... Be perfect, therefore, as your heavenly Father is perfect" (Matt. 5:43–5, 48; cf. Luke 6:27–8). God's perfect moral character thus sets the moral standard for following Jesus, and the love commanded by Jesus should form the motive for following him. A higher moral standard for humans is hard to imagine.

Evidently, humans lack the power on their own to love as Jesus commanded. They seem too weak morally to adopt God's perfect moral character on their own. In particular, loving God as commanded requires a singular and primary commitment to God that often eludes humans. So, they need help, from a source able to empower them to love as Jesus commanded. Human "flesh" is "weak," as noted (Mark 14:38), but divine power can overcome its weakness through due human cooperation with God in putting God's will first.

Faith in God is not offered as an alternative to loving God as Jesus commanded. Instead, such faith is to be motivated by such love, given Jesus's love commands. Paul, as Chapter 2 noted, captured the result: "In Christ Jesus neither circumcision nor uncircumcision matters; the only thing that matters is faith energized [ἐνεργουμένη] by love" (Gal. 5:6, my translation). He meant divine righteous love *from* God (cf. Rom. 5:5, 2 Cor. 5:14–15) that should motivate human love. Faith in God is thus the human response of cooperation, with a trusting commitment, toward God in the divine righteous love on offer. Such a cooperative response to divine challenges in a human life is a means to appropriating the needed divine love that can empower faith in God "energized by love." So, God has the initiative in prompting human faith and love toward God. Divine grace is thus secure, being prior to any human response.

Chapter 2 noted Jesus's naming himself as the source of knowing God, while acknowledging a role for divine hiding (Matt. 11:25–7; cf. Luke 10:21–2; see also John 17:25–6). In referring to himself as "the Son," Jesus acknowledged his submission to his Father. He was the obedient child who put his Father's will first in all things, and Gethsemane demonstrated as much. As a result, Jesus could serve as the trustworthy filial revealer of his Father. Since his obedience was unmatched and without defect, he could serve as the unique revealer of God for the sake of human redemption by God.

According to the synoptic Gospels, as noted, the revelation of God from Jesus was selective in going to some people but being "hidden" from others (such as "the wise and the intelligent"). This divine hiding makes sense if it comes from God's aim in self-revelation for redemption as reconciliation, and not for the mere satisfaction of human intellectual curiosity. Given that aim, God and Jesus offer what Chapter 2 called "reconciliatory knowledge and evidence" of God's reality. This is knowledge and evidence intended to prompt, attract, sustain, and deepen the reconciliation, including the volitional reconciliation, of humans to God, on the basis of divine goodness in human experience.

Typically it would not serve God's redemptive aim for God to provide (potentially) reconciliatory evidence in cases where recipients are unresponsive or oppositional. Usually, then, God would hide the relevant evidence in such cases until a better redemptive opportunity arises. The same applies to Jesus in his role as the unique filial revealer of his Father. So, there is no need to interpret the previous passage from Matthew's Gospel about the parables as implying that God or Jesus initially chose to exclude some people from the divine kingdom.

The "Messianic secret" represented in Mark's Gospel fits with the kind of divine hiding we have characterized in

connection with Jesus's storytelling.[4] Jesus tended to avoid
public talk of himself as Messiah, because his audience was
not ready for his distinctive conception of Messiah grounded
in reconciliatory power antithetical to the coercive domination and triumph of typical royal power. His audience
tended not to cooperate with the expectations of such an
atypical conception of power, as Peter showed at Caesarea
Philippi (Mark 8:32). A general tendency of his audience was
to want God's Messiah to remove their oppressors without
delay. Jesus showed a different approach, and thus rebuked
Peter. Their clash was over divine power: Would it aim
ultimately for cooperative reconciliation rather than domination? The cross of Jesus offered a hint, and it would not win
a popularity contest, then or now.

The storytelling of Jesus fits with the Messianic secret
directed at divine–human reconciliation. His short stories,
we have suggested, seek more than intellectual understanding because they seek volitional cooperation with
the message of God. They thus seek volitionally sympathetic understanding that leads to obedience. Madeleine
Boucher has rightly characterized the parables of Jesus:

What the parables teach are the implications of the coming of the
kingdom for the situation of the audience. They convey not
secret information, but the requirements made of the hearer.
The mystery has to do entirely with one's willingness to receive
the eschatological and ethical teaching of Jesus. The word "willingness" is used deliberately here: Mark's theory is that the
meaning of a parable is perceived only by those disposed to
appropriate its teaching; those who do not understand are those
who will not allow its lesson to impinge on their existence.[5]

"Willing" or sympathetic understanding is indeed important because it bears on the audience of Jesus's parables as

---

[4] On the historical plausibility and intention of the Messianic secret, see Barrett, *The
Holy Spirit and the Gospel Tradition*, pp. 120, 142–3, 158–9.
[5] Boucher, *The Mysterious Parable*, pp. 83–4.

responsible hearers. They are responsible for their decisions regarding the moral challenges before them, and their decisions will reveal their attitude toward Jesus and divine–human reconciliation. Those decisions also will determine whether God's redemptive power comes to fruition as intended in their cooperation with it. This perspective fits with the theistic accountableism introduced in Chapter 1.

The ultimate divine goal represented by Jesus is the redemption of people in uncoerced reconciliation, not the exclusion of people. Even so, we should settle for explaining how God *typically* supplies or withholds evidence in self-manifestation. As suggested, we should not presume to have full explanatory coverage of God's purposes in self-manifestation to humans. This lesson is analogous to our lacking full understanding of God's purposes in allowing evil. We thus must acknowledge God's freedom in supporting exceptions to what is typical in divine revelatory practice.

Gethsemane-oriented epistemology characterizes the evidence from divine self-revelation in terms of the kind of volitional response to God shown by Jesus in Gethsemane. It portrays such evidence to be typically volitionally sensitive in a manner corresponding to the volitional receptivity of a human relative to God's expressed redemptive will. This sensitivity results from God's redemptive aim to use self-revelation typically to attract and sustain the reconciliation of humans to God. The latter reconciliation would be not just intellectual but volitional and affective as well. It would bring a whole person, and not just an intellect, into cooperation with God without coercion of a will.

We saw how God seeks reconciliation of a whole person in connection with the parable of the prodigal son. The focus is on the volitional and active cooperation of a person *with God*, for the sake of *interpersonal* reconciliation, and not on actions apart from such reconciliation. A corresponding lesson applies to Gethsemane-oriented epistemology. According to such epistemology, not all actions disobeying God's commands trigger divine hiding from the people performing those actions. We should expect not a simple mechanical account of divine hiding, but an approach sensitive to human attitudes to a cooperative relationship with God as morally authoritative.

As suggested, we lack an algorithm for explaining all cases of divine hiding, and we should not expect to have one, given our limitations in knowledge of divine purposes. It is clear, however, that we can disobey a divine command without disowning a broader cooperative relationship with God. In Paul's language, the broader relationship would be a *koinōnia* relationship with God, and it would be an intended part of divine–human redemption as reconciliation to God (2 Cor. 5:16–21, 13:14; cf. Col. 1:19–21).[6]

In neglecting or opposing a reconciled relationship with God, we would risk God's "giving us up" to our own anti-God tendencies, and that can include divine hiding from us for the sake of our coming to see the futility of our ways. Indeed, Paul held that God has subjected creation in general to futility on its own for the sake of revealing our need to be children *of God*, in a relationship of reconciled dependence on God (Rom. 8:21).[7] God would hide and seek to benefit that kind of relationship, even beyond our explanatory resources. We need to clarify further the role of the post-resurrection Jesus in Gethsemane-oriented epistemology, and we can do so with further aid from Paul.

5.4 ATTRACTING CONVICTION

The storytelling of Jesus aimed to bring receptive hearers into the presence of divine reconciliatory power, God's

---

[6] For discussion of *koinōnia* in New Testament theology, see A. R. George, *Communion with God in the New Testament* (London: Epworth Press, 1953), and Lehmann, *Ethics in a Christian Context*. For a broader discussion, with attention to the interpersonal impact of Jesus, see Wilhelm Herrmann, *The Communion of the Christian with God*, ed. R. T. Voelkel (Philadelphia: Fortress Press, 1971 [1903]), and Baillie, *The Place of Jesus Christ in Modern Christianity*, chap. 3.
[7] See Cranfield, *A Critical and Exegetical Commentary on the Epistle to the Romans*, vol. 1, pp. 413–14.

power, in the way that an intellectual treatise would not. As Chapter 3 suggested, Paul thought of the power of Jesus's obedient life as being central to the gospel as "the power of God for salvation to everyone who has faith" (Rom. 1:16, Phil. 2:8–9), to be received by "the obedience of faith" (Rom. 1:5, 16:26). So, in his thinking, obedience to God is integral to the kind of faith or belief that, as a receptive means, conveys God's power for salvation. Paul thus used talk of obeying (ὑπήκουσαν) interchangeably with talk of believing (ἐπίστευσεν) (Rom. 10:16), and this fits with our portrait of Gethsemane in the reception of the power of God's will. The role of faith in God as "the obedience of faith" requires what Paul, as noted, called our "living to God," rather than to just a law (Gal. 2:19). This agrees with our emphasis on a reconciled cooperative relationship with God as crucial to redemption.

Coupled with Gethsemane, the storytelling of Jesus enables us to make sense of *how* contemporary people can experience God and the risen Jesus. Experiencing God and the risen Jesus through Jesus's storytelling is experiencing firsthand the cooperative will of the obedient Jesus toward God as one submits to his and God's will. In such *imitatio Christi*, a person experiences and imitates the submission of Jesus's will to God's will, Gethsemane-style. Jesus thus remains as the obedient Son of his Father even after his resurrection. In his wake, his disciples are to follow suit, even if they do so imperfectly, in ways needing divine forgiveness.

Robust obedience to God includes what we have called "reconciliatory evidence and knowledge," because it includes the *koinōnia* of reconciliation with God in volitional cooperation. Gethsemane-oriented epistemology accommodates a previously mentioned lesson of John's Gospel in connecting our knowledge of the authoritative relation of Jesus to God with our resolve, or willingness, to obey God: "Anyone who resolves to do the will of God will know whether the teaching is from God or whether

I am speaking on my own" (John 7:17). Our intentional direction thus can bear on whether we are suitably positioned to receive evidence from God, given God's redemptive aim. It thus can bear also on our response to the storytelling of Jesus on behalf of divine goodness.

Gethsemane-oriented epistemology implies that the presence and power of God and the risen Jesus can be experienced, courtesy of divine self-manifestation, by cooperative people duly attentive to their moral experience of God. The self-revelation of God and the risen Jesus seeks the cooperative reconciliation of people in divine love. So, human indifference or opposition to such revelation would make it a pointless revelation regarding what it typically seeks: redemption as divine–human reconciliation in willing cooperation with God's will. Suitable recipients of divine self-revelation thus must be *willingly conformable* to the nature of the divine reconciliatory power being offered. The nature and the corresponding evidence of this power are best understood, we have noted, as *reconciliatory* by intent, in keeping with God's redemptive moral character. Jesus's parables challenged his audience to face the implications of such distinctive power and to respond appropriately.

Jesus's storytelling aimed to attract, without coercion, a redemptive kind of *conviction* in his hearers. This is *cooperative* conviction, attracted but not forced by divine moral power. Stories tend to be better than intellectual treatises as instruments for such conviction, because stories, at least as told by Jesus, tend to offer and to attract a kind of felt participation from their hearers. In that sense, stories akin to those from Jesus tend to have life-forming existential value, beyond mere intellectual value.

God's Spirit, understood as God in active goodness, can use uncoerced conviction in conscience to attract and guide a person toward God's will (and related truth) and away from counterfeits. Such conviction will reflect, via divine self-manifestation, God's perfect moral character, and therefore what is morally corrupt will be challenged by one's moral experience. Even if God's will is unclear in some cases, it does not follow that it is unclear in all or even most cases. In addition, if God aims to promote cooperative trust in Jesus, we have Jesus's distinctive moral character to clarify God's will and to attract receptive people to it.[8]

God's will can arise as a challenge in human moral experience, if permitted, and it can convict people, as suggested, *both* against anti-God ways *and* toward God's moral character of righteous *agapē*. The effort toward moral conviction comes from God's Spirit (as God in active goodness), and this Spirit is the direct reflection of the risen Jesus, sometimes overlapping in role with the risen Jesus (Rom. 8:9–11; cf. John 14:16–18, 16:8–15). The Spirit's desired conviction in moral conscience can be a means of *attracting* and *leading* people in cooperation with God. Paul thus considered such leading as central to being a child of God (Rom. 8:14; cf. Gal. 5:16–18).

The Spirit's conviction and leading are subject to rejection by humans as accountable agents, and when rejecting such conviction and leading, they are rejecting *God*, including God's presence and moral power. They then are rejecting reconciliation with God, the heart of divine redemption for humans. So, as suggested, human neglect or rejection of God's convicting will can send God and the risen Jesus into redemptive hiding, waiting for an opportune time for corrective intervention and conviction.

Given his ongoing obeyance of his Father, the risen Jesus can show in an attentive moral conscience the submission of his will to God's will, as God's obedient child. He thus can prompt cooperative co-willing from humans. As

---

[8] On the importance of the moral character of Jesus in Paul's thought, see Stanton, *Jesus of Nazareth in New Testament Preaching*, pp. 99–110, and Elias Andrews, *The Meaning of Christ for Paul* (New York: Abingdon Press, 1949), pp . 28–39. On the importance of the moral character of Jesus in the Gospel traditions, see Stanton, *Jesus of Nazareth in New Testament Preaching*, pp. 137–71.

humans cooperate with God's desired intervention in moral conscience, Gethsemane-style, the joint will of God and the risen Jesus emerges in their experience and they come to know them, intentional person to intentional person, in a reconciliatory manner.

If God is worthy of worship, and thus inherently morally perfect, humans should expect to know God in a morally beneficial way, rather than in a morally neutral way. As Chapter 2 explained, the relevant evidence will represent God's unique moral character for the sake of divine–human reconciliation. The same holds for the evidence central to knowing the risen Jesus, the life-giving Spirit as the unique filial revealer and advocate of God. The story-telling of Jesus aimed to engage hearers in a way that challenged and attracted them toward the desired reconciliation. It aimed to build a society of cooperative hearers reconciled to and reflective of the God behind the short stories.

A focus on moral conscience as the motivational avenue of the risen Jesus's intervention in human experience can acknowledge the key role of (a) a Gethsemane-style challenge regarding the priority of God's will and (b) human co-willing with the risen Jesus in favor of God's will. We then will have an interpersonal model for willingly receiving the self-revelation of God and the risen Jesus, as an alternative to divine hiding from human indifference or opposition. Gethsemane moral experience, in this perspective, is the motivational interpersonal context for the self-revealing of God and the risen Jesus in human moral cooperation.

Jesus gave the parable of the sower to explain why he faced widespread rejection in bringing the good news of God's arriving kingdom. His explanation has the common thread of identifying how anti-God *wills* take misplaced priority over God's will. Such wills result in the rejection of cooperation with Jesus in Gethsemane; they thus disobey God as moral authority and thereby demote God's supreme status. Demoting God in that way entails a kind of idolatry, and it thus obstructs reconciliatory knowledge of God and the risen Jesus.

The reconciliation of cooperative humans to God emerges when human wills end their indifference or opposition to God and cooperate with God's will. In their cooperation with God's will, they gain the power of God's will to obey a superior, perfect will, in reconciliation with God. They thus resist the anti-God power familiar in human interactions that hinder and even destroy relationships reflective of divine goodness. Following Jesus, then, leads to a divine–human reconciliation that can overcome much destructive power at large in the world.

Divine–human reconciliation leads to *koinōnia* with God, attracted and led uncoercively by divine *agapē*. The desired reconciliation and *koinōnia*, however, come with a price: dying to our anti-God wills. This is dying to anti-God ways on the basis of Gethsemane cooperation with God and the risen Jesus. It is dying in order to live with God, dying into God's lasting life with the risen Jesus (cf. 2 Cor. 4:11, Rom. 8:13). It also anchors knowledge of God and the risen Jesus in the kind of offered reconciliation and willing obedience faced and embraced by Jesus in Gethsemane, thus endorsing what we have called "reconciliatory knowledge."

The hiddenness of God and the risen Jesus often prompts a question about human wills: To obey or not to obey the perfect will of God? This is a direct effect of the reconciliatory nature of redemptive evidence and knowledge of God and Jesus. Because the expected obedience is Gethsemane oriented, as Chapter 3 explained, it is not *mere* obedience. Instead, it is prayer-guided obedience with an I–Thou interpersonal center: Not my will, but Thy will, be done. Such will-to-will interaction is interpersonal interaction, and irreducibly so. It amounts to being "face-to-face" with God, whose perfect will motivates God's perfect moral life.

The outstanding question for Jesus the storyteller was whether humans are willing to share in God's life, cooperatively and resolutely. This pressing question led him to ask: "When the Son of Man comes, will he find faith on earth?" (Luke 18:8). The latter question remained open because his role as the Son of Man was tied up with redemptive suffering for God and humans. Some of his stories had indicated as much, but we need to identify the troublesome but central role of suffering in his self-understanding and mission in relation to divine goodness.

6

~

Suffering for Divine Goodness

We cannot understand Jesus adequately without an understanding of his suffering or without an understanding of his own understanding of his suffering. A key issue is thus: What led Jesus to refer to himself using talk of "son of man" with the implication that he should suffer and die for God? This issue is initially puzzling if the basis for his self-reference is the exalted figure of Daniel 7. The perspective of Jesus in the synoptic Gospels goes beyond exaltation, with a role for suffering and death for the "son of man" that is not obvious in Daniel 7. We shall see how Jesus fits with Daniel 7 after all, and how he thought of his suffering as redemptive in attracting people to divine–human reconciliation and thus to divine goodness.

6.1 DANIEL'S VISION

We shall consider that, whatever role Jesus acknowledged for the suffering "servant" of Isaiah, he intentionally *complemented* the "son of man" talk of Daniel 7 as his template in order to highlight suffering and death in his mission for the sake of divine goodness. We shall see that, in his understanding of the suffering son of man, Jesus enhanced Daniel's image by a *shared-destiny assumption*, regarding suffering and rejection for himself and his disciples. This assumption is attributed to him repeatedly in the synoptic Gospels. Given that assumption, Jesus sought to bring the focus of inquirers to himself and to God rather than to just a previous figure or image. Commentators have neglected the central importance of the shared-destiny assumption to Jesus's understanding of the Danielic Son of Man and thus of himself.

However skeptical we are about the synoptic Gospels' portraits of Jesus, we cannot plausibly deny that he had a message of "good news" regarding the "kingdom of God." As Chapter 4 noted, Mark's Gospel introduces Jesus, after his baptism by John, as follows: "Now after John was arrested, Jesus came to Galilee, proclaiming the good news of God, and saying, 'The time is fulfilled, and the kingdom of God has come near [ἤγγικεν]; repent, and believe in the good news'" (Mark 1:14–15).

Some commentators have asked whether Jesus was prompted by a statement in the Book of Daniel: "The time arrived when the holy ones gained possession of the kingdom" (Dan. 7:22).[1] Even if an answer is underdetermined by our available evidence, Mark's introduction assumes an important connection between the kingdom of God and the good news. We need to identify this connection to understand a key motivational component for Jesus as "son of man" in his mission of obedience under suffering for divine goodness.

The good news, according to Mark's Jesus, is connected to the kingdom of God having come near.[2] We should not infer, however, that the kingdom has arrived *in full* according to the message of Jesus; instead, we should ask *how* it has come near in his message. In particular, we should ask how Jesus, in his self-understanding in the synoptic Gospels, relates to the drawing near of this kingdom, particularly in his distinctive actions for his mission of

---

[1] On the coming of God in the Book of Daniel, see G. R. Beasley-Murray, *Jesus and the Kingdom of God* (Exeter: Paternoster Press, 1986), pp. 26–35, and John E. Goldingay, *Daniel*, WBC (Dallas, TX: Word, 1987), pp. 59–60, 330–2. See also David Wenham, "The Kingdom of God and Daniel," *Expository Times* 98 (1987), 132–4.

[2] See Chapter 7 on two phases of the kingdom's arrival in Jesus's message.

suffering as "son of man." Those actions can reveal his presumed rationale and motivational power for his mission for divine goodness.

The synoptic Gospels prompt us to consider an apparent connection between Jesus and the Book of Daniel. They have him using a cryptic locution for himself amounting to "the son of man" (in their Greek: ὁ υἱὸς τοῦ ἀνθρώπου). Despite extensive controversy,[3] a key issue is whether some of Jesus's uses of this locution echo some Aramaic language from chapter 7 of the Book of Daniel.[4] The Aramaic of Daniel 7 for "one like a son of man" (כְּבַר אֱנָשׁ) has no definite article, and in some ancient uses it means simply "one like a human being" (as assumed, for instance, in the text of the NRSV and the REB).[5]

Daniel reports his night vision:

I saw one like a son of man [כְּבַר אֱנָשׁ]
    coming with the clouds of heaven.
And he came to the Ancient One

---

[3] For a critical overview of the controversy, see Delbert Burkett, *The Son of Man Debate*, SNTSMS (Cambridge: Cambridge University Press, 1999).

[4] For support, with some variations, for a positive answer, see Manson, *The Teaching of Jesus*, pp. 211–34, T. W. Manson, "The Son of Man in Daniel, Enoch, and the Gospels," in *Studies in the Gospels and Epistles* (Philadelphia: Westminster Press, 1962), pp. 123–45, Manson, *Jesus the Messiah*, pp. 113–19, Morna D. Hooker, *The Son of Man in Mark* (Montreal: McGill University Press, 1967), Hooker, "Is the Son of Man Problem Really Insoluble?," in *Text and Interpretation*, eds. Ernest Best and R. M. Wilson (Cambridge: Cambridge University Press, 1979), pp. 155–68, Moule, *The Origin of Christology*, pp. 11–22, Moule, "The Son of Man: Some of the Facts," *New Testament Studies* 95 (1984), 277–9, Matthew Black, "Aramaic Barnāshā and the 'Son of Man'," *Expository Times* 95 (1984), 200–6; Chrys C. Caragounis, *The Son of Man*, WUNT (Tübingen: Mohr Siebeck, 1986), pp. 174–90; John Donahue, "Recent Studies on the Origin of 'Son of Man' in the Gospels," *Catholic Biblical Quarterly* 48 (1986), 484–98; W. D. Davies and Dale C. Allison, Jr., "The Son of Man," in *A Critical and Exegetical Commentary on the Gospel According to Saint Matthew*, vol. 2, pp. 43–50, Christopher Tuckett, "The Son of Man in Q," in *From Jesus to John*, ed. M. C. De Boer, JSNTSS (Sheffield: JSOT Press, 1993), pp. 196–215, Darrell Bock, "The Use of Daniel 7 in Jesus' Trial," in *Who Is This Son of Man?*, eds. Larry Hurtado and Paul Owen, LNTS (Edinburgh: T&T Clark, 2011), pp. 78–100, and Crispin Fletcher-Louis, *Jesus Monotheism* (Eugene, OR: Cascade Books, 2015), vol. 1, pp. 101–27.

[5] For some philological background of "son of man," see Joseph A. Fitzmyer, *A Wandering Aramean: Collected Aramaic Essays* (Chico, CA: Scholars Press, 1979), pp. 143–52, and Maurice Casey, *The Solution to the "Son of Man" Problem* (London: T&T Clark, 2007), pp. 56–81.

and was presented before him.
To him was given dominion
and glory and kingship,
that all peoples, nations, and languages
should serve him.
His dominion is an everlasting dominion
that shall not pass away,
and his kingship is one
that shall never be destroyed. (Dan. 7:13–14, with "son of man"
from NRSV margin)

Daniel's "one like a son of man" is thus given the dominion
or power [שׁלְטָן] of lasting kingship by God. In that regard,
this son of man reigns over and in a divine kingdom, the
kingdom of God. So, this is no ordinary human being,
given his lasting kingly status from God.

The kingdom in question need not be a specific location,
but it can be a reign, rule, or dominion of God, a divine *power
of reigning* for kingship (cf. Psalm 145:13). Arguably, the
relevant power includes a motivational power for human
action suited to manifesting God's kingdom, and it thus
could bear on how Jesus understood divine power for his
own action, in the light of Daniel 7. We shall consider this
option, and identify its importance for a central redemptive
purpose of Jesus as suffering son of man, for the sake of
advancing, and attracting people to, divine goodness.

The divine kingdom of Daniel 7 is complicated by two
factors. First, it is given by God not only to one like a son of
man but also to the people of God: "The holy ones of the Most
High shall receive the kingdom and possess the kingdom
forever – forever and ever" (Dan. 7:18). Similarly: "The kingship and dominion and the greatness of the kingdoms under
the whole heaven shall be given to the people of the holy ones
of the Most High; their kingdom shall be an everlasting
kingdom, and all dominions shall serve and obey them"
(Dan. 7:27). So, *if* Daniel's "one like a son of man" is an
individual person, the kingdom power of God is shared by

this person with the holy people of God. This mysterious person thus would be closely associated with God's people, at least in their sharing the kingdom power of God.

Second, the people of God undergo persecution and suffering despite their being given the kingdom of God. Daniel's vision includes beasts as kings with horns, and one of them "made war with the holy ones and was prevailing over them" (Dan. 7:21). In addition, one of them "shall speak words against the Most High, shall wear out the holy ones of the Most High, … and they shall be given into his power for a time" (Dan. 7:25). The kingdom opposed to God "shall devour the whole earth, and trample it down, and break it to pieces" (Dan. 7:23; cf. 7:19).

The vision suggests that the recipients of God's kingdom (including, it seems, one like a son of man who shares this kingdom with them) undergo persecution, suffering, and perhaps even death from one opposed to God.[6] An opponent of God, according to the vision, will "prevail over" and "wear out" the holy people of God. The vision thus suggests a conflict of power sources between God and enemies of God. Even so, the persecution of God's people is not forever but only "for a time" or "until the Ancient One came" (Dan. 7:22, 25). Daniel suggests that the suffering of God's "holy ones" is redemptive and ultimately vindicated by God (Dan. 11:35, 12:2–3). As C. K. Barrett notes regarding suffering in Daniel: "Here is the conviction that the people of God will be vindicated, not in terms of historical development but by a divine act at the end of history, involving the resurrection of the dead, or at least some of them. Here too is the notion, in embryonic form, of

---

[6] This consideration figures in C. H. Dodd's remark that "to say, as it is often said, that the Old Testament knows nothing of a suffering Son of Man is inaccurate," although Dodd suggests that the suffering of the Son of Man must be combined with Isaiah's Servant to be "redemptive." See Dodd, *According to the Scriptures* (London: Nisbet, 1953), chap. 4. One could doubt the latter suggestion, however, if Jesus assumed that righteous suffering for God is "redemptive" in being good for some people (courtesy of God), as acknowledged by Psalms 22 and 107. Section 6.3 returns to the matter of redemptive suffering.

vicarious and atoning suffering."[7] We shall see how Jesus approached this suffering in a redemptive manner.

6.2 JESUS AND DANIEL

Given the close association in Daniel 7 of "one like a son of man" with "the holy ones" of God, one naturally can include this son of man with the people of God who receive the divine kingdom in their suffering for God. Daniel's "one like a son of man" thus may be (at least in part) a *representative individual* for the people of God who shares their destiny, including their being persecuted and suffering on behalf of God. The relevant idea is that in sharing his kingdom from God, "one like a son of man" represents (in standing for) the people sharing that kingdom and thus their destiny.

Jesus may have drawn from Daniel 7 in his self-attribution of the "son of man" as one who must suffer for God. Indeed, this would be a natural move if he thought of himself as sharing in the kingdom suffering of God's holy ones. In any case, it would be unduly skeptical now to insist that all ascriptions of "the son of man" to Jesus in the synoptic Gospels result just from the early church and not from Jesus. Our historical literary evidence does not support common or widespread use of "the son of man" for Jesus by the early church. In almost all cases, the evidence has Jesus using the phrase for himself. Acts 7:56 is a rare exception that highlights the pattern of our relevant literary evidence (cf. John 12:34, Rev. 1:13).

Our question about what Jesus *meant* with his talk of "son of man" amounts to the issue of what he *intended to signify or convey* with such talk, and he may have intended different things in different contexts. In addition, he may have built up specificity over time to express an increasingly definite meaning. Linguistic use can be variable in

---

[7] Barrett, *Jesus and the Gospel Tradition*, p. 44.

that way, and it can be *allusive* in a way that intends to evoke something that is not yet adequately understood or identified by hearers. It also can be *elusive* in a way that intentionally puzzles hearers for the sake of their giving careful attention to what is being expressed. Jesus's speaking of himself with a locution in the third person could serve such a purpose of aiming to increase attention from his audience. In any case, "son of man" need not have been a widely acknowledged title to figure in allusive and elusive meaning formed by the linguistic intentions of Jesus.

In some of his uses, Jesus could have had in mind, in a partly demonstrative manner, *that* mysterious son of man involved in Daniel 7.[8] This would not have to be a *purely* referential use,[9] however, because it could express some semantic content, if allusively and elusively, having to do with some distinctive features of the mysterious figure of Daniel 7. One relevant use, making reference to Daniel 7, is: "The high priest asked him, 'Are you the Messiah, the Son of the Blessed One?' Jesus said, 'I am; and you will see the Son of Man seated at the right hand of the Power, and coming with the clouds of heaven'" (Mark 14:61–2). We obscure the key reference to Daniel 7 if we remove the *status-assigning* function of "the Son of Man" here, whether by proposing that "son of man" is just (a) a circumlocution for "I," (b) a term with a generic sense of "man" in general, or (c) a term with an indefinite sense of "a man" or "someone."[10]

---

[8] See Moule, *The Origin of Christology*, p. 13.

[9] On such a use, as a first-person pronoun, see Larry W. Hurtado, *Lord Jesus Christ: Devotion to Jesus in Earliest Christianity* (Grand Rapids, MI: Eerdmans, 2003), p. 293. For critical discussion, see Fletcher-Louis, *Jesus Monotheism*, pp. 101–27.

[10] For criticisms of such deflationary interpretations of "son of man," with special attention to the proposals of Geza Vermes, Maurice Casey, Barnabas Lindars, and Richard Bauckham, see Delbert Burkett, "The Nontitular Son of Man: A History and Critique," *New Testament Studies* 40 (1994), 504–21, and Burkett, *The Son of Man Debate*, pp. 82–96. On Vermes and Lindars on "son of man," see also Donahue, "Recent Studies on the Origin of 'Son of Man' in the Gospels." Moule recommends consideration of the option that the unusual Greek phrase in the Gospels for "the son of man" "preserves something in the traditions of the sayings of Jesus which is more distinctive than simply an Aramaic phrase meaning 'a man' or 'somebody' or even 'I'." Moule, "Neglected Features in the Problem of 'the Son of Man'," in

Acknowledging a status-assigning function does not require assuming "son of man" to be a widely acknowledged or widely understood title among Jesus's audience. Morna D. Hooker rightly notes that "any satisfactory solution to the problem of the Son of Man must demonstrate not only why Jesus was thought to be referring to himself but also how the term came to be interpreted as denoting a figure who exercised superhuman authority and who would play a central role in the future as judge."[11] We evidently need, then, a status-assigning function for "son of man" in the case of some of Jesus's uses.

The New Testament Gospels supply our only evidence regarding the relevant linguistic intentions of Jesus, and this evidence is piecemeal rather than systematic. Even so, we do find a pattern sketched in the synoptic Gospels. Mark's Gospel, for instance, presents Jesus as being familiar not only with Daniel's announced "desolating sacrilege" or "abomination of desolation" in the temple (Mark 13:14; cf. Dan. 8:13, 9:17, 27, 11:29–31, 12:11) but also with Daniel's son of man "coming in the clouds" (Mark 13:26, 14:62; cf. Dan. 7:13). The latter exalted role for the synoptic Gospels' son of man (in the oldest interpretation of the locution in the Gospels) coexists with their role for suffering by the son of man. If Jesus's use of "[the] son of man" for himself echoes Daniel 7 in some cases, we can make some sense of his intention. In that case, he suggested that he in particular is Daniel's son of man who receives a kingdom from God, including "kingship, that all peoples, nations, and languages should serve him" (Dan. 7:14). We shall see, however, that this is just one side of a historically plausible two-sided story about Jesus as "the son of man."

Essays in New Testament Interpretation (Cambridge: Cambridge University Press, 1982), p. 83.
[11] Hooker, "Is the Son of Man Problem Really Insoluble?," p. 165.

6.3 SHARED REDEMPTIVE DESTINY

Daniel did *not* say of the "holy people" of God anything close to his following statement about his elusive "son of man" figure: "I saw one like a son of man coming with the clouds of heaven, and he came to the Ancient One." The "holy people" as a group did not come "with the clouds of heaven" or "to the Ancient One" in Daniel's story; this exalted status is reserved for "one like a son of man." Even so, Daniel portrayed the holy people as sharing God's kingdom with the one who does thus come to God. Despite his exalted status, this kingly son of man is represented as reigning over and with the holy people who suffer from opposition to God.

We cannot exclude on the basis of our literary evidence that Jesus thought of himself as Daniel's "one like a son of man" who, as God's appointed representative, would share the destiny of the "holy ones" in their suffering for God. Daniel's figure can illuminate, we shall see, the reference to "the Son of Man" in this striking remark: "[Jesus] began to teach them that the Son of Man must undergo great suffering, and be rejected by the elders, the chief priests, and the scribes, and be killed" (Mark 8:31; cf. Mark 10:33–4, Luke 9:22, Matt. 16:21).[12] Similarly, we need to elucidate this surprising comment: "[Jesus] said to them, 'Elijah is indeed coming first to restore all things. How then is it written about the Son of Man, that he is to go through many sufferings and be treated with contempt?'" (Mark 9:12; cf. Matt. 17:10–12). If Daniel's "son of man" is in mind here, that figure in the perspective of the synoptic Jesus cannot be understood as *merely* triumphant and exalted because he is engaged in suffering for God.

---

[12] C. K. Barrett refers to this teaching of Jesus as "a revolution in thought," as a "creative moulding of the older tradition [that probably] was the work of Jesus himself." See Barrett, *The Holy Spirit and the Gospel Tradition*, p. 119; cf. p. 154.

A pressing issue concerns where Jesus got his idea of a suffering son of man, including his view that "the Son of Man goes as it is written of him" (Mark 14:21; cf. Matt. 26:24, Luke 18:31, 22:22, 17:25). The reference to what is "written of him," as Chapter 4 noted, suggests a textual biblical origin for his idea of a suffering son of man. Daniel 7, as indicated, is arguably the most plausible textual basis for this key idea for Jesus in the synoptic Gospels, and the gospel passages just cited indicate that all three synoptic Gospels, and not just Mark's Gospel, represent the idea. The issue now concerns how suffering as persecution for God is derivable from, or at least related to, Daniel's "son of man" figure.

The textual basis in Daniel 7 is suitably open-ended and subtle for Jesus's purpose in uniquely characterizing himself, his authority, and his mission for God. It thus allows for his sharp contrast with anything like familiar kingship or lordship (Mark 2:10–11, 3:23–7, 12:1–11; cf. John 6:15, 18:36–7). It also prompts the challenging question: Who then is this man? (Mark 4:41, 8:27, Matt. 16:13). The synoptic Gospels suggest that Jesus preferred a notion of a suffering son of man, in contrast with a notion of a dominating Davidic king, to guide any notion of authority applied to him (Mark 8:29–35; cf. Mark 12:35–7). Daniel 7 itself does not offer a notion of Messiah (we shall return to this matter), but it does offer an elusive notion of "son of man" that Jesus could complement to serve his purposes in embracing and manifesting redemptive suffering and authority for divine goodness.

C. F. D. Moule comments:

The fact remains that in Daniel 7:21, 25, the specially aggressive "horn" on the beast's head "made war with the saints, and prevailed over them" and was destined to "wear out the saints of the Most High"; and it is precisely with these saints of the Most High that the Son of Man is identified ... [T]his interpretation of the Son of Man vision ... was in Daniel 7 as Jesus and his disciples knew it – and I know of no evidence to the contrary. But, if so, the Son of Man, in the only document known to have been available then, stands for a loyal, martyr-group who are brought to glory and vindicated *through persecution*. There is no need to invoke Isaiah 53 (a questionable procedure anyway). The Danielic Son of Man is itself a sufficient symbol for martyrs who are to be vindicated.[13]

Regarding Isaiah's suffering "servant," we can be open to its influence on Jesus, even though the evidence is inconclusive, and Jesus refrains from calling himself "the suffering servant" or even "the servant." I suspect, in any case, that Isaiah's conception of a servant who suffers was too thin by itself to capture the kind of kingly authority suggested by Jesus, and thus that Jesus found better service overall from Daniel's image of "son of man."[14]

We need not preclude, at least as a live option, an influential perspective of Vincent Taylor, commenting on Jesus's prediction of his persecution and rejection in Mark 8:31–2: "The teaching is based on a unique combination of the idea of the Suffering Servant of Isaiah 53 with that of the Son of Man."[15] A clear echo of this influential perspective occurs in Chrys Caragounis: "[Jesus] conflated the Son of Man concept with that of the Suffering Servant, and thus opened the way for him to draw upon Isaianic and other materials at will."[16] Peter Stuhlmacher also finds an influence of Isaiah 53 on Jesus, in connection with Mark 10:45

---

[13] C. F. D. Moule, "Review of H.E. Tödt, *The Son of Man in the Synoptic Tradition*," *Theology* 69 (1966), 174.

[14] Here I agree with Manson, *Jesus the Messiah*, p. 111. Chapter 7 returns to the distinctive kind of kingly authority valued by Jesus.

[15] Vincent Taylor, *The Gospel According to St. Mark*, 2nd ed. (London: Macmillan, 1966), p. 378. For a similar view, see Matthew Black, "Servant of the Lord and Son of Man," *Scottish Journal of Theology* 6 (1953), 1–11, and R. T. France, *Jesus and the Old Testament* (London: Tyndale Press, 1971), pp. 121–6. In the same vein, with some qualification, see Goppelt, *Theology of the New Testament*, pp. 190–3.

[16] Caragounis, *The Son of Man*, p. 229.

(Matt. 20:28).[17] A key issue, however, is whether we need to acknowledge the alleged combination to account for the role of the suffering "son of man" in Jesus. Notably, as suggested, the synoptic Gospels do not represent Jesus as calling himself "the servant," and this has added to doubt among some scholars about the alleged combination, in the absence of better supporting evidence.[18]

I agree with C. K. Barrett that "it is not necessary to interpret 'Son of Man' in terms of 'Servant of the Lord' in order to understand the predictions of the passion, and the passion itself."[19] We shall see that Jesus's complemented use of Daniel 7 serves this purpose without invoking Isaiah's "servant." In addition, we lack definite evidence that Jesus thought of himself in terms of Isaiah's "servant." The claim is not that Jesus was unaware of the servant poems of Isaiah; instead, it is that the New Testament does not supply definite evidence that he regarded Isaiah's "servant" as a model for himself. As Donald Juel has noted, "there seems to have existed no Suffering Servant or Servant of the Lord as a distinct figure or even vocation in Jewish tradition which would serve as a paradigm [for Jesus]."[20] Given that Jesus repeatedly referred to himself as "son of man," we should look for a more defensible influence on his self-understanding from Daniel 7.

[17] Peter Stuhlmacher, "Vicariously Giving His Life for Many, Mark 10:45 (Matt. 20:28)," in *Reconciliation, Law, and Righteousness*, pp. 16–29.
[18] For grounds for such doubt, see C. K. Barrett, "The Background of Mark 10:45," in *New Testament Essays*, ed. A. J. B. Higgins (Manchester: Manchester University Press, 1959), pp. 1–18, Morna D. Hooker, *Jesus and the Servant* (London: SPCK, 1959), pp. 74–9, and Hooker, "Did Jesus Use Isaiah 53?," in *The Servant of God in Practice*, eds. J. W. Rogerson and J. J. Vincent (Blandford Forum: Deo Publishing, 2017), chap. 5.
[19] Barrett, *Jesus and the Gospel Tradition*, p. 45.
[20] Donald Juel, *Messianic Exegesis* (Philadelphia: Fortress Press, 1988), p. 130. Juel adds: "Believing Jesus to be the promised Messiah and following accepted principles of interpretation, his followers were led to the servant poems as potentially messianic texts, since the Messiah is called 'God's servant' in Zech. 3:8 and Ps. 89:39, passages traditionally understood as messianic in postbiblical Jewish circles" (p. 131). Isaiah's servant poems themselves do not have a definite messianic status, and, as suggested, their servant lacks the authoritative status of Daniel's "son of man."

Moule proposes that the best account of our literary evidence has Jesus himself using "the son of man" (at least in some cases) as a symbolic demonstrative phrase: in effect, *that* son of man, the one portrayed in Daniel 7. He comments: "In Daniel 7, the seer sees *a* human figure *(kebar 'enosh'* – 'what looked like a man'); but Jesus, referring back to this symbol, with all its associations, speaks of his own vocation and that of his friends in terms of '*the* Son of Man': it is for him and for them to be or to become that figure."[21]

Contrary to Moule's suggestion, the synoptic Gospels do not talk of Jesus *becoming* the son of man, and we need not rely on such talk. In addition, Jesus does not represent his followers as *becoming* the son of man, as if a community understanding of this goal is at work in his teaching. Similarly, we cannot capture the elusive figure of Daniel 7 as *simply* one that "stands for a loyal, martyr-group," given that an apparent *individual* has a significant role. So, we need to improve on Moule's interpretation of Jesus on the "son of man." As an alternative, we shall see, a neglected idea can illuminate the self-understanding and mission of Jesus: that of Jesus's *complementing* Daniel's image of one like the "son of man" with his own understanding of redemptive suffering, in terms of a shared redemptive destiny with his followers.

We need special caution about the relation between Daniel's "one like a son of man" and the "holy ones of God." The relation is representative, at least with the former representing the latter in terms of what the kingdom of God brings, but the "holy ones" similarly can represent "one like a son of man." This is not a relation of strict identity, however, where the one like a son of man is reducible to the holy people of God. We have noted a key difference in that *only* the one like a son of man (and *not* the holy ones of God) comes "with the clouds of heaven" or "to the Ancient One."[22] Neglected in much of the literature,

---

[21] Moule, *The Origin of Christology*, p. 16; cf. Moule, "The Son of Man," p. 278.

[22] It is thus misleading for R. T. France to claim: "In Daniel 7 . . . the Son of man . . . is never set over against [the people of God] as an individual against a community.

this important difference blocks a claim to strict identity, and it calls for a special kind of representation instead. It also fits with W. G. Kümmel's judgment regarding Daniel 7 that "'the one like a man' must originally have been [deemed] an individual heavenly figure," and not a social group.[23] We have noted evidence for the latter contrast in Daniel 7.

Hooker notes that "the problem which concerns the author of Daniel 7 is that of the suffering of 'the saints of the Most High' who are clearly represented by the man-like figure in the vision. We find in this chapter [of Daniel] precisely the theme of suffering–vindication which characterizes the Markan understanding of the Son of Man."[24] Our key issue now, however, concerns *how* Jesus understood the Danielic "son of man" (as himself) to be related to the suffering people of God and thus to be implicated in their persecution, suffering, and rejection. The synoptic Gospels portray Jesus as understanding his representative role from God to include a shared redemptive destiny with the people of God, in a way fitting with the "son of man" of Daniel 7 but also in a way irreducible to membership in a community of God's people.

Matthew's Gospel offers a statement of the shared redemptive destiny in the role of Jesus as both "the Son of Man" and "king" (Matt. 25:31–46). An assumption of *shared redemptive destiny*, including either persecution and rejection or blessing and vindication, figures in the king's announcement that "just as you did it to one of the least of these who are members of my family, you did it to me" (Matt. 25:40; cf. Mark 9:37, Matt. 18:5, Luke 9:48). Matthew's

He *is* the people, represented in a visionary form." France, *Jesus and the Old Testament*, p. 129. For a similar claim needing qualification, see Hooker, "Is the Son of Man Problem Really Insoluble?," p. 166.

[23] Kümmel, *The Theology of the New Testament*, pp. 77–8. Similarly, see John J. Collins, *Daniel*, Hermeneia (Minneapolis: Fortress Press, 1993), pp. 304–10, and, with attention to 1 Enoch and 4 Ezra, Collins, *The Scepter and the Star*, ABRL (New York: Doubleday, 1995), pp. 176–9. See also Goldingay, *Daniel*, pp. 167–72.

[24] Hooker, "Is the Son of Man Problem Really Insoluble?," p. 166.

Gospel sets this principle in the context of the coming of Jesus as "the Son of Man" (Matt. 25:31).[25]

Persecution or rejection of the king's followers, according to the principle, is shared by the king (and thus by "the Son of Man") himself. Jesus, of course, could have recognized this principle in connection with the destiny of John the Baptist. The relevant "shared redemptive destiny" includes the destiny regarding the world's response to people identifying with God in obedience. It is *redemptive* at least in being preparatory for being "blessed" and vindicated with entering God's kingdom in its fullness (Matt. 25:34, 46). Jesus as the sender of God's people would share the destiny of the sent people, including being vindicated by God, thus going beyond the matter of the sent sharing in his status as sender. Here we have a parallel with the suffering noted in Daniel's vision.

Jesus's assumption of shared redemptive destiny figured in his following remark to his disciples: "Whoever listens to you listens to me, and whoever rejects you rejects me, and whoever rejects me rejects the one who sent me" (Luke 10:16; cf. Matt. 10:40). Joseph Fitzmyer observes: "The principle implied in it is that of representation, akin to the institution of *shaliah* of contemporary Judaism."[26] It implies representation owing to the disciples' representing Jesus in their being accepted or rejected, but Jesus assumed more.

Jesus assumed a shared redemptive destiny in *his* being accepted or rejected when his disciples are accepted or rejected. He assumed that *God* likewise shares in this destiny in a redemptive manner, including in divine vindication of the rejected disciples. Notably, however, a person's

---

[25] For considerations in favor of historical authenticity, see J. A. T. Robinson, "The 'Parable' of the Sheep and the Goats," *New Testament Studies* 2 (1956), 225–37, and David Catchpole, "The Poor on Earth and the Son of Man in Heaven," *Bulletin of the John Rylands Library* 61 (1979), 355–97. Similarly, see Théo Preiss, "The Mystery of the Son of Man," in *Life in Christ*, trans. Harold Knight, SBT (Chicago: Allenson, 1954), pp. 43–60.

[26] Fitzmyer, *The Gospel According to Luke*, vol. 1, p. 857. Fitzmyer finds it likely that Luke derived the saying from the Q tradition.

acceptance or rejection of Jesus or God, according to
Matthew 25:37–40, does not require that person categoriz-
ing or describing this as accepting Jesus or God. It could
function, in terms of a medieval distinction, as *de re* rather
than *de dicto*, as causally direct without theological description. This consideration bears importantly on divine
redemption working in intellectually diverse people,
including agnostics and even atheists.[27]

The assumption of shared redemptive destiny would
have made it natural for Jesus to understand the suffering
of the persecuted "holy ones" of Daniel 7 as shared by him
in his role as the anticipated "son of man" of that section of
Daniel. This sharing, however, does not entail the kind of
redemptive "substitution" attributed by some scholars to
Jesus as "son of man"; nor does it entail the reductive
"community" approach to "son of man" in Daniel suggested by some commentators.[28] We can make do without
those questionable assumptions.

Given the shared-destiny interpretation of the "son of
man" in Daniel 7, Jesus would have considered his own
persecution in terms of its being "written about the Son of
Man that he is to go through many sufferings and be
treated with contempt" (Mark 9:12). His understanding of
his destiny as "son of man" could have included death as
well as persecution and suffering, particularly as
a suggestion of Daniel's talk of the "wearing out" of the
holy ones of God (Dan. 7:25). We need to consider what
such a self-understanding included, in the light of his
assumption of shared redemptive destiny.

---

[27] On this matter, see Moser, *Understanding Religious Experience*, pp. 46–9, 316–20, Moser, "God *De Re et De Dicto*: Kierkegaard, Faith, and Religious Diversity," *Scottish Journal of Theology* 74 (2021), and Moser, "Responsive Phenomenology of God," *Expository Times* 132 (2021).

[28] On a substitution approach, see Preiss, "The Mystery of the Son of Man," p. 53, Stuhlmacher, "Jesus the Reconciler," pp. 1–15, and Caragounis, *The Son of Man*, pp. 200–1. On a reductive community approach in Daniel, see Manson, *The Teaching of Jesus*, pp. 227–34, Moule, *The Origin of Christology*, pp. 20–1, and Hooker, "Is the Son of Man Problem Really Insoluble?," p. 166.

New Testament scholars have overlooked the relevance of Jesus's shared-destiny assumption in the synoptic Gospels to his understanding of Daniel 7. This omission has blocked awareness of the straightforward explanation of the suffering "son of man" offered here. As suggested, a noteworthy benefit of the explanation on offer is that it does not require a uniform "corporate" or "community" understanding of "son of man" that runs afoul of non-corporate uses in the synoptic Gospels, such as in the characterizations of the exaltation and authority of "the Son of Man" that are not shared by God's people in general.[29] Similarly, it avoids the shortcoming of a deflationary self-referential use, amounting to "I," that attributes no special status to Jesus. An additional benefit is that is does not require a controversial assumption of an influence on Jesus as suffering "son of man" from material in Isaiah, Ezekiel, 1 Enoch, or 4 Ezra. Our literary historical evidence does not clearly recommend any such assumption. From the standpoint of our literary historical evidence, the explanation offered here is on firmer ground. It best explains our relevant data, with due parsimony.

Daniel's narrative can shed some further light on the self-understanding of the synoptic Jesus. Mark's Gospel, as noted, portrays Jesus as being familiar with Daniel's announced desolating sacrilege in the temple. Perhaps this is part of Mark's redaction, but Jesus would have needed some understanding of Daniel's announced desolation of the temple to make adequate sense of the divinely appointed role of Daniel's "one like a son of man." This desolation, in Daniel's narrative, called for the kind of divine judgment involving the divinely empowered vindication and triumph of one like a son of man (Dan. 7:9–14).

If Jesus was familiar with Daniel's narrative on the desolation of the temple, as Mark's Gospel suggests, he likely

---

[29] See Hooker, *The Son of Man in Mark*, p. 181, and Burkett, *The Son of Man Debate*, p. 49.

would have considered the following characterization, directly or indirectly:

Seventy weeks are decreed for your people and your holy city: to finish the transgression, to put an end to sin, and to atone for iniquity, to bring in everlasting righteousness, to seal both vision and prophet, and to anoint a most holy place. Know therefore and understand: from the time that the word went out to restore and rebuild Jerusalem until the time of an anointed prince, there shall be seven weeks ... After the sixty-two weeks, an anointed one [מָשִׁיחַ] shall be cut off and shall have nothing, and the troops of the prince who is to come shall destroy the city and the sanctuary. (Dan. 9:24–6)

Daniel 7 is not explicitly messianic, but Daniel 9 is in its talk of "anointed one" (מָשִׁיחַ).[30] The reading or hearing of these sections of Daniel together, in combination, may have prompted the association of the Danielic "son of man" with the Messiah in the synoptic Gospels and even in the mind of Jesus (Mark 8:29–31, Matt. 16:13–16, Luke 9:20–2). At least, we cannot exclude this.

Chapters 7 and 9 of Daniel supply an available literary basis for associating the "son of man" with the Messiah. In any case, our literary evidence in the synoptic Gospels indicates that Jesus was familiar with at least part of that basis, directly or indirectly, given his talk of "son of man" regarding himself. In addition, if Mark 13 is to be trusted in this connection, he was also familiar, directly or indirectly, with the messianic deliverance (from temple sacrilege) announced by that literary basis. We should not rest a case for Jesus's self-understanding mainly on the latter conditional, but that conditional is true to the synoptic narrative.

The potential contribution of Daniel 9 to the self-understanding of Jesus as "son of man" goes further. It

---

[30] For relevant discussion of Daniel 9, see Fitzmyer, *The One Who Is to Come*, pp. 56–64, and Goldingay, *Daniel*, pp. 266–8.

sets the following redemptive goal in connection with the promised "anointed one": "to finish the transgression, to put an end to sin, and to atone for [וּלְכַפֵּר] iniquity, to bring in everlasting righteousness" (Dan. 9:24). Perhaps this goal was suggestive to Jesus about his mission as the Danielic "one like a son of man," and he may have understood "atoning for iniquity" in terms of divine–human reconciliation. We cannot exclude this option, and it helps us to make sense of some portrayals of him in the synoptic Gospels.

The authors of the synoptic Gospels wanted readers to think of the "son of man" as a messianic redemptive figure. This includes the author of the Gospel of Luke: "The Son of Man came to seek out and to save the lost" (Luke 19:10). The authors of the Gospels of Mark and Matthew put the redemptive language for the son of man in different terms: "The Son of Man came not to be served but to serve, and to give his life a ransom for many" (Mark 10:45, Matt. 20:28; cf. Luke 22:27). Their general idea of "serving," however, need not take us to the book of Isaiah, and, as suggested, it does not include calling Jesus "the servant." We find an idea of serving in Daniel 7:14, but Jesus offered a reversal: The Son of Man would seek to serve rather than to be served.[31] This reversal fits with the humility of sharing the redemptive destiny of God's suffering people.

James D. G. Dunn has offered a sober response to the relation of Mark 10:45 to Isaiah 53: "There is a clear danger that both sets of suggested allusions (Isaiah 53; Daniel 7) are more in the eye of the beholder than contrived or intended by the initial tradents. But at least the latter [Daniel 7] has the support of a more extensive motif, including other clear allusions, whereas the case for seeing here evidence that Jesus himself was influenced by Isaiah 53 is not much strengthened."[32] Dunn thus shares the skepticism of

---

[31] On some of the relevant philology, see Stuhlmacher, "Vicariously Giving His Life for Many, Mark 10:45," pp. 21–2.

[32] Dunn, *Christianity in the Making*, vol. 1, p. 815. See also Dunn, *Jesus, Paul, and the Gospels*, pp. 16–17.

Hooker, Moule, and others about the place of Isaiah 53 in the thought of Jesus. Our definite literary evidence, as suggested, makes it difficult to counter that skepticism.

Notably, we find the idea of servant in Daniel 9, as applied to the prophets in general, who are "servants" of God (Dan. 9:10). In Daniel 9, this idea is associated with divine mercy, forgiveness, and judgment. If the synoptic Jesus took himself to be at least a prophet of God (Mark 6:4, Matt. 11:9, Luke 24:19), the relevant idea from Daniel of redemptive serving for God, for the sake of divine–human reconciliation, would have applied to him in his prophetic mission. So, we need not look to the servant songs of Isaiah for Jesus's notion of redemptive service for God.

6.4 VINDICATION THROUGH SUFFERING

Some commentators have questioned the relevance of Daniel 7 to Jesus's suffering as "son of man" on the ground that Daniel's figure represents the holy ones of God only after their triumphant deliverance from persecution.[33] The charge implies that we do not find explicit talk of a suffering son of man in Daniel and therefore we need to look elsewhere for the source of such talk. Such an approach to biblical interpretation for Jesus is, however, too rigid at best, especially given what we know of Jesus's original handling of the Jewish scriptures, as represented in the synoptic Gospels (see, e.g., Mark 12:35–7, Matt. 22:41–6, Luke 20:41–4).[34]

We have no reason to think that Jesus would have limited his understanding of Daniel's "son of man" as representative of God's people to a status of triumph and exaltation. On the contrary, given the shared-destiny

---

[33] See, for instance, Burkett, *The Son of Man Debate*, p. 49, citing H. H. Rowley, *The Servant of the Lord*, 2nd ed. (Oxford: Blackwell, 1965), p. 64, France, *Jesus and the Old Testament*, pp. 128–30, and Wayne Meeks, "Asking Back to Jesus' Identity," in *From Jesus to John*, pp. 45–6.

[34] See also Joel Marcus, *The Way of the Lord: Christological Exegesis of the Old Testament in the Gospel of Mark* (Louisville, KY: Westminster Press, 1992).

assumption repeatedly assigned to Jesus in the synoptic Gospels, we should think more broadly of his self-understanding for his representing the people of God in connection with Daniel's "son of man." We should consider that he may have recognized what was implicit in Daniel's portrait of the "son of man."

We have noted suggestions of redemptive suffering in Daniel's elusive figure, and we have identified passages from the synoptic Gospels that associate Jesus's representative role, via the shared-destiny assumption, with redemptive suffering. That assumption, therefore, can illuminate an understanding of Daniel's "son of man" as one of whom it is "written ... that he is to go through many sufferings and be treated with contempt" (Mark 9:12). The book of Isaiah does not mention a suffering *son of man*; so, we would be hard put to find a source there for the synoptic Jesus's notion of a suffering "son of man." (A similar concern bears on relevant appeals to material in Ezekiel, 1 Enoch, or 4 Ezra.)[35]

According to Mark's Gospel, as suggested, Jesus predicted to the high priest, with reference to Daniel 7:13, that "you will see the Son of Man seated at the right hand of the Power [τῆς δυνάμεως], and coming with the clouds of heaven" (Mark 14:62; cf. Mark 13:26, Matt. 26:64, Luke 22:69). God is thus, in the mind of Mark's Jesus, "the Power" and the power for the vindication of God's people, including Daniel's "son of man." Mark's Gospel leaves its readers with no doubt about this divine vindication involving the "son of man" (Mark 13:26–7; cf. Matt. 24:30–1).

The synoptic Jesus set the power of divine vindication in a context of shared redemptive destiny under persecution

---

[35] The author of Mark's Gospel clearly endorsed the relevance of the book of Isaiah to the ministry of Jesus. See Watts, *Isaiah's New Exodus and Mark*. Even if Jesus saw his ministry foreshadowed in parts of the book of Isaiah (Luke 4:17–19, reflecting Isaiah 61:1–2), it is a separate issue whether he found there a basis for his understanding of the suffering "son of man." This chapter contends that we need not assume so, given the chapter's proposed approach to Daniel 7 and Jesus's shared-destiny assumption.

and suffering with the people of God. For this reason, Jesus arguably chose to characterize himself by reference to the enigmatic "son of man" of Daniel 7. This reference allowed him to associate with God's kingly status of authority while exemplifying the power of redemptive *agapē* that shares the suffering of the vulnerable and persecuted people of God for the sake of deepening their attraction and loyalty to God. Suffering for what is good tends to attract many people in that way. Jesus was attracted by divine goodness, including God's love for him, to seek and suffer for the attraction and realization of that goodness and love for others, including his enemies. As Chapter 3 noted, some of his parables, including the parables of the lost sheep and the wicked tenants, confirm this lesson.

The combination of kingship and shared redemptive destiny under suffering has seemed strange to many observers, including to Peter at Caesarea Philippi (Mark 8:31–2, Matt. 16:21–2). Even so, the synoptic Gospels embrace the combination and assign it, at least in the case of the Gospels of Mark and Matthew, to the teaching of Jesus as the "son of man" (Mark 10:42–5, Matt. 20:25–8; cf. Luke 22:24–7). That combination, we have seen, is foreshadowed in the Book of Daniel and thus offered a memorable template for Jesus.

The Gospels of Mark and Matthew portray Jesus as calling Peter "satan" (adversary) for taking exception to his shared-destiny assumption as suffering "son of man" (Mark 8:33, Matt. 16:23). They add that Jesus chastised Peter, in that context, for "setting your mind not on divine things [οὐ φρονεῖς τὰ τοῦ θεοῦ] but on human things." We have an indication here of how seriously the synoptic Jesus took his shared-destiny assumption. He used it to draw a clear line between what is of God and what is not of God. So, his assumption appears to be central to his understanding of how God works in human affairs, including in his own redemptive mission.

The Gospels of Matthew and Luke suggest that Jesus located the distinctive combination of kingship and shared redemptive destiny in the divine goodness of the moral character of God (Matt. 5:43–8, Luke 6:27–8, 32–6). He portrayed God as seeking shared redemptive destiny in righteous *agapē* with humans, including with people persecuted for God (Mark 10:29–30), and even with God's enemies. The synoptic Gospels thus picture Jesus as called by God to "seek and save" humans, even in the midst of persecution and suffering, for their redemption as cooperative reconciliation to God. His parables of the lost sheep, the lost coin, and the prodigal son highlighted his distinctive redemptive picture of God and of his mission given by God and vindicated by God (Luke 15; cf. Matt. 18:12–14). We have noted passages from all strata of the synoptic Gospels to clarify his striking picture of God as redemptive through suffering.

We now can see why the synoptic Jesus worked with his Danielic self-conception of the "son of man," instead of offering something transparent and convenient for his audience. He talked of the "son of man" with self-reference to indicate, on the basis of Daniel 7, that he came from God to share the redemptive destiny of God's persecuted people, a destiny of shared vindication in divine goodness. In addition, he sought to encourage his hearers to puzzle over not only *who he is* in representing God and divine goodness (Mark 8:27–33, Matt. 16:13–23, Luke 9:18–22) but also *who God is*, in terms of the divine goodness of God's redemptive character and purpose (with his parables of the kingdom highlighting the latter).

Jesus challenged his audience not only to acknowledge but also *to share* in God's motive of righteous *agapē* toward people in need of reconciliation. This kind of self-reflective challenge regarding one's motive in interpersonal relations can indicate one's fitting or not fitting with God's character of redemptive *agapē* under persecution and thus with God's persecuted kingdom. Even so, the trial for endurance under persecution does not come with a full theodicy that comprehensively explains the divine rationale for allowing persecution in the first place. Instead, divine power is portrayed as being vindicated, as powerfully good, *in the midst of* unexplained evil. The Gospels of Mark and Matthew offer Jesus's cry of dereliction on Calvary, in the absence of an explanatory response, as confirmation of this hard-learned lesson. (Chapter 8 returns to the topic of unexplained evil.)

Jesus's parable of the sower expresses the intended value of an agreeable shared motive between humans and God, in connection with the "good soil." The Gospel of Luke, as Chapter 5 suggested, captures the intention explicitly, with the following language: "As for that in the good soil, these are the ones who, when they hear the word, hold it fast in an honest and good heart, and bear fruit with patient endurance" (Luke 8:15; cf. Mark 4:20, Matt. 13:23).[36] The relevant "holding fast" (κατέχουσιν) includes enduring, obediently (with a "good heart") through suffering, because the divine vindication comes *through* obedient suffering, and not in place of it. Such suffering confirms the "good heart," including the fruitful motivation, sought by Jesus in his use of parables. God makes it redemptive in bringing divine vindication with divine goodness to it, including deeper reconciliation with God.

The synoptic Jesus is consistent on the lesson that the Gospel of Luke captures as follows: "By your endurance you will gain your souls" (Luke 21:19). The Gospels of Mark and Matthew, drawing a connection with Daniel's sacrilege in the temple, provide a somewhat different formulation: "The one who endures to the end will be saved" (Mark 13:13, Matt. 24:13; cf. Matt. 10:22). The relevant "gaining your souls" and "being saved" include redemptive vindication by God through suffering, in particular, obedient suffering in the face of persecution. The synoptic Jesus was able to capture this lesson with his distinctive

---

[36] See Chapter 5 on the importance of audience motive for the teaching of the synoptic Jesus in connection with his parables.

perspective on the Danielic "son of man," coupled with his shared-destiny assumption.

We have suggested a connection between a motive sought by Jesus in a hearer and the hearer's being "fit" for the kingdom of God. The Gospel of Luke uses such talk of being fit (εὔθετός) for the kingdom of God in a context of its statement of the shared-destiny assumption we have ascribed to Jesus (Luke 9:62; cf. Luke 10:16). This is no coincidence. The motive of righteous *agapē* sought by Jesus fits *God's* kingdom because it fits *God's* moral character, the character that defines and empowers the kingdom with divine goodness.

The divine vindication in the kingdom includes divine approval of the kind of human endurance that manifests, even under persecution, God's perfect moral character, the center of divine goodness. The synoptic Jesus gave undivided homage to that character and goodness with his aforementioned striking remark that "no one is good but God alone" (Mark 10:18, Luke 18:19; cf. Matt. 19:17). Arguably, Jesus intended an understanding of God's moral character, as the center of divine goodness, to be required for an understanding of his mission as "son of man." I suspect that this is so, given the ways in which the synoptic Jesus tended to be elusive but nonetheless focused on God's unique moral character as the center of divine goodness and of his mission.

The good news announced by Jesus included God's coming near to humans, with a divine kingdom of righteous power, to attract, sustain, and vindicate them in their obedient response, even under persecution. Daniel's figure of the "son of man" summed up this message for the synoptic Jesus, particularly given his shared-destiny assumption. Human obedience to God, in Jesus's teaching, is required for inclusion and vindication in the divine kingdom (Matt. 7:21; cf. Luke 6:46), but this is not a matter of "earning" God's approval; instead, it is a response that enables one to (become "fit" to) appropriate the good power that is God's kingdom. Indeed, it is part of God's goodness and thus of the good news from God that humans need not earn their approval with God (Matt. 20:1–16; cf. Luke 12:32).

When the synoptic Jesus interpreted the Danielic "son of man" in terms of his shared-destiny assumption, he gained a distinctive template for his redemptive mission from God. He thus came to understand himself as called by God to suffer, redemptively, for God's people, in order to call and attract them to God's kingdom in renewed obedience, to receive divine goodness. His shared redemptive destiny with them included his and their eventual vindication by God with divine goodness. For wayward humans, it found illustration in the running by the father to his troubled son in the parable of the prodigal son. (As suggested, Jesus did not identify himself with the wayward son.)

The divine vindication, in Jesus's self-understanding, came through his sharing in the suffering of the people of God and thereby attracting and leading them, through obedient endurance, to ever-deepening reconciled life in God's kingdom. It also included God sustaining him through his rejection in Jerusalem, via divine resurrection. We thus have a straightforward explanation, grounded in the synoptic Gospels, of Jesus as the suffering "son of man." The explanation clarifies the self-understood mission of the synoptic Jesus, the redemptive mission that prompted, and continues to prompt, the understandable question, "Who is this Son of Man?" (John 12:34). We turn to a related signature role for Jesus as moral-kingmaker in God's mysterious kingdom of divine goodness.

7

❧

Kingdom of Divine Goodness

If we know anything about Jesus, we know that he had a message about the "kingdom of God." The synoptic Gospels confirm this, if they confirm anything. A challenge arises, however, in our identifying (a) what Jesus thought of the arrival of this kingdom, especially regarding its timing and its role for divine judgment, and (b) what he considered its intended impact to be on a person's experience, beyond talk about it. If the kingdom in question is just talk, with no intended impact on human experience, it will lack needed supporting evidence (for its reality) and motivational power (for being compelling).

This chapter examines (a) and (b) in order to arrive at Jesus's core understanding of the kingdom of God. It contends that Jesus presented a dual, two-phased kingdom, with the first phase anchored in a distinctive redemptive experience and the second phase to include the completion of God's desired society. This dual status prompted widespread misunderstanding among his audience, including puzzlement over the culmination of God's society. We shall identify a neglected self-understanding of Jesus as a moral-kingmaker and gatekeeper for God who portrays divine judgment as postponed for the sake of God's redemptive reign in divine goodness.

7.1 KINGDOM ARRIVAL

The Book of Daniel offered an influential vision of God's coming kingdom for the social context of Jesus and his Jewish contemporaries: "The God of heaven will set up a kingdom [מַלְכוּ] that shall never be destroyed, nor shall this kingdom be left to another people. It shall crush all these kingdoms and bring them to an end, and it shall stand forever" (Dan. 2:44). Daniel's vision of the coming of God's kingdom has it crushing all opposing kingdoms on earth and bringing them to an end. Given this vision of divine judgment, many contemporaries of Jesus had a clear test for the arrival of God's promised kingdom: The powers on earth opposed to God would be destroyed, crushed and brought to an end, by God. For instance, the opposing Roman kingdom over Israel would be wiped out by God's arriving kingdom. Some of Jesus's contemporaries shared this expectation from Daniel.[1]

John the Baptist, according to the synoptic Gospels, served as a prophet of God's arriving kingdom with a relationship to Jesus. Matthew's Gospel introduces John as follows: "In those days John the Baptist appeared in the wilderness of Judea, proclaiming, 'Repent, for the kingdom of heaven has come near'" (Matt. 3:1–2). This portrait of John raises the question of how he understood the arriving kingdom "of heaven" (= of God). The Gospel of Matthew leaves no doubt: God's kingdom arrives with divine judgment. It, along with Luke's Gospel, has John proclaim to his audience: "Who warned you to flee from the wrath to come? . . . Even now the ax is lying at the root of the trees; every tree therefore that does not bear good fruit is cut down and thrown into the fire" (Matt. 3:7, 10; cf. Luke 3:7, 9). The "wrath to come" announced by John brings divine judgment to people at odds with God's arriving

---

[1] For relevant discussion, see Collins, *The Scepter and the Star*, pp. 173–214, Beasley-Murray, *Jesus and the Kingdom of God*, pp. 26–35, 46–51, and Meier, *A Marginal Jew*, vol. 2, pp. 243–70.

kingdom. In addition, John claimed that this wrath was coming in his day, already "lying at the root of the trees."

According to the Gospels of Matthew and Luke, John announced a coming figure, mightier than himself, who would effect divine judgment: "I baptize you with water; but one who is more powerful than I is coming; I am not worthy to untie the thong of his sandals. He will baptize you with the Holy Spirit and fire. His winnowing fork is in his hand, to clear his threshing floor and to gather the wheat into his granary; but the chaff he will burn with unquenchable fire" (Luke 3:16–17; Matt. 3:11–12). Luke describes this as part of John having "proclaimed the good news to the people" (Luke 3:18). Evidently Luke had in mind the offer of God's Spirit, if not the promise of divine judgment, as good news.

All three synoptic Gospels have John's announcement of a coming one point to Jesus and his baptism as God's "beloved Son" (Mark 1:9–11, Matt. 3:13–17, Luke 3:21–2). By implication, the Gospels of Matthew and Luke also have John portray Jesus to come with divine judgment on "the chaff" of this world. In the case of Matthew's Gospel, this means that the kingdom of heaven arrives, by John's lights, with divine judgment. This expectation fits with the Book of Daniel on the coming of God's kingdom with judgment on opposing powers of the world. We need to ask whether Jesus agreed with this expectation of John regarding divine judgment in the arrival of the kingdom of God.

We shall see that Jesus observed a duality in the kingdom, owing to a distinction between (a) the kingdom as *God's hidden redemptive reign* among people and (b) the kingdom as *a visible culminating society of God's people*. This is a distinction between God's *manifesting divine power* among people for their redemptive benefit and God's *completing the formation of a society* of people under divine kingship. The former does not logically entail the latter.

God could manifest redemptive power to people at present while the complete formation of an ordered society

under divine kingship awaits a future time. The *full* kingdom of God could depend on both phases, with the first,
hidden phase leading to the second. The delay of the complete society, however, would not preclude the (incomplete
and hidden) redemptive reign of divine power in human
history. The latter reign, including a postponement of final
divine judgment, need not be readily visible to humans,
even if it is morally discernible by them as they apprehend
divine redemptive power at work. This kind of duality
figured, we shall see, in Jesus's understanding of the two-
phased kingdom of God.

Jesus claimed that the kingdom of God had become
actual in human history, in his lifetime, and did not simply
await a future arrival. Luke's Gospel makes this clear:
"Once Jesus was asked by the Pharisees when the kingdom
of God was coming, and he answered, 'The kingdom of
God is not coming with things that can be observed; nor
will they say, "Look, here it is!" or "There it is!" For, in fact,
the kingdom of God is among you [ἐντὸς ὑμῶν ἐστιν]'"
(Luke 17:20–1). The Gospels of Luke and Matthew portray
Jesus as acknowledging the arrival of God's kingdom in his
ministry: "If it is by the finger of God that I cast out the
demons, then the kingdom of God has come to you
[ἔφθασεν ἐφ' ὑμᾶς]" (Luke 11:20; cf. Matt. 12:28). In
a similar vein, Mark's Gospel has Jesus report: "Truly
I tell you, there are some standing here who will not taste
death until they see that the kingdom of God has come with
power" (Mark 9:1).[2] Such remarks indicate the presence of
God's kingdom in the time of Jesus, rather than merely
a future arrival of it. Even so, Jesus could recommend
praying "Thy kingdom come," in hope of the *full* realization of the kingdom of God (Matt. 6:10, Luke 11:2; cf.
Didache 8:2).

---

[2] Section 7.3 returns to the issue of the kind of power promised. I agree with
T. W. Manson that the natural interpretation of the passage has the event described
to occur in the lifetime of the people addressed. See Manson, *The Teaching of Jesus*,
pp. 278–84. See also Meier, *A Marginal Jew, vol. 2*, pp. 341–4.

If God's kingdom "is not coming with things that can be observed [παρατηρήσεως]," then its arrival must be discerned in a special way. Jesus denied that it can be apprehended by sensory observation of the kind involved with pointing: "Here it is." In that respect, it is hidden, subtle, and elusive, and not a commodity for casual inspection or spectator access. The hiddenness of the kingdom is featured in Jesus's parable of the leaven: "He told them another parable. 'The kingdom of heaven is like leaven which a woman took and hid [ἐνέκρυψεν] in three measures of flour, till it was all leavened'" (Matt. 13:33, RSV; cf. Luke 13:21). A similar theme is found in his parable of the hidden treasure: "The kingdom of heaven is like treasure hidden [κεκρυμμένῳ] in a field, which someone found and hid; then in his joy he goes and sells all that he has and buys that field" (Matt. 13:44; cf. Gospel of Thomas 109).

The hiddenness of the arriving kingdom is a key feature of what Mark's Gospel calls "the mystery of the kingdom of God": "[Jesus] said to them, To you has been given the mystery [μυστήριον] of the kingdom of God, but for those outside, everything comes in parables" (Mark 4:11, using "mystery" from the NRSV margin). The mystery, or secret, concerns how God works in a hidden, less-than-obvious manner to inaugurate the divine kingdom in human history.

Mention of the mystery of the kingdom arises in the context of Jesus's parable of the sower. This parable illustrates that God works through human cooperation with the good news brought by Jesus ("the word of the kingdom," according to Matthew 13:19), but this divine effort meets human rejection on many fronts. So, divine coercion or destruction of humans is not the source or the center of the kingdom's first phase, and the first phase does not enjoy full success among humans. This phase goes unremarked in Daniel's aforementioned vision of the kingdom's arrival on earth, but it had center stage in Jesus's understanding of the presence of God's kingdom in his ministry.

Both the first, hidden phase and the second, visible phase of the kingdom are captured by Jesus's parable of the weeds. As in the parable of the sower, the kingdom of God comes with the sowing of seed. An enemy of the householder-master, however, sows weeds among the wheat, and this results in weeds appearing with the wheat. The master commands: "Let both of them grow together until the harvest; and at harvest time I will tell the reapers, Collect the weeds first and bind them in bundles to be burned, but gather the wheat into my barn" (Matt. 13:30). The talk of "the harvest" is illuminating because it separates the two phases of the kingdom: its hidden inauguration (with incomplete redemptive reign) and its visible culmination (with completed divine judgment). The kingdom of God is present in both phases, but in different ways, with different manifestations. Jesus gave due consideration to both phases, in a way that puzzled his audience and continues to puzzle many interpreters.[3]

Matthew's Gospel includes an interpretation of the parable of the weeds, with reference to the harvest for the kingdom of God:

The harvest is the end of the age [συντέλεια αἰῶνός], and the reapers are angels. Just as the weeds are collected and burned up with fire, so will it be [ἔσται] at the end of the age. The Son of Man will send his angels, and they will collect out of his kingdom all causes of sin and all evildoers, and they will throw them into the furnace of fire, where there will be

[3] For some indication of the controversy, see Norman Perrin, *The Kingdom of God in the Teaching of Jesus* (Philadelphia: Westminster Press, 1963), Perrin, *Jesus and the Language of the Kingdom* (Philadelphia: Fortress Press, 1976), George Eldon Ladd, *The Presence of the Future* (Grand Rapids, MI: Eerdmans, 1974), G. R. Beasley-Murray, *Jesus and the Kingdom of God*, and Mark Saucy, *The Kingdom of God in the Teaching of Jesus* (Dallas, TX: Word Publishing, 1997).

weeping and gnashing of teeth. Then the righteous will shine like the sun in the kingdom of their Father. (Matt. 13:39–43)

The predicted harvest will be at "the end of the age," and it will be a harvest "out of [the divine] kingdom." So, the kingdom already exists when the harvest occurs. It also follows that if the harvest will be part of the kingdom, the kingdom includes a duality of two phases: the phase before the harvest, and the phase including the harvest and its aftermath. The parable of the weeds puts the harvest judgment in the future, describing how the situation will be at the end of the age.

The visible kingdom-phase of harvest judgment is postponed, according to Jesus, for the sake of extending the invisible phase of God's redemptive reign, so that the wheat of the kingdom can "grow" (συναυξάνεσθαι), if with the weeds (Matt. 13:30). Similarly, according to the parable of the seed growing secretly, the harvest awaits the grain becoming "ripe" enough to permit (παραδοῖ) harvest (Mark 4:29). The parable of the wedding banquet likewise suggests delay in divine judgment, in allowing time for invitations to go out for the feast of the divine kingdom (Matt. 22:1–4; cf. Luke 14:16–17).

A later New Testament writer reflects the theme of delay in commenting on "the day of judgement": "The Lord is not slow about his promise, as some think of slowness, but is patient with you, not any to perish, but all to come to repentance" (2 Pet. 3:9). The invisible, hidden stage of the kingdom stems from a divine purpose: to attract people over time to decide agreeably and cooperatively for God's reign. Its being hidden from human sight serves that purpose by bringing attention to the key invisible characteristics of divine goodness found in God's moral character and kingdom (Mark 7:14–23, Matt. 15:15–20; cf. Matt. 23:23–8). Those moral characteristics figure in an intended redemptive encounter with God in divine goodness and an informed decision regarding God's kingdom goodness.

7.2 SHARED KINGSHIP

The normative, motivating center of the divine kingdom is the divine goodness in the moral character of the divine king, the God of Jesus. In various ways, Jesus sought to illustrate this lesson. All three synoptic Gospels, as well as John's Gospel, present Jesus's entry into Jerusalem on a donkey, and the Gospels of Matthew and John describe the entry with reference to Zechariah's king coming on a donkey:

Rejoice greatly, O daughter Zion! Shout aloud, O daughter Jerusalem! Lo, your king comes to you; triumphant and victorious is he, humble and riding on a donkey, on a colt, the foal of a donkey. He will cut off the chariot from Ephraim and the war-horse from Jerusalem; and the battle bow shall be cut off, and he shall command peace [שָׁלוֹם] to the nations; his dominion shall be from sea to sea, and from the River to the ends of the earth. (Zech. 9:9–10; cf. Matt. 21:5, John 12:15)

Mark's Gospel alludes to Zechariah with this response to the entry: "Blessed is the coming kingdom of our ancestor David!" (Mark 11:10), and Luke's Gospel follows suit with this response: "Blessed is the king who comes in the name of the Lord! Peace in heaven, and glory in the highest heaven!" (Luke 19:38). If Jesus had Zechariah 9 in mind, as suggested by the four Gospels, he would have had in mind the aim to "cut off . . . the war-horse . . . and the battle bow" and to "command peace." Luke's Gospel makes the role of intended peace, or reconciliation, explicit. In any case, this is no portrait of a militant Davidic king of Israel.

The donkey suggests a humble king, in accordance with Zechariah 9, but it also suggests a mission of peace if we take Zechariah 9 and Luke's suggestion at face value. The peace sought by the divine kingdom, according to Jesus, is not just the absence of war because it seeks the reconciliation of humans with God, as illustrated by the parable of the prodigal son (Luke 15:11–32). God, according to that parable, aims to bring people into a relationship of positive filial peace with God, despite their wayward tendencies. This divine aim does not include the coercion of people; instead, it extends pardon to people while showing patience in waiting for their coming to their senses and turning to God cooperatively. In such pardon, people can be reconciled to God as they yield to divine goodness, including God's moral character and redemptive purpose. Some people will resist, according to the parable, but this does not undermine God's good intention for filial peace in divine–human reconciliation.

Humans resistant or indifferent to God's arriving kingdom can opt out, as the parable of the sower confirms. The kingdom reaches its redemptive goal, according to this parable, in a way attentive to the motivational attitude of a hearer. God comes, in the first phase of the kingdom, without coercing hearers to comply or even to pay attention. The parable, as Chapter 4 noted, identifies the need for "good soil" in the intended divine–human reconciliation, and such soil corresponds to humans who "hear the word and accept [παραδέχονται] it and bear fruit, thirty and sixty and a hundredfold" (Mark 4:20).

Without human acceptance, the word of the kingdom misses its mark and does not yield redemption. Luke, we have noted, is more explicit, referring to humans who "hear the word, hold it fast [κατέχουσιν] in an honest and good heart, and bear fruit with patient endurance" (Luke 8:15). The needed acceptance calls for holding fast to the word in a good heart, with a motivational commitment of cooperation with it. The kingdom thus has redemptive success only in human cooperation with the arriving king. The redemptive, moral power of the kingdom, then, is not coercive.

The divine aim in the kingdom's first phase is, according to Jesus, human *co-ownership* of the kingdom with the king, in shared kingship under the authority of Jesus. This

feature has received inadequate attention from commentators and theologians, but it was central to Jesus's understanding of the divine kingdom and its king. As appointed
king under God as supreme king, Jesus serves as the moral-
kingmaker for God, as the one who appoints moral kings
for God. "Moral" modifies "king" in "kingmaker," thus
indicating the moral status of the kingship.

Jesus announced to his apostles: "You are those who
have stood by me in my trials; and I confer on you, just as
my Father has conferred on me, a kingdom, so that you
may eat and drink at my table in my kingdom, and you will
sit on thrones judging the twelve tribes of Israel" (Luke
22:28–30; cf. Matt. 19:28, 16:19, Psalm 122:4–5).[4] These are
thrones of kings, moral kings with special moral authority
and responsibility, and they figure in the inauguration of
phase two of God's kingdom. They illustrate Jesus's
announcement that, having received a kingdom from
God, he is a *moral*-kingmaker for God in conferring
a divine moral kingdom on his disciples.

The book of Revelation echoes the idea of shared kingship with Jesus: "I am standing at the door, knocking; if you
hear my voice and open the door, I will come in to you and
eat with you, and you with me. To the one who conquers
I will give a place with me on my throne, just as I myself
conquered and sat down with my Father on his throne"
(Rev. 3:20–1). Jesus's entry into Jerusalem on a donkey
suggests that his royal "conquering" is moral rather than
coercive or dominating toward his audience. His hearers
can reject him. In agreement, the present passage sets
a condition for his entrance: "if you ... open the door."
Jesus sought to *invite* and to *attract* human cooperation with
God and himself rather than to force it.

The theme of responsible co-ownership of God's kingdom, under the authority of Jesus, bears on a potential wide

---

[4] On the background and historicity of this passage, see Marius Reiser, *Jesus and
Judgement*, trans. L. M. Maloney (Minneapolis: Fortress Press, 1997), pp. 258–62, and
Fitzmyer, *The Gospel According to Luke*, vol. 2, pp. 1418–19.

audience, beyond the twelve apostles. It arises from Jesus's teaching regarding the faithful and wise slave: "Blessed is that slave whom his master will find at work when he arrives. Truly I tell you, he will put that one in charge of all his possessions" (Matt. 24:46–7; cf. Luke 12:43–4). The parable of the talents echoes this theme, with a comment from the master: "Well done, good and trustworthy slave; you have been trustworthy in a few things, I will put you in charge of many things; enter into the joy of your master" (Matt. 25:21; cf. Luke 19:17). This parable of Jesus suggests the aforementioned idea of Jesus that God shares owner-ship of his kingdom with his disciples. So, this is not a kingdom with an exclusive king. As a result, Jesus remarked of his disciples: "Blessed are the poor in spirit, for theirs is the kingdom of heaven" (Matt. 5:3; cf. Luke 6:20, 12:32).

The Book of Daniel figures in the best explanation of the source of Jesus's idea of the co-ownership of God's king-dom. A vision in Daniel 7, as Chapter 6 noted, has "one like a son of man" receive kingship and a kingdom from God (Dan. 7:13–14), but the kingdom is to be shared with the people of God. Thus:

The holy ones of the Most High shall receive the kingdom [from God] and possess the kingdom forever – forever and ever ... Judgement was given for the holy ones of the Most High, and the time arrived when the holy ones gained posses-sion of the kingdom ... The kingship and dominion and the greatness of the kingdoms under the whole heaven shall be given to the people of the holy ones of the Most High; their kingdom shall be an everlasting kingdom, and all dominions shall serve and obey them. (Dan. 7:18, 22, 27)

The people of God thus receive a lasting kingdom, the kingdom of God given initially to "one like a son of man." In receiving "possession of the kingdom," the people of God receive co-ownership of God's kingdom from "one like a son of man." This approach to the co-ownership of kingship under God was reflected in the teaching of Jesus even though it is neglected widely by interpreters.

As Chapter 6 explained, Jesus thought of himself and his shared destiny with the people of God in the light of Daniel 7. He added, however, an important consideration: The people of God must be considered by God to be *worthy* of God's kingdom. So, Luke's Gospel has Jesus refer to "those who are considered worthy of a place in that age [καταξιωθέντες τοῦ αἰῶνος ἐκείνου] and in the resurrection from the dead" (Luke 20:35). Similarly, Jesus spoke of one being "fit for the kingdom of God": "No one who puts a hand to the plow and looks back is fit for the kingdom of God [εὔθετός ἐστιν τῇ βασιλείᾳ τοῦ θεοῦ]" (Luke 9:62; cf. 2 Thess. 1:5). In that connection, Luke's Gospel suggests that there is a preparation for the kingdom in being trained: "A pupil is not above his teacher; but everyone, after he has been fully trained [κατηρτισμένος], will be like his teacher" (Luke 6:40, NASB).

The first phase of the kingdom provides, according to the ministry of Jesus, an opportunity for (broadly moral) training toward fitness for the kingdom. It offers an opportunity for the time needed by disciples for training, on the assumption that being trained and learning to train others take time. According to Luke's Gospel, Jesus aimed to train witnesses to the divine forgiveness in his ministry: "He said to them, 'Thus it is written, that the Messiah is to suffer and to rise from the dead on the third day, and that repentance and forgiveness of sins is to be proclaimed in his name to all nations, beginning from Jerusalem. You are witnesses [μάρτυρες] of these things'" (Luke 24:46–8).

The first phase of the kingdom brings an offer of divine forgiveness, or pardon, to all hearers. One's response to this offer is a key factor in whether one will, or is willing to, enter the kingdom, and the response, in relating to God, should include shared forgiveness toward all other people: "Whenever you stand praying, forgive, if you have anything against anyone; so that your Father in heaven may also forgive you your trespasses" (Mark 11:25; cf. Matt. 6:14–15, Luke 6:37, 11:4). Jesus thus grounded training for the kingdom in shared divine forgiveness for the sake of having witnesses to divine goodness, including God's merciful character and will. Such forgiveness is to hold together the kingdom of morally imperfect agents seeking to please God, given their ongoing moral failures.

The Gospel of Luke identifies the kind of kingship for which Jesus trained his disciples: "[Jesus] said to them, 'The kings of the Gentiles lord it over them; and those in authority over them are called benefactors. But not so with you; rather the greatest among you must become like the youngest, and the leader like one who serves'" (Luke 22:25–6). Jesus here used *kingship* as a standard for his disciples, and this confirms the interpretation of Jesus's kingmaker role being developed here. He did not, however, have in mind the kingship typical for the world's kings. Instead, as indicated, he suggested for his disciples a shared *moral-kingship*, with moral authority and responsibility from God, oriented toward serving others. In his serving as self-giving for others, he offered what he had: his moral-kingship under God's moral authority.

The disciples' moral-kingship and authority would arise from their sharing in the moral-kingship and authority of God and Jesus. Jesus thus appealed to his own moral example as a basis: "I am among you as one who serves" (Luke 22:27; cf. Mark 10:44–5, Matt. 20:27–8). This teaching led to his aforementioned conferral of a moral kingdom on his disciples as his Father had conferred such a kingdom on him (Luke 22:29). Because the kingly service in question aimed at divine–human reconciliation, a later New Testament writer can refer to "a royal priesthood, ... God's own people" and link this status to a message of reconciliation in divine mercy (1 Pet. 2:9–10, echoing Ex. 19:6 in its talk of a "priestly kingdom").

The main concern of Jesus was to abide in and reflect divine goodness, including God's merciful moral character as supreme king. The corresponding moral authority of Jesus in God's kingdom is reflected not in coercion but in an obedient response to his moral challenge (Mark 1:27). This fits with the startling remark of Jesus that "whoever becomes humble like this child is the greatest in the kingdom of heaven" (Matt. 18:4; cf. Luke 18:17). This kingdom, as suggested by Daniel 7, does not fit with the power characteristic of the kingdoms of the world.

7.3 CONFLICT AND IMPACT

Jesus, we have seen, announced the arrival of the kingdom of God (if not fully) in his lifetime, and he did not restrict it to the future. In his perspective, the kingdom of God *has come*, in drawing near and becoming present to humans with redemptive power in his ministry. It has come in a way fitting to the divine goodness, including the redemptive character and purpose, of the king who draws near and becomes present in the ministry of Jesus.

The king's redemptive reign, to the surprise of some observers, has arrived without the social order, the society, of the kingdom being fully in place. The latter society in its fullness takes more time and thus awaits a future fulfillment, according to Jesus, but the kingdom still is present in virtue of the redemptive presence of its divine king. So, Jesus announced that God was present as king, while many of his critics took exception in assuming that the kingdom of God's presence is altogether future. This conflict about the present kingdom marked the ministry of Jesus, and it resulted in significant social division and, ultimately, in the demise of Jesus. His turbulent actions of conflict in the temple may have triggered concerted efforts toward his demise (Mark 11:18, Luke 19:47–8), including a subsequent trial before Pilate that included the question of whether he actually is "king of the Jews" (Mark 15:2, Matt. 27:11, Luke 23:5).

Jesus announced the conflict surrounding him, with some hyperbole: "Do not think that I have come to bring peace to the earth; I have not come to bring peace, but a sword. For I have come to set a man against his father, and a daughter against her mother, and a daughter-in-law against her mother-in-law; and one's foes will be members of one's own household" (Matt. 10:34–6). Luke's Gospel confirms this theme from Jesus: "I came to bring fire to the earth, and how I wish it were already kindled! I have a baptism with which to be baptized, and what stress I am under until it is completed! Do you think that I have come to bring peace to the earth? No, I tell you, but rather division! From now on five in one household will be divided, three against two and two against three" (Luke 12:49–52). These remarks do not contradict the message of peace given by Jesus's aforementioned entry into Jerusalem. He intended to bring peace in reconciliation with God, but the response to him included conflict, division, and strife with such definiteness that they *seemed* inevitable, if not ultimately intended (as in his hyperbole of intended division).

The original conflict over the significance of Jesus and his kingdom ministry raised the question of how God's kingdom would arrive, particularly in its intended impact on human experience. Some of Jesus's critics alleged that he was consorting with demons to oppose God (Mark 3:22).[5] Jesus, however, thought of his ministry as representing the impact of divine goodness, including God's moral character and purpose, on human experience, if in an elusive manner at times. He acknowledged that the divine impact could be overlooked, neglected, or opposed by humans, and his parable of the sower illustrated this consideration

---

[5] See Stanton, *Jesus and Gospel*, pp. 127–47, and Graham Stanton, *Gospel Truth?* (Valley Forge, PA: Trinity Press International, 1995), pp. 156–63.

in response to the uneven reception of his mission by his audience.

Jesus indicated the uniqueness of his role in the arrival of the divine kingdom: "Turning to the disciples, Jesus said to them privately, 'Blessed are the eyes that see what you see! For I tell you that many prophets and kings desired to see what you see, but did not see it, and to hear what you hear, but did not hear it'" (Luke 10:23–4; cf. Matt. 13:16–17, 12:41–2). His disciples experienced, according to Jesus, the fulfillment of the hope of ancient Israel in what he was doing. In his ministry, Jesus suggested, the kingdom of God had arrived, although in an unexpected manner without immediate final judgment or completion. His role in its arrival set him above past prophets and kings and even the temple (Matt. 12:6, 41–2).

Given the uniqueness of his kingdom mission, Jesus showed due caution about using familiar titles for self-representation, including the title "Messiah." His unique mission called for redefining familiar titles for himself as God's authoritative representative, and that effort would take time. He was willing, nonetheless, to claim authority over various biblical injunctions and laws, including Sabbath law (Matt. 5:21–2, 12:8), and over extending divine forgiveness to people (Mark 2:10–12).[6] In addition, he was willing to signal, if cryptically, his unique status to John the Baptist (Luke 4:17–19), but this status called for recasting various theological categories in circulation, including those of God's moral character and purpose and thus of the category of divine goodness (Matt. 5:39–48, Luke 6:27–36).

The unique role assigned to Jesus in the kingdom of God called for a special understanding of its credibility, at least

[6] On Jesus's authority in relation to divine forgiveness, see Kümmel, *The Theology of the New Testament*, pp. 44–6, 51–3, Sanders, *Jesus and Judaism*, pp. 38–40, 200–11, Moule, "The Gravamen against Jesus," pp. 108–12, and Tobias Hägerland, *Jesus and the Forgiveness of Sins*, SNTSMS (Cambridge: Cambridge University Press, 2012), chaps. 5–6.

for his disciples. Some interpreters have asked whether that role is at best a matter of wishful thinking by later followers. In response, an illuminating understanding of how Jesus conveyed his kingdom message has focused on the intended impact of Jesus on his hearers. John Baillie has remarked:

It was the impression made upon his disciples by the spirit and the words of the historic Jesus which first suggested to them that higher view of his significance to which the church has ever since clung; and it is only so far as the historic Jesus, as portrayed in the existent records, can still make that impression upon us, that we of today can hope to share that view and find it reasonable.[7]

This position fits with our previous observation that if God's kingdom "is not coming with things that can be observed," then its arrival must be discerned in a special way. The same holds for discerning the status of Jesus, given his role in the kingdom, and this bears on identifying a feature that supported a "higher view of his significance." The issue concerns what kind of influence or impact prompted and supports the latter view. Jesus himself, we have noted, suggested a self-status beyond being just one king among many in God's kingdom.

As Chapter 4 noted, E. P. Sanders has suggested that Jesus thought of himself as higher than Messiah, as the "viceroy of God, and not just in a political kingdom but in the kingdom of God."[8] Our aforementioned evidence from the synoptic Gospels supports this position, but we have noted that it goes further: to a role for Jesus as the moral-kingmaker for the kingdom of God. This includes a role as the gatekeeper for the divine kingdom, thus anticipating an interpretation in John's Gospel: "Jesus said to them, 'Very

---

[7] Baillie, *The Place of Jesus Christ in Modern Christianity*, p. 100.
[8] Sanders, *The Historical Figure of Jesus* (London: Penguin, 1993), p. 242. See also Sanders, *Jesus and Judaism*, p. 321.

truly, I tell you, I am the gate for the sheep ... Whoever enters by me will be saved, and will come in and go out and find pasture'" (John 10:7–9). Being a moral-kingmaker for God presumes being a *morally qualified* gatekeeper for the kingdom of God, lest opponents of God be made kings for God and the kingdom be divided and destroyed.

The role of moral-kingmaker as gatekeeper for God rests on the kind of aforementioned authority claimed by Jesus as the ultimate *filial cognitive guardian* for God: "All things have been handed over to me by my Father; and no one knows the Son except the Father, and no one knows the Father except the Son and anyone to whom the Son chooses to reveal him" (Matt. 11:27; cf. Luke 10:22). Since knowledge of God is required for entrance to God's kingdom, Jesus, as avowed filial cognitive guardian for God, has authority over such knowledge from God. Luke's version of this statement is followed by the previously noted remark: "Blessed are the eyes that see what you see! For I tell you that many prophets and kings desired to see what you see, but did not see it, and to hear what you hear, but did not hear it" (Luke 10:23–4). Jesus thus claimed to bring something unique to his audience: the powerful redemptive presence of God's kingdom in his ministry. In doing so, he avoided any suggestion that he is just one among many *ultimate* gatekeepers or cognitive guardians for God, even though, as ultimate kingmaker for God, he envisaged multiple kings with moral authority *under* his royal authority and God's in a shared kingdom.

Jesus's role of ultimate kingmaker (including ultimate gatekeeper and filial cognitive guardian) for God's kingdom is summed up in the synoptic Gospels by calling him "(the) Lord."[9] Luke's Gospel represents Jesus as asking: "Why do you call me 'Lord, Lord,' and do not do what I tell you?" (Luke 6:46). Matthew's Gospel has a similar

---

[9] On the Semitic background of various New Testament uses of the term "κύριος," see Fitzmyer, *A Wandering Aramean: Collected Aramaic Essays*, pp. 115–42, and Moule, *The Origin of Christology*, pp. 35–46.

theme, portraying Jesus as gatekeeping Lord under God, for God's kingdom: "Not everyone who says to me, 'Lord, Lord,' will enter the kingdom of heaven, but only the one who does the will of my Father in heaven. On that day many will say to me, 'Lord, Lord, did we not prophesy in your name, and cast out demons in your name, and do many deeds of power in your name?' Then I will declare to them, 'I never knew you; go away from me, you evil-doers'" (Matt. 7:21–3). As gatekeeping Lord, Jesus aimed to attract and lead people to obey his redemptive message from God, for the sake of their doing God's will and thereby living in God's kingdom. This aim is a key require-ment of being Lord under God, for God's co-owned kingdom.

A striking claim of many New Testament writers is that Jesus not only was Lord during his ministry but still *is* Lord under God, even after his death. The historical story is complicated, given its astonishing effects on some people (such as the apostle Paul), but we can identify some import-ant coherence in it. Prior to his death, Jesus had an impact on his disciples that led to their calling him "Lord" in a way that exalts him above other humans and closely associates him with God.

In Jesus's intended impact on his disciples, they found a distinctive intervention by God, as if Jesus were a moral-kingmaker and gatekeeper for God's kingdom. We have some initial indication of this in Peter's confession at Caesarea Philippi about Jesus as Messiah (Mark 8:29, Luke 9:20, Matt. 16:16; cf. John 6:68–9) and in his statement that the disciples have "left everything" to follow Jesus (Mark 10:28, Matt. 19:27; cf. Luke 18:28). We also find a general indication of the uniqueness of Jesus's impact in the amazed disciples' question about him, "Who then is this?" (Mark 4:41, Luke 8:25; cf. Matt. 8:27) and in his critics' response to him regarding his forgiving sins (Mark 2:7, Luke 5:21).

According to the Gospels of Luke and Matthew, the disciples came to a better understanding of the intended impact of Jesus after his death. Luke's Gospel portrays Jesus as the authoritative revealer of God in his impact on them after his death: "[Jesus] opened their minds to understand the scriptures" (Luke 24:45). Matthew's Gospel likewise highlights his special authority from God for them after his death: "All authority in heaven and on earth has been given to me. Go therefore and make disciples of all nations, ... and teaching them to obey everything that I have commanded you. And remember, I am with you always, to the end of the age" (Matt. 28:18–20). Similarly, the book of Acts has the apostle Peter proclaim: "God has made him both Lord and Messiah, this Jesus whom you crucified" (Acts 2:36), with a connection drawn to an offer of divine pardon and reconciliation (Acts 2:38–41).

The exalted claims of the disciples about the status of Jesus, with regard to his unique filial authority under God, did not arise apart from human experience. Those claims would be ungrounded talk, and perhaps even misleading fiction, apart from a footing in human experience. This is true of such claims about the pre-crucifixion Jesus as well as the post-crucifixion Jesus. In addition, the claims about the post-crucifixion Jesus would need support from a basis in experience that indicates some continuity with the pre-crucifixion Jesus, specifically in his bringing the kingdom's arrival among his hearers. Otherwise, the prospect of two different figures would arise in a person's evidence, one pre-crucifixion and the other post-crucifixion, with the latter perhaps being simply imaginary. Some continuity of impact on human experience must figure in holding the two together for humans, despite any discontinuity between them.[10] The needed continuity is in the distinctive interpersonal goodness experienced in Jesus.

---

[10] C. F. D. Moule has rightly emphasized the importance of continuity here; see his "The Gravamen against Jesus," pp. 106–13.

A question needing an answer from the disciples before and after the crucifixion of Jesus was: *What kind* of intentional impact would Jesus seek and have as filial moral-kingmaker and gatekeeper for God's kingdom? Here it is easy to give a misleading answer, and Jesus himself identified a misguided approach calling for a misplaced "sign" (Mark 8:11–12, Matt. 16:1–4, Luke 11:29–30). If we sum up his royal role as being lasting *Lord* under God, we may expect that Jesus would want to have an impact on people as their living Lord, as one who attracts and leads them uncoercively to God in obedient love, in an *ongoing* authoritative way (as suggested by Matthew 28:18–20; cf. Luke 24:46–4). To that end, he would attract and lead people to face God's moral character directly and to conform to it (Matt. 5:44–8, Luke 6:35–6, Mark 12:29–30). He could self-hide or self-reveal accordingly, with the goal of aiding his intentional impact *as Lord* on a person's experience. In that regard, we should expect his self-revelation to be elusive, at least at times, given its morally robust aim to challenge people uncoercively to cooperate with him in his redemptive mission for God's kingdom.

The needed role of human cooperation with God emerges, as suggested, in Jesus's parable of the rich man and Lazarus: "If they do not listen to Moses and the prophets, neither will they be convinced even if someone rises from the dead" (Luke 16:31). "Listening to" Moses and the prophets here includes cooperating with the redemptive message from God. We saw this factor at work in the parable of sower, particularly with Luke's version in its talk of those who "hear the word, hold it fast in an honest and good heart, and bear fruit with patient endurance" (Luke 8:15). Such holding fast is no matter of mere observation; it includes a cooperative moral commitment to God.

Seeking cooperative moral commitment, Jesus would direct his moral impact toward the *moral attracting and leading* of people to God, including to their agreeably doing God's will. Such attracted commitment would be

the way to enter God's kingdom and to recognize Jesus as
Lord (as suggested previously by Matthew 7:21–3). It also
signifies the moral nature of the kings sought by Jesus as
kingmaker for God, after his moral self-example aimed at
receiving, reflecting, and being empowered by God's
unique moral character (Luke 22:25–6). Jesus acknowledged his being empowered by divine goodness in his
ministry (Matt. 12:28, Luke 11:20), and he expected the
same moral empowerment from God for his disciples as
central to the kingdom's arriving "with power" (Mark 9:1).

Many of the first disciples of Jesus regarded his intended
impact on them as the intended impact of *God* through him.
They also regarded the moral character of Jesus as uniquely
reflective of, and empowered by, the moral character of
God, the latter character being central to the distinctive
quality of the relevant experience. Such considerations
were decisive for these disciples in acknowledging Jesus
as the Lord under God. They thus made the best available
sense of their experience of Jesus with regard to God.

A key question for the disciples became: Does Jesus have
a post-crucifixion intentional impact on our experience *as
one resurrected by God and now alive?*[11] If so, he would not be
merely historical, because a deceased merely historical person no longer has an intentional impact as one now alive.
Deceased people can influence subsequent memories and
feelings, but they do not have the current intentions needed
for an intentional impact as one now alive. Socrates, for
instance, has no *current intentional* impact on our experience now, even though we can appreciate his past intentions and contributions. His death marked the end of his
current intentions and thus the end of his current intentional impact. The same holds for other merely historical
persons, whatever their broader influence on our
experience.

---

[11] C. F. D. Moule has attended to this question; see his *The Origin of Christology*, chap. 2,
and "Jesus of Nazareth and the Church's Lord," in Moule, *Forgiveness and
Reconciliation*, pp. 81–94.

An appeal to Jesus's current intentional impact on our experience, as one resurrected and now alive, would be an appeal to an impact that occurs in our history of experience, in the sense that it occurs at some time or other in our experience. Its source, however, would not be limited to our *past* history if the source exists *currently*. In addition, an adequate assessment of such an appeal would take us to the matter of ethical challenges for us now that are not merely "historical," in terms of our past, but are central to our now being morally responsible agents with lives to live. Evidence for a resurrected Jesus now, rather than merely in the past, would go beyond evidence regarding past history, and it would have continuity with the moral character of the historical Jesus.

An adequate assessment of Jesus's impact would involve the nature of our moral experience, including our moral conscience and its ethical challenges for our current lives. A living Lord under God would deliver the latter kind of challenges for our moral good in relation to God's perfectly good moral character. So, our question about the intentional impact of Jesus bears on the nature of what our moral experience delivers, or does not deliver, to us regarding challenges from the moral character of Jesus and God.

A main issue becomes whether our moral experience, including our moral conscience, represents current activity of a living Jesus-like Lord. If it does, it represents, if elusively, a living Lord who aims to challenge our moral complacency in order to instill in us, with our cooperation, divine goodness, including the goodness of God's moral character, kingship, and authority of righteous *agapē* toward all agents.[12] If it does not, our evidence for a living Lord in Jesus will be inadequate, whatever our evidence indicates about the *past* history of Jesus. We have, then, an evidential

---

[12] On the epistemological background for this position regarding divine moral challenge, see Moser, *Understanding Religious Experience*, chaps. 7–8.

basis for deciding on a resurrected living Lord, even if the evidence can vary among people.

The required evidence would not be at our control because a living Lord in Jesus would not be at our control. It would be evidence intended to attract and lead us, cooperatively, not only to enter God's kingdom but also to take the next step into the future in realizing that kingdom. This evidence would stem from divine goodness, and it would manifest such goodness, including for our future. If Jesus is, under God, Lord of the future as well as the present, we would be challenged to enter that future under his lordship, in keeping with God's moral character. So, we would face, in an ongoing manner, a *next* decision about our future in the kingdom; the scope of the divine challenge, then, would not be limited to the present.[13]

A cooperative next decision would reflect a divine challenge in our conscience, indicating God's challenging redemptive character, and it would commit to divine lordship for our future, under God's future. We thus straddle, in Jesus's perspective as living Lord, a duality of two phases of the divine kingdom: the realized and the forthcoming, the present and the future. From the standpoint of the present, the divine kingdom thus offers hope in God, owing to the divine goodness of the future. In this regard, at least, the divine kingdom is eschatological and irreducible to the past or the present.

Moral experience of Jesus as living Lord can be, and arguably is, variable among people, owing in part to variable potential and actual responses from them. This is one lesson of the parable of the sower and of Jesus's statement,

---

[13] For a variation on this theme, see Manson, *Jesus the Messiah*, pp. 145–56. For an effort to relate past and future in connection with the resurrection of Jesus, and to make some sense of the elusiveness of its evidence, see Rowan Williams, *Resurrection*, 2nd ed. (London: Darton, 2002), pp. 23–44, 82–90. On an abductive approach to the resurrection of Jesus, with attention to the relation between history and faith, see Alan Richardson, *History Sacred and Profane* (London: SCM Press, 1964), pp. 195–217, and George Eldon Ladd, *I Believe in the Resurrection of Jesus* (London: Hodder and Stoughton, 1975).

as filial cognitive guardian, of God's hiding divine self-revelation in the face of human resistance (Matt. 11:25, Luke 10:21). By ignoring or rejecting a divine challenge in moral experience, we would ignore or reject God's self-presented moral character and thereby unique evidence of God's presence. That would be to ignore or reject *God*, even if unwittingly. In such a case, as suggested, God could withdraw from moral intervention, with redemptive intent, until one is prepared to respond more cooperatively.

A moral experience of Jesus as living Lord, like the experience of God, need not be shared by all people, given variability in human tendencies to respond. It follows that the absence of such an experience for some people does not entail a similar absence for all people. A basis for agnosticism does not arise so easily for all people. In seeking a cooperative role, God would allow human freedom to result in variability in potential and actual responses to divine challenges in experience. One result would be variability among humans in evidence of God's presence and reality.

7.4 A ROYAL MORAL

Jesus told parables of divine judgment *postponed*, and now we see why: They leave room for him to serve as redemptive moral-kingmaker for God. They thus provide an opportunity to build God's society, with freely offered and freely received shared moral-kingship under divine moral authority. As suggested, this moral authority would be fully exercised by Jesus's disciples in the fullness of time, when divine judgment arrives. Even so, like the kingdom itself, it would be exercised in a partial manner before the kingdom's culmination. Jesus thus remarked to his disciples: "Truly I tell you, whatever you bind on earth will be bound in heaven, and whatever you loose on earth will be loosed in heaven" (Matt. 18:18; cf. Matt. 16:19, John

20:23). He had in mind the exercise of moral power representative of God, and this confirms his role of moral-kingmaker for God.

Measuring Jesus by a standard of a kingdom as a completed society under God misses the redemptive point.[14] It thus misses the point of the mission of Jesus in human history, including the need to launch the universal society of God to be completed later. (Prior manifestations of God's people lacked the needed universality for a God of all people, gentiles as well as Jews.) Our distinction between the two phases of the kingdom should save us from any such mistake. It also should save us from the mistake of thinking that Jesus expected an immediate arrival of the kingdom in its fullness, as if the first phase would not take some time for its redemptive purpose.[15] Jesus himself expressed ignorance of when the kingdom would arrive with final judgment; he affirmed that only God knows (Mark 13:32, Matt. 24:36). Similarly, we lack knowledge of the details of the kingdom in its fullness, but Jesus offered experienced divine goodness as indicative of its nature and as a ground for human hope in it.[16]

Once we recognize Jesus's redemptive effort to call, attract, and prepare co-owners of God's kingdom, under his lordship and under divine moral authority, his talk of a two-phased kingdom makes sense. Indeed, neglect of that effort leaves interpretive incoherence in its wake. We do well, then, to restore to center stage the neglected role of Jesus as moral-kingmaker for God, in a co-owned kingdom of two distinct phases with judgment postponed. In doing so, we will gain a heightened, and fitting, appreciation of

---

[14] This point is missed by Joseph Klausner, *Jesus of Nazareth*, trans. Herbert Danby (New York: Bloch Publishing, 1922), pp. 398–407.

[15] Many interpreters have made such a mistake since the time of Albert Schweitzer, *The Quest of the Historical Jesus*, 2nd ed., trans. W. Montgomery (London: A&C Black, 1911). For discussion, see Meier, *A Marginal Jew*, vol. 2, pp. 336–48.

[16] On such hope, see Paul K. Moser, "Grounded Hope in God: Epiphany and Promise," forthcoming, taking exception to the neglect of religious experience in Jürgen Moltmann, *Theology of Hope*, trans. James Leitch (London: SCM Press, 1967), among others.

the moral role of Jesus and his disciples in the kingdom of God. We then will have needed perspective on Jesus's motivation by and aim for divine goodness anchored in God's unique moral character. We turn to the result of this perspective for our responding to divine goodness as represented by Jesus.

8

⁓

God's Gambit for Divine Goodness

Talk of God tends to be ambiguous and elusive – even when associated with Jesus. A helpful option, as suggested by Chapter 2, uses the term "God" as a perfectionist title connoting worthiness of worship and hence perfect moral goodness. Such a title can have good semantic sense but fail to refer to an actual object. So, even atheists can use it with a good conscience. We shall see that this title, owing to its moral perfectionist implications, involves a notion of offered companionship, and that this notion is morally robust in demanding a rigorous kind of moral self-reflection and decision.

The relevant companionship is intended to be *redemptive* for persons in supplying divine–human interpersonal reconciliation. It thus differs from what many people understand to be "companionship" or "friendship." We shall identify how this consideration bears on divine goodness, including in connection with Jesus, and on a gambit pursued by God for the sharing of divine goodness.

8.1 REDEMPTIVE DURESS

God's overarching goal for humans in divine–human reconciliation would include some kind of divine communication with humans for the sake of that reconciliation. A conflict would arise, however, between the perfect moral character of God and the inferior moral character of humans at odds with God. This conflict would obstruct human reception of divine goodness expressed in revelation from God. Seeking divine–human reconciliation, God would adopt a strategy with risk, a gambit, to challenge human resistance to divine goodness.

God's gambit would be a strategy of risk and perhaps even sacrifice aimed at gaining an advantage for the good of humans. One prospect is that God would use a risky strategy of duress for humans and for God in the process of redemption. A divine aim with this duress would be to manifest the moral seriousness of the divine redemptive effort. The duress in the risk would include the risked suffering of God and humans who face various kinds of evil in the process aimed at reconciliation. God, in this perspective, would not sacrifice a redemptive effort in order to avoid a risk of suffering that results from evil.

Righteous *agapē* toward others would be part of divine goodness. In a world of personal conflict, it would be "suffering love" in many situations, given one's frustrated goals for the good of other persons and the resulting pain for oneself. Such love would motivate God and humans committed to a life of perfect *agapē* in interpersonal relationships. If God is perfectly loving toward morally imperfect humans, suffering as frustration would be part of God's own moral life. It also could underlie a divine offer of forgiveness to wayward humans, for the sake of divine–human reconciliation. Related suffering could underlie the human reception of forgiveness as a means to such reconciliation.

As morally perfect, God would not cause all suffering or any evil. As all-knowing Lord, however, God intentionally would *allow*, for some purpose or other, the suffering and the evil that occur. It would be odd if human suffering and evil had no divine purpose while God could stop it. God could allow suffering and evil in order to participate in it and thus to *redeem* it by bringing good out of it. God's suffering would be self-chosen in general, and not a case of a greater power imposing it on God. So, divine suffering would not threaten God's lordship. Divine lordship would include a rationale for allowing divine and human suffering, even if humans do not fully understand it.

The suffering of Jesus, including the evil inflicted on him by humans, can illustrate how God could use redemptive duress toward humans. The pattern is that of evil opposing divine goodness, including God's blameless representative, to create tragic loss while God responds to transform the tragedy by bringing divine goodness out of it. Such redemptive transformation would counter selfish human power in order to make room for life-giving divine power, even in the midst of suffering, evil, and death. This kind of redemptive effort captures what lies hidden in some conceptions of the warrior God of Israel. It replaces evil violence in the warrior God with divine redemptive goodness for the benefit of all concerned. Jesus manifested this morally improved conception of a God of conflict for divine goodness, and he instructed his disciples accordingly (Matt. 5:38–48, Luke 6:27–36).

The divine pattern of redemptive transformation finds its high point in the death-and-resurrection of Jesus, but this is not its only manifestation. It would emerge wherever divine redemption is at work for the sake of divine goodness in a context of evil. We might wonder why this is the pattern for divine redemption when something less severe seems preferable to us. We lack a complete answer, but we can find a partial answer in the ultimate motive and goal of divine redemption: *righteous agapē* among persons in relating to God and others, as something needed for meeting and living with God in a good society.

Paul comments that God "did not withhold his own Son, but gave him up for all of us" (Rom. 8:32), and that "God proves his love for us in that while we still were sinners Christ died for us" (Rom. 5:8). The writer of 1 John concurs: "God's love was revealed among us in this way: God sent his only Son into the world so that we might live through him. In this is love, not that we loved God but that he loved us and sent his Son to be the atoning sacrifice for our sins" (1 John 4:9–10; cf. John 3:16–17). The sacrificial suffering of Jesus thus may reflect the sacrificial suffering of *God* in sending Jesus to die for the benefit of humans, for the sake of attracting them to God. In that case, the divine sending of Jesus would manifest redemptive duress on God's part.

God's sending Jesus to attract humans to a reconciled life with God would manifest divine self-sacrificial love for the sake of humans. Jesus's self-giving death-and-resurrection thus would offer a distinctive model for the unique divine love at work for humans. Such love would call for the end of all competing human power, for the sake of lasting, reconciled human life in *God's* power. Paul identified part of the divine aim in redemptive suffering: "We have this treasure in clay jars, so that it may be made clear that this extraordinary power belongs to God and does not come from us" (2 Cor. 4:7). This scenario would manifest redemptive duress in the lives of people undergoing reconciliation to God.

Paul identified God's aim in a case of his own redemptive suffering: "We felt that we had received the sentence of death so that we would rely not on ourselves but on God who raises the dead" (2 Cor. 1:9). This divine aim bears on what we ultimately *trust* or *rely on*: either God or ourselves. Human power competing with divine power will eventually confront God's self-sacrificial love that calls for a reordering of typical human priorities, including what and how we trust and love. This confrontation seeks, in God's gambit, death to anti-God human ways for the sake of new, divinely empowered ways. If we cooperate in trust, our ultimate self-trust would give way to ultimate trust in God, and our self-inadequacy or collapse in suffering could encourage us to welcome this shift toward God and divine goodness in reconciliation.

God's gambit of redemptive duress emerges from Jesus's aforementioned parable of the wicked tenants (Mark 12:1–12, Matt. 21:33–46, Luke 20:9–19). Matthew's Gospel offers the parable as a model of how "the kingdom of God" approaches and challenges people who resist God's plan for reconciliation through obeying God. The divine kingdom is, courtesy of God's goodness, on loan to people, but it comes with God's expectations for their conforming to it rather than abusing it. The parable illustrates that, for the sake of reaching people with divine goodness, God takes a risk of abusive and murderous freedom among humans, including such freedom toward God's well-intentioned representatives.

The parable suggests that God risks abusive human freedom by allowing providential distance between God and humans. God thus "went away" from the accountable humans (Mark 12:1, Matt. 21:33) but still expected responsible behavior from them. The divine gambit includes taking the risk of human abuse for the sake of showing divine goodness, including the goodness of God's faithfully redemptive character and action under duress. The redemptive death of Jesus is, according to the main New Testament message (and the parable of the wicked tenants), central to this divine gambit. It is part of the redemptive risk of rejection that God takes in order to manifest and give divine goodness, including divine self-giving love, to humans.

Jesus put himself at risk of rejection by the Jewish leaders and death by the Roman officials in Jerusalem. He did this with what E. P. Sanders has called his "self-claim" and with his public actions, including his protest actions in the temple, and the result was his demise in Jerusalem.[1] He suggested, according to the synoptic Gospels, a unique status for himself as God's beloved son with divine authority not

---

[1] See Sanders, *Jesus and Judaism*, pp. 153–5, 306–8, 333–4, and Moule, "The Gravamen against Jesus," pp. 95–114.

only to forgive sins and to supervise God's kingdom but also to recast and fulfill the Mosaic law (see Chapters 3 and 7).

Jesus's assumed filial status with God, joined with his talk of himself as Daniel's exalted "son of man" (see Chapter 4) indicated special intimacy and authority from God, to such an extent that he was accused by Jewish leaders of blasphemy, along with seeking to destroy the temple (Mark 14:55–64, Matt. 26:59–66; cf. Luke 22:66–71). In addition, his enacted parable of Zechariah's arriving king (see Chapter 7) enabled the Roman officials to regard him as a political threat who must be removed (Mark 15:2–5, 12–15, Matt. 27:11–14, 22–6, Luke 23:2–5, 20–4). Jesus's enacted parable of the Last Supper indicates that he was aware of his fate, while he assumed authority from God to launch a new covenant with his resulting death (Mark 14:22–5, Matt. 26:26–9, Luke 22:15–20). We thus can make sense of the trajectory of his life toward its demise in Jerusalem, even in the absence of a full biography.

Jesus was content to regard himself as God's unique beloved son, without any claim to be God. Our evidence counts against any alleged self-claim of Jesus to be God, despite the contrary suggestion of some theologically conservative commentators.[2] It is a historical and theological mistake to read later trinitarian theology, even in an incipient form, into the mind of the historical Jesus. Notably, the theologically developed Gospel of John avoids an unqualified claim that Jesus is God (John 17:3), while claiming that the Father is "greater" than Jesus (ὁ πατὴρ μείζων μού ἐστιν) (John 14:28) and "has given life to the son [τῷ υἱῷ ἔδωκεν ζωὴν]" (John 5:26; cf. John 8:28–9).

We should not infer that Jesus is just a deceased historical founder of the Christian movement or that he is not worthy of worship. His goodness and corresponding

---

[2] See, for instance, N. T. Wright, "Jesus and the Identity of God," *Ex Auditu* 14 (1998), 42–56.

authority depend on his Father, in his own understanding, but it can be *divine* goodness and authority nonetheless, in a manner that merits worship of him (Matt. 28:16–20, Luke 24:44–53). Paul thus thought of Jesus as uncreated and worthy of worship but nonetheless dependent on, and subjected to, his Father, even lastingly (Phil. 2:5–11, 1 Cor. 15:27–8).[3] The Jewish leaders opposing Jesus saw the problem he posed for a strict, untiered monotheism, even though he did not call himself "God."

Given Jesus's worthiness of worship, his divine goodness as uncreated Son of God calls for a tiered monotheism, with his divine status subjected to, and dependent on, his Father's divine status. Their divine *unity* includes their perfectly sharing uncreated perfect goodness worthy of worship, even given Jesus's self-avowed dependence on his Father's goodness. The Gospel of John struggled with this matter, resorting to a notion of Jesus as "begotten [μονογενοῦς]" by God (John 1:14, with textual variation between "begotten son" and "begotten God"). The latter notion, however, is left unclear, and a detailed metaphysics of the relation is underdetermined by our available evidence.

The evidence in the New Testament is, as suggested, largely concerned with functional, rather than metaphysical, aspects of redemption and Christology. In addition, the previous considerations recommend against trinitarian speculation regarding the Jesus of history. Nothing in the mission of Jesus is lost, however, in following Jesus in calling him "the Son of God," rather than "God," and in settling for tiered monotheism rather than trinitarian speculation.[4] In staying close here to the language of the

---

[3] On the worship of Jesus in early Christianity, see Hurtado, *Lord Jesus Christ*, pp. 134–53, 605–19. See also Raymond E. Brown, "Did New Testament Christians Call Jesus God?," in *An Introduction to New Testament Christology* (New York: Paulist Press, 1994), pp. 171–95.

[4] This position of tiered monotheism goes beyond any suggestion that Jesus is a human who functions in divine roles. For relevant discussion, see J. R. Daniel Kirk, *A Man Attested by God: The Human Jesus of the Synoptic Gospels* (Grand Rapids,

Gospels and of the historical Jesus, we help to maintain their focus on relating to God and Jesus in trust, love, and obedience, rather than metaphysical speculation.

God's redemptive gambit undermines any naïve story of a "quick-fix-it" god who does not leave time or opportunity for redemptive duress. It presents instead a God who risks, and patiently monitors, human opposition, failure, and collapse for the sake of human redemption as reconciliation to God. It thus presents a God who values interpersonal goodness over hedonic pleasure.

As Chapter 2 noted, Paul put the gambit thus: "The creation was subjected to futility, not of its own will but by the will of the one who subjected it, in hope that the creation itself will be set free from its bondage to decay and will obtain the freedom of the glory of the children of God" (Rom. 8:20–1). Paul suggested that God, without causing evil, subjects various human efforts and plans to futility or frustration in order to attract people to receive the freedom of becoming children of God. In their failure and suffering, according to this perspective, people can find in God's goodness, including in reconciliation with God, a better alternative for their well-being.

Helmut Thielicke has summed up the divine gambit in relation to Jesus:

In setting over against himself a being to whom he gave freedom and power, [God] risked the possibilities that the [human] child would become a competitor, that the child would become a megalomaniacal rival of the Creator ... This venture of God in which he bound himself to man – and exposed himself to the possibility of being reviled, despised, denied, and ignored by man – this venture was the first flash of his love. God ventured, as it were, his own self. He declared himself ready to suffer the pain the father

MI: Eerdmans, 2016), and, in contrast, Richard Bauckham, "Is 'High Human Christology' Sufficient?," *Bulletin for Biblical Research* 27 (2017), 503–25.

endured when he let the prodigal son go into the far country, when he allowed deep wounds to be inflicted upon his
heart, and still would not give up his child of sorrows. This
line reaches its end in Jesus Christ. There God exposed
himself to his rebellious children, put himself at their
mercy, and let his most beloved die by their hand but for
them.[5]

This portrait of God's purpose fits with Thielicke's suggestion of divine risk in the consideration that "the
afflictions of your life and mine are the hollow ground
under our feet which gives way because God wills to
catch us."[6] The purpose may not be obvious at times,
but it still could be discernible through due attention
and cooperation.

Perhaps God would want reconciliation and fellowship with humans "through good and bad." So, there
would be both good and bad as a context for God to
test for the effectiveness of the divine redemptive gambit (see the book of Job). As a result, people would face
a test of what *they will do* by way of response in relation
to God, given the duress and the evil they face, however tragic. For better or worse, our learning trust and
love that endure toward God under redemptive duress
can call for tragic suffering on our part, and on God's
part too.

Many people naturally will wonder whether the
redemptive effort is worthwhile in the end. Perhaps it
would have been better not to have lived at all. Job thus
responds in protest: "Why was I not buried like a stillborn
child, like an infant that never sees the light? There the
wicked cease from troubling, and there the weary are at
rest" (Job 3:16–17). Somehow, Job's painful protest gave

[5] Thielicke, *How the World Began*, trans. J. W. Doberstein (Philadelphia: Muhlenberg
Press, 1961), pp. 60–1.
[6] Thielicke, *Out of the Depths*, trans. G. W. Bromiley (Grand Rapids, MI: Eerdmans,
1962), p. 20.

way to his cooperative response to God: "I have uttered what I did not understand, things too wonderful for me, which I did not know. I had heard of you by the hearing of the ear, but now my eye sees you; therefore, I despise myself, and repent in dust and ashes" (Job 42:3–6). A transformative religious experience seems to have intervened for Job, and it led to a changed attitude toward God.

The difficulty of redemptive duress, including the duress of the cross of Jesus, offends many people, but it is not altogether unintelligible. A relevant difference is between a quick-fix-it God and a God who patiently seeks reconciliation and fellowship with people in righteous *agapē*. The reconciliatory God would monitor and guide redemptive duress for the good of all concerned, even in cases of human despair and collapse. The redemption would come ultimately from divine restorative power, even in the absence of human success and progress, and perhaps with resurrection. The evidence supporting a human response of cooperative trust would come in the context of one cooperatively knowing the God in question, via divine goodness, even if one cannot confirm many details of God's redemptive plan for the future.

A God worthy of worship would seek a reconciled relationship with humans, but we should not expect constant experience of God by them. Such experience can become an idol in relation to God, because God would not be a religious experience and would be distorted and even neglected in some religious experiences. The history of religion shows that religious experiences, even allegedly of God, include many counterfeits and can divert attention from God and divine goodness. God would seek loyal and cooperative human commitment to God's goodness, including God's morally perfect character and will, for the sake of human benefit. God would seek and value such commitment even while one is not having a religious experience of God. Perhaps, as suggested, this lesson figures in the significance of Jesus's cry of dereliction from the cross. In any case, we can probe further in what the divine gambit seeks.

8.2 REDEMPTIVE COMPANIONSHIP

If God is worthy of worship, then divine goodness includes morally perfect goodness, without moral defect. God then merits the full loyal commitment and love suited to worthiness of worship. In addition, if God is morally perfect, then God is perfectly caring and redemptive toward people needing redemption as interpersonal reconciliation to God. Being thus caring and redemptive, God would seek what is morally good for those people for the sake of their reconciliation to God. This effort would be central to God's gambit, and it would seek to build a universal society of people motivated by and reflective of divine goodness.

The reconciliation intended by God would attract some people to cooperate willingly with divine goodness, including God's morally perfect character and will, at least to some extent. It would seek *companionship* as caring and willing cooperation between God and humans without divine condoning of human wrongdoing. Such companionship would morally involve reconciled humans with God in a caring and cooperative way foreign to some understandings of companionship. God's moral character and will, we shall see, would have distinctive implications for *redemptive* human companionship with God, and this fits with the mission of Jesus for divine goodness.

Going beyond a hypothetical situation of what God would do, we should ask whether human history offers actual reports of a God who seeks redemptive companionship with some humans. The book of Isaiah refers to the patriarch Abraham as a companion of God, and this idea is repeated in some Jewish and Christian writings.

You, Israel, my servant, Jacob, whom I have chosen, the offspring of Abraham, my friend; you whom I took from the ends of the earth, and called from its farthest corners, saying to you, "You are my servant, I have chosen you and not cast you off"; do not fear, for I am with you, do not be afraid, for I am your God; I will strengthen you, I will help you, I will uphold you with my victorious right hand. (Isa. 41:4, 8–10; cf. 2 Chron. 20:7, James 2:23)

This passage does not explain what divine companionship includes. It does suggest, however, that God is favorably disposed toward Israel, the offspring of Abraham, perhaps as a result of friendship with him. A related reference occurs in Exodus 33:11, with regard to Moses: "The Lord used to speak to Moses face to face, as one speaks to a friend." Here, too, the verse does not explain what the companionship includes; its concern is the directness of God speaking to Moses. We need to look elsewhere for clarification of divine redemptive companionship.

John's Gospel offers an approach to companionship with Jesus that bears on our concern. It portrays Jesus as saying:

This is my commandment, that you love one another as I have loved you. No one has greater love than this, to lay down one's life for one's friends [φίλων αὐτοῦ]. You are my friends if you do what I command you. I do not call you servants any longer, because the servant does not know what the master is doing; but I have called you friends, because I have made known to you everything that I have heard from my Father. (John 15:12–15)

The companionship suggested here has three important features. It stems from a redeemer's self-giving love for his companions; it requires that his companions obey what the redeemer commands; and it depends on the redeemer revealing something from God to the companions. We shall consider how Jesus aimed to make God known in redemptive companionship, with a unique moral gift and challenge. The moral superiority of God and Jesus relative to typical humans allows for the kind of caring cooperation integral to companionship, including redemptive companionship.

Given the central role of love in the passage, Raymond E. Brown translates the Greek word *philoi* as "those he loves." He explains: "The English word 'friend' does not capture sufficiently this relationship of love (for we have lost the feeling that 'friend' is related to the Anglo-Saxon verb 'frēon', 'to love')."[7] This is true of a typical use of "friend," but the passage itself requires more than being loved.

The passage calls for a kind of responsiveness in relationship that talk of merely "being loved" omits. It calls for the friends of Jesus to do what he *commands* them to do; it thus demands obeying Jesus. The simple idea of being loved does not include this demand, and therefore it falls short of the relevant notion of being a friend of Jesus. So, the familiar translation using "friends" is preferable to the alternative of "those he loves," as long as we think of the relevant kind of friendship as grounded in divine love and requiring obedience to Jesus. This is *redemptive* companionship, because it is caring in seeking what God deems best, all things considered, for its recipients. Self-giving love governs such companionship, given Jesus's mention of "laying down his life" for his friends. So, we are not talking about friends as selfish partners in crime, because redemptive companionship is anchored in unselfish love aimed at moral goodness.

John's Jesus claims that his kind of love in redemptive companionship is akin to the kind of love *God* shows to him and thereby to others: "As the Father has loved me, so I have loved you; abide in my love" (John 15:9). In addition, God is portrayed as seeking not to condemn the world but

---

[7] Brown, *The Gospel According to John*, p. 664.

to save it through Jesus – that is, to redeem it in reconciliation to God (John 3:16–17; cf. John 17:3). In this regard, the companionship represented by Jesus is divine redemptive companionship. We thus may explore, as an approach to redemptive companionship from God, how Jesus intended to present divine companionship and the kind of love it includes. If God seeks redemptive companionship with humans, this goal may bear on how God self-reveals to them and thus on how God responds to human inquiry about God.

Luke's Gospel anticipated John's Gospel in portraying Jesus as talking of his "friends": "I tell you, my friends [φίλοις], do not fear those who kill the body, and after that can do nothing more" (Luke 12:4).[8] This talk of friends occurs in a context where Jesus advised his disciples: "Even the hairs of your head are all counted. Do not be afraid" (Luke 12:7). So, this is companionship anchored in divine goodness and love. The use of the particular term "friend," however, is not as important as the representation of the *idea* and the *example* of friendship in the teaching and the conduct of Jesus.

The present context in Luke's Gospel includes this remark by Jesus: "Do not be afraid, little flock, for it is your Father's good pleasure to give you the kingdom" (Luke 12:32). The idea of *giving* the kingdom here is that of a *gift* – something unearned or unmerited, from God. It includes the gift of an interpersonal kingdom *relationship* where the king is a self-giving friend. The ideas of gift and interpersonal relationship are brought together in this context in Luke as follows: "If you then, who are evil, know how to give good gifts to your children, how much more will the heavenly Father give the Holy Spirit to those who ask him" (Luke 11:13). The gift of God's Spirit to a human, according to various writers in the New Testament, is

---

[8] In addition, the Gospels of Luke and Matthew leave the impression that Jesus was considered by some people to be a "friend" (φίλος) of "tax collectors and sinners" (Luke 7:34, Matt. 11:19).

central to the most important interpersonal relationship possible. It is the gift of an interpersonal relationship of uncoerced fellowship as redemptive companionship with God.

The divine king in Luke's Gospel is a friend who, as king, gives guidance to people. In the present context in Luke's Gospel, the announcement of the gift of a kingdom thus leads to a gift of *guidance* from Jesus. That guidance concerns focused use of a human will toward properly valuing God and God's ways: "Sell your possessions, and give alms. Make purses for yourselves that do not wear out, an unfailing treasure in heaven, where no thief comes near and no moth destroys. For where your treasure is, there your heart will be also" (Luke 12:33–4; cf. Matt. 6:19–21). The notion of a "heart" here includes the idea of a human will, and thus the gift of God's kingdom includes a gift of guidance for a human will, in the context of a companionship grounded in unselfish love. The guidance is for one willingly to treasure God and God's ways as an alternative to any priority in things that "wear out."

Luke's Gospel (along with the other Gospels) captures the guiding attitude of Jesus, as Chapter 3 explained, with the case of his prayer in Gethsemane: "Father, ... not my will but yours be done" (Luke 22:42; cf. Mark 14:36). Typically, we do not think of God's primary gift to include personal guidance for a human will, but this approach to the divine gift recurs in the New Testament, including in the teachings of Jesus. God's main redemptive purpose is that humans receive this gift of divine guidance in redemptive companionship. The guidance enables humans to appropriate the companionship, thus receiving God as *their* Lord, the one who *leads* them with uncoercive authority. In the absence of such leading, we may have talk of lordship, but we do not have genuine lordship realized, including lordship in action (Luke 6:46; cf. Matt. 7:21).

Our cooperative redemption by God, in interpersonal reconciliation to God, would require our being aware of the kind of human *motivation* agreeable to God's perfect will and character. For instance, as Chapter 2 suggested, human motivation by a hateful or grudging attitude toward God would be misplaced. Our direct awareness of God's perfect redemptive will would serve well, because this perfect will would display the kind of motivation suited to God. In meeting firsthand with this will in our direct experience, we would go beyond mere talk of a perfectly good will that is just theoretical, reflective, or speculative. We then would have an experiential basis for our talk and reflection about this morally perfect will.

The will of a redemptive God would challenge us in our direct experience, and the challenge would be for us willingly to conform it. It also would be a gift in our experience because it would offer us invaluable, needed guidance by God. Even so, this challenging gift would not coerce our will to conform to it. Instead, it would nudge us, at God's preferred time, toward God's moral character, but it would allow for our ignoring, suppressing, or rejecting the nudge. God's will, then, would not extinguish our personal agency. It thus would allow for a genuine interpersonal interaction and relationship between humans and God.

God would seek to have us guided by the divine will as a gift and a challenge *as we willingly value it*, beyond our merely experiencing it or reflecting on it. In willingly valuing it, we would become suited, in our own will, to conform to God's will, and we thus would allow ourselves to be befriended by God. If we do not value God's perfect will, we will not welcome it or God's perfect redemptive companionship stemming from it. In that case, we would not value *God*, and we would, in effect, opt out of companionship with God. God's redemptive gambit thus would seek opportunities for befriending people who will value God's perfect will. Our decision to opt out would frustrate God's redemptive will, at least until we reverse our response.

In failing to value God's perfect will, I would block myself from not only appreciating but also apprehending firsthand its value and the reality of what it intends: my cooperating with God in redemptive companionship. God thus could withhold self-revealing of the divine redemptive will from humans who fail to value it. Otherwise, people could tend toward, or at least be at risk of, deeper alienation from God, in facing God's will without valuing it. Chapter 5 suggested that such redemptive withholding of divine self-revealing fits with Jesus's statement of the purpose for his use of parables (Luke 8:9–15; cf. Luke 10:21–2).

8.3 EXPLAINING GOOD AND EVIL

We have been explaining Jesus through divine goodness, and this is arguably the best available means of doing so. It fits well with our historical evidence, and it illuminates some important features of the moral experience of many people. It thus makes Jesus historically and morally credible in relation to divine goodness.

A "problem of goodness" asks whether we can adequately explain the goodness in human lives without the reality of a good God. A corresponding "problem of evil" asks whether the evil in human lives disconfirms the reality of a good God. Both problems bear on an understanding of Jesus in relation to divine goodness, but the problem of evil challenges the reality of the divine goodness central to understanding Jesus.

We can have *some* understanding of God's moral perfection and purposes without having an adequate understanding to explain *fully* why God allows various instances of suffering and death. Our inability to explain fully is illustrated, for instance, by the horrifying case of the Holocaust. God could redeem even the Holocaust, but we are not in a position to explain fully why it was allowed in the first place. Our understanding some general things about God's purposes in allowing suffering does not supply a full theodicy for us. As Paul notes, we now "know only in part" (1 Cor. 13:12). God could have a redemptive reason in not giving us a full theodicy now.

Our own understanding of some matter or other easily becomes an idol in relation to God, because we often give it an authoritative status that rivals God. We sometimes assume that God must, or at least should, conform to our own understanding. So, if God reveals divine purposes in allowing suffering, and they do not conform to our prior understanding, we may be inclined to fault those purposes. In doing so, we can alienate ourselves from redemptive companionship with God.

The underlying problem is that our moral character falls short of God's, given that God is worthy of worship while we are not. As a result, our understanding will fall short of God's, at least on various moral matters, including some matters of righteous *agapē* for the world and its redemption. So, we would need moral humility in relation to a God worthy of worship. Our moral understanding would not match God's in depth but would function at a less profound level. The same holds for our moral goodness itself.

We should not expect to understand fully all of God's ways or purposes in permitting human suffering and death. So, the following issue arises if a person objects: Why suppose that we cognitively limited humans *should* be able to answer questions about God's unrevealed purposes that fail to meet the expectations of some humans for God's activity? Another issue emerges in response: Why *should* one expect that God would reveal divine purposes to us for the sake of answering such unanswered questions? I doubt that we have a good reason for having such an expectation, even though many people do have such an expectation and use it to challenge God's reality or goodness.

We should be prepared to say that "we do not know" with regard to some of God's purposes toward humans. If *God* is Lord of human understanding while we are not (and we have no reason to exclude the area of our understanding), then we should not expect our understanding to comprehend God's ways fully, even if we have some understanding. This epistemic limitation is a reflection of our cognitive shortcoming, but it does not challenge God's moral character in any way. It would be a confusion, between human understanding and divine character, to suggest otherwise.

Seeking our best, all things considered, God would have us learn that divine–human companionship can flourish in a context of human suffering and tragedy, including death, and in their aftermath. Indeed, God would value redemptive companionship enough to invite it, and wait for it, even under extreme suffering, including God's. Perhaps some humans, at least, need to learn this lesson the hard way, not out of divine punishment but out of the felt exposure of their inadequacy to flourish on their own, without companionship with God.

We may think of God aiming to help in our inadequacy as God seeking to launch or to deepen redemptive companionship with us, as we acquire a felt need of it and of God. The divine goal would be for us to give priority in our lives to God and our redemptive relationship with God. God's allowing our suffering can contribute to this goal by encouraging proper focus in our lives toward our need of God, above our having a life free of suffering.

God, we have noted, would allow for our rejection of redemptive companionship with God, for the sake of having such companionship with genuine *agents* rather than coerced pawns. So, God would not coerce human cooperation with God in the matter of redemptive companionship. Even so, God could allow for severe challenges to people, including through suffering and evil, to invite them to value God and their need of God, if more deeply.

Divine goodness does not require that God give humans immediate protection from everything bad in their lives. God thus could decide not to spare people from suffering and evil but instead to seek restoration for them in the aftermath, such as in a subsequent resurrected life. God then would bring good out of bad, after allowing something bad, perhaps even extremely bad, in human lives. The New Testament portrays God as proceeding accordingly in the life, death, and resurrection of Jesus, and it promises something similar for his disciples.

Some people hold that if God intentionally allowed all of this world's extreme suffering in human lives, then God would be too severe to be morally good. They assume that it is not morally justifiable to allow such evil, regardless of one's intentions toward bringing about something good as a result. This position may seem plausible at first glance, but the matter is complicated.

An immediate problem is that we do not have the overall picture of the ultimate moral good planned by God. The Holocaust itself is, of course, extremely evil and not good, but we do not have the full picture of the ultimate good God will bring out of it. We are not in a position now, given human limitations in relevant evidence, to examine that full picture of planned ultimate good in any detail. So, a charge of excess severity from God, it is arguable, would be premature. Withholding judgment about such severity would be better suited to our actual evidence regarding divine plans.

Leslie Weatherhead has remarked: "To make the point that God allows what he does not will should be followed immediately by the insistence that the *measure* of what he allows is the *measure* of his purpose in bringing good out of evil. [God] would not allow anything to happen which could finally defeat his plans."[9] We can understand divine power to include God disallowing things that undermine the ultimate divine purpose for humans. Even so, our evidence does not give us a full understanding of God's ultimate purpose in allowing extreme human suffering.

[9] Leslie Weatherhead, *The Christian Agnostic* (New York: Abingdon Press, 1965), p. 210.

Arguably, some of our evidence includes a divine promise that God will redeem this world's evil in satisfying a good ultimate purpose (Rom. 8:18, 28, 1 Cor. 2:9, 2 Cor. 4:17). So, a key issue is whether God is trustworthy with this promise. If our evidence supports that God is trustworthy with promises of this kind, we can have grounded hope that God somehow will redeem the world's suffering and evil with divine goodness, even if the details now elude us. Humans can vary in the evidence they have on this matter, and this is to be expected given the divine redemptive purposes we have identified.

8.4 REDEEMING EVIL WITH GOOD

Philosophers such as A. N. Whitehead and Edgar Sheffield Brightman have suggested that God lacks the power to end the world's suffering and evil.[10] In their perspective, God's power and will are "finite," and God is not omnipotent in being able to do everything that is logically doable. Brightman rejects the view that "God regards all so-called evils as instrumental goods and therefore approves of them." He adds that "a wise finite God ... judges [some evils] to be unjustifiable as well as unavoidable, yet in spite of the dross of creation, he creates because gold may be obtained."[11] God thus faces evil that does not come from God's will and cannot be avoided by an act of God's will. So, God's power and will, in this perspective, are finite.

Brightman rightly suggests that we have no good reason to suppose that worthiness of worship logically requires the omnipotence of God. Some attempts to show otherwise confuse the goodness of God's *character* with the (possibly limited) goodness of what God is *able to enact*. Even so, in

---

[10] A. N. Whitehead, *Process and Reality*, eds. David Ray Griffin and D. W. Sherburne (New York: Free Press, 1929 [1978]), p. 342, Edgar Sheffield Brightman, *The Problem of God* (New York: Abingdon Press, 1930), chap. 7.

[11] Edgar Sheffield Brightman, *A Philosophy of Religion* (New York: Prentice Hall, 1940), p. 334.

responding to the world's suffering and evil, we should be cautious about favoring divine finitude in power over divine hiding regarding ultimate purposes in allowing suffering and evil. Such hiding, we have suggested, can save some people from deepening opposition to such purposes and to God. Our relevant evidence, in any case, does not clearly recommend the finitude of divine power.

Notably, we have no clear indication of divine finitude from the acknowledged prophets or revelations of traditional monotheism, including from Moses, Jesus, Paul, or Muhammad. We might have expected some indication of this perspective, if it were true, given its alleged importance in exonerating God from a charge of excess severity toward human suffering. A prime opportunity for such an indication arises in the book of Job, but the author does not move toward divine finitude. Similarly, Jesus does not endorse such finitude, but appears to go against it, in his remark at his arrest: "Do you think that I cannot appeal to my Father, and he will at once send me more than twelve legions of angels?" (Matt. 26:53). He assumes that God has the power to free him but opts not to do so.

Perhaps we should sympathize with a good God who sought to avoid the actualization of evil in the world but lacked the power to do so. That would be a regrettable misfortune for a good God who sought to avoid evil. Traditional monotheism, however, does not supply clear evidence, in its acknowledged prophets or revelations, that recommends our sympathizing with God in that regard. Instead, it consistently recommends that God does not cause evil but can be trusted to bring ultimate good out of evil in the fullness of time. It also suggests that any tragedy for God comes from God's intentionally creating and allowing for free agents who frustrate God's will.

Arguably, it would be a moral defect in God if God had limited power toward removing suffering and evil but did not make this limitation *clearly knowable* by humans. This would be a moral failure in revealing something that could exonerate God and remove widespread misgivings about God among humans. Evidently, God would be able to reveal this clearly to humans if there were such a limitation in divine power.

Our inability to *explain why* the proposed God does not clearly reveal the suggested limitation to humans shows that we lack a *full* theodicy for this God, given the epistemic shortcoming at hand. A process theodicy in terms of divine inability suffers from the absence of a clear divine confirmation of that inability, and thus itself lacks needed epistemic clarity on that front. So, such a process approach has an epistemic defect in any proposed full theodicy, and thus its theodicy would not be truly *full*.

We should ask whether a finite God's suggested finite power has met its match in the world's evil. God's will lacks the power to dismiss evil now, according to finitism, but one might hope for a better future. One might hope that God's will gets the needed power in the future, but on what ground can a finitist have this as a *well-grounded* hope? What evidence enables us to suppose that the power situation will change in relation to God and evil? Perhaps optimism here depends on supposed evidence we do not actually have.

It would be *ad hoc* to recommend the finitude of divine power on the ground that a finite God would be exonerated from excess severity toward human suffering. We should not let a desired exoneration of God drive our understanding of our *evidence* regarding God's character and power. Instead, we should let our evidence take the lead in our understanding of God's character and power.

It would be misleading to endorse Brightman's aforementioned remark, concerning a traditional view, that "God regards all so-called evils as instrumental goods and therefore approves of them." God can allow and use evils for the sake of what is ultimately good, and thereby redeem them, without "approving" of them or deeming them to be "goods." Redeeming an evil does not make it something other than an evil; it does not make it something good. So, God can redeem evils for good without making them good. The goodness is in what God *brings out* of the evil; it is not in the evil itself.

Redeeming evil without explaining evil is a live option for a good God. In representing God in his mission, Jesus refrained from explaining God's full purpose in allowing unjust suffering and evil. Luke's Gospel gives an example:

There were some present who told [Jesus] about the Galileans whose blood Pilate had mingled with their sacrifices. He asked them, "Do you think that because these Galileans suffered in this way they were worse sinners than all other Galileans? No, I tell you; but unless you repent, you will all perish as they did. Or those eighteen who were killed when the tower of Siloam fell on them – do you think that they were worse offenders than all the others living in Jerusalem? No, I tell you; but unless you repent, you will all perish just as they did." (Luke 13:1–5)

Jesus rejected a bad theodicy here, but he gave no hint of why God allowed the unjust suffering and evil in question. In addition, he did not suggest that God should reveal the relevant divine purpose now to humans.

Jesus redirected the topic to how humans relate to God. He suggested that the inquirers about evil should focus on turning toward cooperative obedience to God, and this focus points to divine–human reconciliation. Jesus thus responded as if God will not now give humans a full explanation of why God allows unjust suffering and evil in human lives. Even so, he identified something more important than such explanation: the redemption of humans in reconciliation with God.

According to Jesus, redeeming persons is more important than explaining the occurrence of evil, even severe evil. Here we find an important priority of Jesus in relation to divine goodness. God's redemptive goodness, in his

perspective, can flourish in the absence of our fully understanding God allowing opposition to it. We may ask why
God allows it, as Jesus himself did in his own suffering, but
we are not in a position to expect an answer from God, as
Jesus learned in his own suffering.

Jesus consistently refrained from any indication of a full
theodicy for humans now. Instead, he suggested that humans
are not in a position now to understand God's full purposes,
including the divine purposes in allowing unjust suffering
and evil. He thus would have rejected any suggestion that
without a full theodicy, one could not have well-grounded
belief that a perfectly good God exists. If a full theodicy is
required for well-grounded belief that God is perfectly good,
then *no* human now would have such belief. We have, however, no good reason to accept the proposed requirement.

People can have experiential evidence adequate for well-
grounded belief that God is perfectly good, but lack a full
theodicy. Undefeated evidence of divine reality and goodness
in their moral experience (as characterized in Chapter 2) can
make their belief about God well-grounded for them, even
though they cannot fully explain all of God's purposes in
allowing suffering and evil. The lack of such a full explanation
is no defeater here. Evidence regarding divine goodness,
including God's good character and will, could indicate
God's perfect goodness in a trustworthy manner, while omitting a full theodicy. This situation would allow for a person's
well-grounded trust in God's goodness and promises, without that person having a full explanation of God's purposes. It
thus would allow for well-grounded and maturing faith
in God.

Faith and hope *in* God are eschatological in pointing to
the fullness of time. So, as suggested, our *present* perspective does not exhaust what God *will* do in response to evil,
including the horrors of the Holocaust. As a result, we
should not assume that God will do nothing in response.
Timing matters in a redemptive effort that honors human
agency, of the kind previously characterized as redemptive

companionship, and we should expect God to have better timing than we do.

We would be presumptuous in assuming that we should be able to set God's schedule for responding to evil. We also would be presumptuous in denying God's moral perfection for divine failure to comply with *our* schedule. If patience is among the fruit of God's Spirit, we would do well to consider it in our quest for a theodicy, even though we now lack a full theodicy.

Regarding epistemic patience, given our actual evidence regarding God, we have a better option in *withholding judgment* on the extent of divine power than in endorsing its finitude. We still could have evidence that God is perfectly good, but we then would be tentative regarding God's limitations in power. We thus could deem God to be worthy of worship, but we would wait for eschatological verification of the extent of God's power. So far as our evidence goes, one might say in that modest scenario, the jury is still out on whether God is unable to eliminate all evil now. In that case, we should not jump to the conclusion, for the sake of a quick theodicy, that God's power is finite. Instead, we should await decisive evidence.

Chapter 1 identified the question of whether we are willing to consider and to cooperate with a divine intervention in our moral experience. Our answer will reveal where we stand in relation to divine goodness. Each of us now has a self-referential question to answer in that regard, courtesy of the question from Jesus as God's inquirer of us: Who do you say that I am? By way of careful reply, we may gain understanding of who Jesus was or is and who we are in relation to his God. So, our inquiry about and from Jesus may matter significantly, especially in relation to divine goodness for ourselves and others. Jesus, in any case, leaves us with vital questions and answers regarding divine goodness. As a result, he merits our careful attention, whatever our theology or philosophy. His value, then, will endure, as long as divine goodness endures.

Index

Milton Keynes UK
Ingram Content Group UK Ltd.
UKHW021048280124
436796UK00011B/42